# SHUT UP
# & SING

# SHUT UP & SING

## How Elites from Hollywood, Politics, and the UN Are Subverting America

# LAURA INGRAHAM

Since 1947
**REGNERY**
**PUBLISHING, INC.**
*An Eagle Publishing Company • Washington, DC*

Library of Congress Cataloging-in-Publication Data

Ingraham, Laura.
  Shut up & sing : how elites from Hollywood, politics, and the UN are subverting America / Laura Ingraham.
       p. cm.
Includes index.
  ISBN 0-89526-101-4 (alk. paper)
  1. Elite (Social sciences)—United States. 2. United States—Politics and government. 3. United States—In mass media. 4. United States—Social conditions. I. Title: Shut up and sing. II. Title: How elites from Hollywood, politics, and the UN are subverting America. III. Title.
  HN90.E4I54 2003
  305.5'2'0973—dc22
                              2003018049

Published in the United States by
Regnery Publishing, Inc.
An Eagle Publishing Company
One Massachusetts Avenue, NW
Washington, DC 20001

Visit us at www.regnery.com

Distributed to the trade by
National Book Network
4720-A Boston Way
Lanham, MD 20706

Printed on acid-free paper
Manufactured in the United States of America

10 9 8 7 6 5 4 3

Books are available in quantity for promotional or premium use. Write to Director of Special Sales, Regnery Publishing, Inc., One Massachusetts Avenue, NW, Washington, DC 20001, for information on discounts and terms or call (202) 216-0600.

*For my father, James, and my brothers,
Jim, Brooks, and Curtis.*

# Contents

# 1

# Who Are the Elites?

They think we're stupid. They think our patriotism is stupid. They think our churchgoing is stupid. They think our flag-flying is stupid. They think having more than two children is stupid. They think where we live—anywhere but near or in a few major cities—is stupid. They think our SUVs are stupid. They think owning a gun is stupid. They think our abiding belief in the goodness of America and its founding principles is stupid. They think the choices we make at the ballot box are stupid. They think George W. Bush is stupid. And without a doubt, they will think this book is stupid.

Meet the elites.

Who are they? Essentially, elites are defined not so much by class or wealth or position as they are by a *general outlook*. Their core belief—embraced with a fervor that does not allow for rational debate—is that they are superior to We the People. They know better. They are way ahead of us in the evolutionary scheme of things—not mere earthlings, but more like the inhabitants of some advanced and super-enlightened planet discovered by the crew of the Starship *Enterprise*. Their brilliance is to be presumed. Their ways are to be emulated, never challenged. And without question, they are right and we are very, very wrong. But not just wrong—our stupidity and our vast numbers make us dangerous.

To them we are a collection of morons with only one thing going for us: There are many more of us than there are of them. And in this land of one person, one vote, that still means something. But not for long—if these elites have their way. To them the fact that their beliefs are not accepted by the masses is a source of both pride and frustration. Ironically, the rejection of their beliefs by the majority of us confirms, to their clouded minds, their intellectual superiority. Yet the elites also know this means they are ultimately impotent, at least in a democracy. This democracy, for them, has become a lumbering dinosaur—all muscle, tiny brain, prehistoric outlook, and largely destructive. They think it needs to be stopped. Or at least reeducated.

But they can't seem to stop us. We keep winning. Our electoral majority keeps growing. They have tried to enlighten us, but we just don't seem to understand. They have tried to instruct us on the right way to think in this interdependent global community. They have enlisted their friends in the media to bombard us with their ideas. They have tried to develop a new generation of elites through indoctrination in the public schools and universities. But we're just not buying any of it.

Somehow, we still believe in one nation under God. We still believe that we are endowed by our Creator with certain inalienable rights, among them life, liberty, and the pursuit of happiness. We think we live in a great country—that "city on a hill." We *love* America, and put our hands over our hearts when "The Star Spangled Banner" is played. And *it drives them crazy!* It makes them angry, bitter, and belligerent. Ask yourself: When is the last time you came across a happy, optimistic liberal?

Indeed, the elites are characterized more by cynicism than optimism. More by arrogance than benevolence. Their hand-wringing, critical, "can't do" attitude is fundamentally un-American. It is certainly not the attitude that built America. They are more interested in restraining America than in continuing to build it. They have embraced a post-Americanism. They are no longer Americans first. They are "citizens of the world." Their brains are too big to be contained within national borders. They are too advanced for patriotism, which they view as a vestige of an antiquated and barbaric culture that they have left behind.

They have outgrown America. They are ashamed of her—and us. We embarrass them. They are constantly having to apologize for our brutish attitudes and policies to their elitist comrades around the world. They can't take us anywhere. We simply refuse to learn.

We still want limited government. We want to pay lower taxes. We want to protect our borders. We fight back when we're attacked. We're suspicious of the UN and other international organizations that threaten our liberty and sovereignty; we don't want to go to them hat-in-hand to bless our foreign policy before acting in America's best interest. We drive huge, gas-guzzling Suburbans. We own guns and don't want to have to check in with Big Brother every time we want to buy a Daisy air rifle at Wal-Mart. We want God acknowledged in our public schools and our public life. We are the troglodytes who demand the protection of children in the womb. We want judges who enforce the law, not invent it. In other words, we want the same America for which our founders pledged their lives, their fortunes, and their sacred honor.

They can't have this. And for all of their empty rhetoric about "peace," the "environment," "privacy," our "standing in the world," "reproductive freedom," and the rest of it, what they are really about is power. And they see their power in this country eroding, along with their ability to win elections and to implement their policies.

So they've chosen a different path. A path aimed at frustrating the will of the people, at blunting the effect of the democratic process, and at turning back the electoral tide that is vanquishing them. They are seeking to make headway primarily through undemocratic, elite-controlled structures both at home and abroad. These include the courts, the media, the universities, the United Nations, the European Union, and other international non-governmental institutions. In short, their numbers make them weak in a representative democracy. So they are playing to their strength, trying to increase the influence of the institutions that they (or their fellow travelers) control.

If they get their way, one day we'll wake up and the America we love will be gone.

## THE ELITE BREAKDOWN

Elitism is a state of mind, not a way of life. It is first and foremost a cult of the self. Elites view themselves as supreme, the center of all things, the highest good in life, and the ultimate judges of right and wrong. Elites come in all political stripes (although they tend to congregate in the Democratic Party). They are less tied to a party label than to a philosophy, the foundational principle of which is that its adherents are better and more enlightened than the poor slobs who make up the rest of humanity. It is this presumption of superiority, this unblinking certainty of personal infallibility, this unexamined arrogance, this unvarnished self-worship that lies at the heart of elitism. With this mentality, elites are able to peddle ideas that are demonstrably false (under even cursory examination) as unquestionably true.

But how can they be wrong if they're so much smarter than the rest of us? Didn't they make good grades? Didn't they go to Princeton? They did, but good grades in the Ivy League—earned taking classes from like-minded professors—have only confirmed their prejudices, against which all unassailable evidence that they are wrong is dismissed. So they cling to their beliefs with the feverish fanaticism of a cult member. They are impervious to reason. They have drunk the purple Kool-Aid, and spent their lives trying to get us to do the same, to get us to accept that they should decide things for we the helots.

Here is a brief overview of the elite Manifesto. Although this list is not exhaustive, it captures the essence of how elites think. It most particularly shows the disdain they harbor for "average Americans."

**WE'RE BRILLIANT.** We are more intelligent and more advanced than everyone else. But we are not only smarter than anyone living— we're smarter than anyone who has *ever* lived! The cemeteries are full of people who were dumber than we! Therefore, our fore-fathers (as the non-elites call them) are not worthy of respect. They did the best they could with their limited intellectual firepower and minds pickled in prejudice. Now it's up to us to overcome their mistakes, to tear down what they built, to replace it with a new set of world communities.

**MORALITY! WHAT MORALITY?** There *is* no objective morality. We are the only judge of what's right and wrong. Freedom means doing whatever we want, whenever we want, with whomever we want. No judgments. No consequences. No guilt. (Unless, of course, we forget to recycle.) We can do no wrong, because there is no wrong unless we say so.

**IMAGINE NO RELIGION.** Enough with this idea that "real religion" means we accept that there is a god out there greater than our-selves (see first two bullet points)! Our real problem with religion is that it teaches objective truth—that God exists, that God created human beings in His image, that God loves us, and that we all have an obligation to love, honor, and serve God. And that whole Ten Commandments thing really cramps our style. The idea that we need to abide by "God's law" in order to be truly happy is laugh-able! Religious people must have never sampled the pleasures available in the world when you seriously commit to pleasing only yourself. Forget heaven—ever been to Hollywood? Who's to say what's right and wrong anyway? All our friends know there is no truth outside of our momentary desires. And we refuse to be judged. Remember what Woody Allen said when they tried to judge him: "The heart wants what it wants." That's our only mantra. We are spiritual, not religious—there's a big difference. Being spiritual means never having to say you're sorry. It means inventing a custom-tailored "religion" all our own—a "religion" that validates all our desires, a "faith" that justifies all our actions, a "church" where we can worship ourselves in peace. That's the real bottom line, isn't it? It's all about self-fulfillment.

And we have great helpers in our effort to keep traditional religions out of our way and out of our public life. The ACLU, Americans United for Separation of Church and State, and other innocuous-sounding groups are always ready, willing, and—with our money—able to censor religious people and force religions to justify even their right to exist. We've chalked up impressive victories—with help from our friends, the elite judges—in censoring voluntary prayer in schools and at public events, shutting down Christmas and Hanukkah displays, outlawing public posting of the Ten Commandments, and on and on. Even the Pledge of Allegiance has been declared unconstitutional (at least by one of the appellate circuit courts). We're on a roll! Next we'll go after America's national motto. In God We Trust? We trust only in ourselves.

**GREEN ACRES IS *NOT* THE PLACE TO BE.** Let's face it, if you don't live in New York, Los Angeles, San Francisco, or D.C., then what's the point? Remember, our only real experience with the "fly-over" people was watching *Fargo*, or CNN's coverage of twisters ripping through a trailer park in Tennessee. It's better not to be subjected to those people on a regular basis. They shop at Wal-Mart. They don't go to the gym. They flew flags *before* September 11. How can it be that their vote counts as much as ours?

**VICTIMS, INC.** We have pity on oppressed minorities. They need us. We need them to need us. (We want them to feel oppressed whether they are or not.) We will be forever committed to "remedying past wrongs" done to various disenfranchised groups. We believe that sex, race, ethnicity, and sexual preference can and should trump merit and entitle you to success—guaranteed and enforced by the government.

**IN KOFI WE TRUST.** We believe that the United States cannot "go it alone," that we should no longer think of ourselves as a "superpower" but as an unselfish member of the global community. We must always strive to work with international institutions, even when those institutions oppose our "national interest." (Remember, we need to move away from thinking *nationally*.) As Bill Clinton said, "Ours is a world without borders." We believe the world hates us and that it's America's fault. We have not acted like a good global neighbor, especially during the Bush years. If only we could be more like France.

There are six native habitats of the elites:

Politics
Media
Ivory tower
Arts and entertainment
Business
International organizations

**POLITICS.** The Democratic Party is the natural home for political elites in the United States, but the GOP has its share of elites, too. Turning to the Democrats first, the populist party of FDR, Harry Truman, and Lyndon Baines Johnson has reinvented itself as a cool hangout favored by Hollywood celebs, media yuppies, trial lawyers, multiculturalists, God-haters, and the race-relations mafia, who look down on the working people who once made up the backbone of the Democratic Party. The elites, in other words, hang with their own except when forced to deal with "ordinary America." The Democrats still depend on the support of blue-collar unions and minorities, but many of these votes now appear to be "legacy" votes cast either out of nostalgia or an obsolete notion that the GOP is still the upper-class party of top-hatted, cigar-smoking Monopoly men grinding their boot heels into the faces of the poor. For the most part, as the Democrats have abandoned real populism, the people have abandoned the Democratic Party.

Nothing illustrates today's Dem-elite mindset better than Tom Daschle's attacks on talk radio in the wake of his party's devastating losses in the 2002 midterm elections. "But what happens when Rush Limbaugh attacks those of us in public life is that people

**One of my listeners summed up the frustration that so many feel when confronted with these elitist attitudes.**

"I admit it. I am one of those who are hated and despised among men who has had the privilege of listening to you defend (what liberals believe is the indefensible) me. I am a fundamental Christian, conservative, gun-owning, Bible-reading, truck-driving, churchgoing, married, heterosexual, non-politically-correct, pro-life white lawyer. I know that any one of these could pronounce the demise of my career as professor at the state college where I teach; in aggregate, forget it. I am a nonhuman in the eyes of many. For the record, I do not wait in the woods wearing military fatigues to ambush those who perform abortions, nor do I drag (or condone such) gays behind my truck. I simply try to work hard, raise my family, pay my taxes, work in my community, and live a good moral life. That said, I wish those who so strongly preach the 'tolerance' mantra would practice it when it comes to those they don't agree with. Thank you for your fresh voice in your defense of the Constitution and for all of us 'normal' people out here." ▪

aren't satisfied to listen. They want to act because they get emotionally invested," Daschle railed. "And so, you know, the threats to those of us in public life go up dramatically, on our families and on us," he added, slandering conservative radio listeners, essentially accusing them of wanting to blow up every left-winger in sight.

Of course Daschle was merely following in the rhetorical footsteps of Bill Clinton, who launched a tirade against Limbaugh back in 1995, linking talk radio to the bombing of the federal building in Oklahoma City. Clinton, still steaming over the drubbing the Dems suffered in the 1994 midterm elections, thought that since he couldn't win over the talk radio audience, he'd vilify it, and then marginalize it. (This of course only energized that audience against Clinton even more.)

Seven years later, after losing the White House and both houses of Congress, the Dem-elites were back, beating the drum against talk radio. But this time Daschle was even more explicit than Clinton: "We see it in foreign countries and we think, 'Well, my God, how can this religious fundamentalism become so violent?' Well, it's the same shrill rhetoric [in talk radio]." Translation: Liberal activists engage in meaningful dialogue. Conservatives engage in opinion terrorism. They are mindless reactionaries. They can't be trusted to engage the fundamental activity of democracy—political debate—because they get "emotionally invested" and then act out in harmful ways. Of course a lot of these people who get "emotionally invested" live beyond the Northeastern corridor, in places that can make Dem-elites uncomfortable.

Massachusetts senator John Kerry sounded like an elite uncomfortable in the heartland when he was running for reelection in 1996. He bemoaned the constant pressure to raise money in American politics: "I'm not suggesting this is a virtuous process. I hate it. I detest it. I hate going to places like Austin and Dubuque to raise large sums of money. But I have to." When cyber-columnist Matt Drudge dug up the story before Kerry traveled to Iowa early in 2003, Kerry spokesman David Wade cried foul. "Obviously, it's such a setup," he charged. It's not small-town America Kerry hates, he said, it's fundraising "that forces senators to spend too much time traveling out of state to raise money." Why Kerry chose to single out Austin and Dubuque rather than simply saying, "I hate going out of state" is perplexing at the very least.

Then there are those pols who allow themselves to be seduced by the elites. "I grew up the son of a teamster and a milk truck driver in St. Louis," Dick Gephardt likes to say on the campaign trail. His parents, Gephardt recalled, saved $20 a month to send him to college. But while Gephardt the candidate claims, "The fight for working families is in my bones," his political life is really an ode to the elites. Both his support of teachers' unions (roadblocks to innovative educational reform that would help the children the Democrats say they care so much about) and his relentless battle against tax cuts, show that Gephardt's views are more in line with professors at Harvard than the people of the American heartland. He pits rich against poor in tax policy, is at the beck and call of labor unions, and touts a "universal health care plan." His claim to fame in the early 1990s was cosponsoring Hillary's socialist health care bill and voting against the Gulf War resolution. And this is supposed to be a guy in tune with working families?

Younger but no less elitist is Democrat John Edwards, big-bucks plaintiff attorney turned North Carolina senator. He describes himself as "moderate" and "somebody who's close to regular people, somebody who understands their problems." Edwards, who made his fortune as a personal injury attorney, branded himself early in the 2004 contest as "a champion" for the "regular folks." You can stop laughing now. No amount of slick marketing will change the fact that Edwards is a liberal (*National Journal* placed Edwards in its "Top 20 Most Liberal Senators List" in 2000), and an inexperienced one at that. His elitism is evident: he is the poster boy for one of America's most pernicious and richest lobbies—the Association of Trial Lawyers of America. It's also evident in that he thinks he's qualified for the presidency after only four years in the U.S. Senate.

Dem-elites sometimes reveal themselves without even knowing it. This happened when Joe and Hadassah Lieberman were on tour to promote their book, *An Amazing Adventure*, about life on the campaign trail. Hadassah, during an interview with radio host Don Imus, mused, "I guess what startled me the most was how incredible a national campaign was, that you had to go out to all of these small towns and see the people. And that is amazing in a democracy, that the people ultimately judge." *Those small towns with all their people . . . and they vote! Can you imagine that? Millions of people out there who have never been to the Museum of Modern Art! They've never browsed the boutiques in SoHo! And they still get to vote! What a country!*

But Democrats are not the only ones with doubts about Middle America. There are also many Republicans who look down on socially conservative, middle-class Americans as being too radical and hard-edged. Elitist "Respectable Republicans" (RRs) pride themselves on their "moderation," "pragmatism," and ability to forge "bipartisan agreements" with their "good friends" the Democrats. The Republican Main Street Partnership was founded in 1998 to give a home to the RRs, of which there are about sixty in Congress, including senators Lincoln Chafee, Olympia Snowe, and Susan Collins. According to its website, the Partnership exists to pursue policies that "reflect a limited, but responsible role for government and that are designed to achieve fiscal responsibility, economic growth, improvements in the human condition and a nation that is globally competitive and secure." It's rumored that they're also for apple pie and motherhood, but they didn't want to get too far out on a limb on those issues, especially motherhood.

The RRs tend to represent comfortably upper-middle-class areas on the coasts and find moral issues such as abortion to be "divisive." As Vermont Senator "Jumpin'" Jim Jeffords announced when he bade adieu to the Republicans: "Looking ahead, I can see more and more instances where I'll disagree with the president on very fundamental issues—the issues of choice, the direction of the judiciary, tax and spending decisions, missile defense, energy and the environment, and a host of other issues, large and small." How profound, especially for a man who six months earlier felt comfortable enough to take money from the Republican Party when he ran for reelection.

Often an RR will identify himself as "fiscally conservative" but "socially liberal," which guarantees him invites to all the right parties attended by all the right people. The RRs are flaming moderates, which means they don't really stand for anything except "pragmatism." This results in favorable press coverage for the RRs. After voting with Senate Democrats to slash the size of the 2003 Bush tax cut proposal, RR Olympia Snowe was the subject of a glowing *Washington Post* profile with the headline: "Maine's Rebel with a Moderate Cause." Reporter Juliet Eilperin described an "unassuming New Englander" whose "determination reflects political savvy." Snowe's "crusade to persuade her peers" will continue despite the "pressure" applied by her party's (dreaded) conservative leadership. You go, girl!

Other RRs include Ohio senators George V. Voinovich and Arizona's John McCain, who sided with Snowe on the budget/tax cut issue. McCain is the king of the "mavericks," the most beloved of the "quirky independents," who forever endeared himself to America's media elite, chatting them up on his "Straight Talk Express" during the 2000 GOP primary campaign. "We are the party of Ronald Reagan, not Pat Robertson," McCain said in a campaign speech in Virginia Beach. "We are the party of Theodore Roosevelt, not the party of special interests. We are the party of Abraham Lincoln, not Bob Jones." You could practically hear the cheers from the elite—finally a Republican was putting those icky religious people in their places.

For elites in both parties, real working people, their way of life, and their beliefs are now the object of ridicule. This is how far we've come in America. Citizens who believe in God, love their country, defend their constitutional rights, protect private property, and want to live free of excessive government intrusion are mocked and suspected. In other words, the kind of people who are the lifeblood of healthy democratic societies—the kind of people most likely to send their kids to fight and die for this country—are now considered by their political elite to be the problem.

**MEDIA.** Others have decisively established that the mainstream media have a pronounced liberal bias. I'm not going to recite their well-known arguments here; what I want to focus on is the sneering attitude displayed by the media elites toward Middle America and its values.

It's bad enough that the majority in major news organizations (newspapers, magazines, television networks) are left-wing, but it's even worse when we the taxpayers are subsidizing the bias. PBS's Bill Moyers is an elite cheerleader who masquerades as a defender of the little guy. One thing that really gets Moyers going is the flag—specifically, when journalists or politicians wear flag pins on their jackets or dresses. "When I see flags sprouting on official lapels, I think of the time in China when I saw Mao's Little Red Book on every official's desk, omnipresent and unread," he intoned during a February 2003 broadcast of his program *Now*. During this program Moyers actually wore a flag pin as a protest of sorts, saying "more galling than anything are all those moralistic ideologues in Washington sporting the flag in their lapels while writing books and running websites and publishing magazines attacking dissenters as un-American." That's your tax dollars at work, Mr. and Mrs. America, because you pay for Moyers's perch at the government-subsidized Public Broadcasting Service. Would the sensitive Mr. Moyers have a problem if reporters or top White House officials wore a UN flag lapel pin instead? And does he have a similar visceral reaction to celebrities who wear colored ribbons for breast cancer or AIDS? Is it any wonder that Moyers is the toast of the New York literary set, a favorite speaker at universities coast to coast?

Moyers may be more obvious in his disdain for American traditions (such as patriotic displays) than most of his colleagues, but his attitude is depressingly representative of their overall dislike of Middle America. Jake Thompson of the *Omaha World-Herald*, who accompanied reporters following then-President Clinton during his first visit to solidly Republican Nebraska in December 2000, captured a fascinating glimpse into the media elite's perception of the rest of the country. It's worth quoting at length:

> The sunrise broke pink along the cloudy horizon when a few sleepy reporters for national newspapers, television and radio networks laid eyes on Nebraska. They saw snow-dusted corn stubble, flat terrain stretching far into the distance. The air was teeth-chattering cold. "This is what I imagine Siberia to be like," said one man who writes for a national newspaper, gazing out the window of the press bus. . . . Others ruminated aloud on the sparse landscape and the outlying neighborhoods of this town of 28,000 [Kearney]. Soon the bus rolled by a police roadblock where a beefy, crew-cut sheriff's deputy stood at the roadside. "His name's Hoss," said one of the press crew. "Yeah, and his partner's name is Big Hoss," another journalist said. "Or just Big-Un." Several reporters chatted back and forth in mock cowboy accents. A writer mused aloud, "What exactly is a cornhusker?" No one answered. The driver, somewhat oblivious to this back-bus critiquing, piped up loudly, "Do you all ever do anything exciting, like go to the Super Bowl?" "This is as good as it gets," a national newspaper writer deadpanned. A few seconds later, one journalist counseled her colleagues, "You know, we have to stop slamming these people when we get to the filing center."

To the elites, "*these people*" might as well live in Turkmenistan. But let's hear from the elites themselves. In the considered opinion of William O'Rourke of the *Chicago Sun-Times*, Bush voters all live in "a large, lopsided horseshoe, a twisted W, made up of primarily the Deep South and the vast, lowly populated upper-far-west states that are filled with vestiges of gun-loving, Ku-Klux-Klan sponsoring, formerly lynching-happy, survivalist-minded, hate-crime perpetrating, non-blue-blooded, rugged individualists."

O'Rourke dubbed this area the "Yahoo Nation," observing that it "contains not one major city, nor one primary center of creative and intellectual density." In contrast, "Al Gore's America is the country's great cities: New York, Boston, Washington, D.C., Chicago, Los Angeles, San Francisco, Philadelphia, Seattle." And so, O'Rourke triumphantly concluded, "if George W. becomes president, he will not have won one center of the thinking America, the teeming centers of creative and intellectual life. It is the clearest rural-cosmopolitan split in modern presidential elections."[1] In other words, the smart elite supports Gore. The stupid people support Bush. Well, all I can say is, give me a rugged, gun-owning, meat-eating, Fox News–watching individualist over an NPR-listening, designer-water drinking, spa-going Manhattanite any day.

**IVORY TOWER ELITES.** The most left-wing of the elites hang their hats, or should I say their berets, at our finest universities and colleges. Both faculty members and administrators tend to believe that America must continually apologize for and make amends for her past. You get the sense that they are always waiting for the next Woodstock. They are obsessed with "diversity"—as long as it's based on race, ethnicity, or sexual preference. Yet intellectual diversity is actually considered by many Ivory Tower elites to be unpleasant and unhelpful. After all, they have worked hard to create and maintain a monochromatic political landscape on campus, and conservative students and faculty have a way of spoiling the politically correct serenity.

At most universities, especially the upper-crust ones, students would be hard-pressed to name five conservative professors out of a faculty of hundreds. The old left-wing guard is still revered for paying its dues at protests and sit-ins. Its members revel in their anti-establishment pasts. But now they *are* the establishment on campus. The real renegades are the conservative students and their handful of professorial patron saints who dare challenge the left-wing pabulum that passes for deep thought.

I thought things were bad when I attended Dartmouth College in the mid-1980s, but today the p.c. police have gone totally bonkers. As liberals have lost ground on key issues such as welfare spending, national health care, the death penalty, and gun rights, the Ivory Tower elites have become angrier, more ruthless, and more intent on maintaining their total domination of political speech on campus. Regardless of what's happening outside their hallowed walls, they are unwavering in their dedication to undermining traditional American values and principles. The type of anti-Americanism popular in elite academic circles refers to Bush as "the real terrorist" and defaces the flag as a symbol of oppression.

The corruption of American scholarship from its original mission of searching for truth in a detached manner into a politicized drive to indoctrinate students *at your expense* was recently summarized by a single comment tacked on to the description for a course at the University of California at Berkeley called "The Politics and Poetics of Palestinian Resistance." It advised that "conservative thinkers are encouraged to seek other sections." In other words, the teacher, Snehal Shingavi, explicitly wished to exclude students who disagreed with his radical anti-Israel views. He had little interest in the pursuit of truth or savoring the cut-and-thrust of open, unfettered debate; to Shingavi, it was all about the politics (and maybe the poetics, I guess).

Unfortunately, most other leftist activists masquerading as "scholars" in academia do not give themselves and their agenda away so clumsily. To these propagandists, America is the enemy and must be "deconstructed" to show that it is nothing but a lie. The professors' duty is to impose their radical views about race, sex, class warfare, history, politics, and philosophy on students, who are taught to reject everything their parents (those not still mired in the slogans of the 1960s) taught them to believe.

**CULTURAL ELITES.** This is a broad category encompassing not only the artistic and literary worlds, but also the class of self-styled intellectuals. Cultural elites regard American values, traditions, and principles as low, embarrassing, and inferior compared with "higher" European ones. Though it's a reach to call some of them "cultured," Hollywood celebrities are also included in this category, because of their touching belief that being famous and rich makes them worth listening to on all issues.

The cultural elites would be funny if they didn't take themselves so seriously. Actually, maybe it's their pomposity that strikes the rest of us as entertaining. Who can resist a smirk at the periodic eruptions from the likes of Barbra Streisand, Sean Penn, and Jessica Lange? David Letterman had it right a few years ago when he observed that Susan Sarandon always seemed angry at *something*. The problem with celebrity elitism is not the idiocy of the ideas that are expressed by the stars—unfortunately, we can't outlaw stupidity—but the blindly arrogant expectation that somehow their views *deserve* to be taken seriously merely because they are famous. Surrounded by phalanxes of bodyguards, hangers-on, and PR flacks, they travel in limousines with blacked-out windows, live in palaces invisible from the road outside, and fly in private jets, while their managers and assistants tell them only what they want to hear. Even those who hail from modest backgrounds, or who toiled for years before "making it," often rapidly transform into spoiled Sunset Boulevard harridans.

Under the circumstances, the metamorphosis of these Cinderellas into Marie Antoinettes is partly understandable, if deplorable. Aspiring actors and actresses who want to hit it big in the biz must follow the rules of the Club. These rules are unwritten, but everyone knows what they are. Rule #1: If you speak about politics, speak as a politically correct liberal. Yes, a few have skirted the rules and still managed to become modern-day megastars (Bruce Willis, Kelsey Grammer, Arnold Schwarzenegger, and Mel Gibson), but their voices are drowned out by their aggressively ignorant colleagues on the left. For the most part, actors, directors, and producers adopt a pre-approved slate of ideological beliefs bearing no resemblance to those of the ordinary Americans who make their lavish lifestyles possible.

Authentic cultural elites—as opposed to semiliterates like Barbra Streisand posing as serious political commentators—are similarly amputated from the "outside world" of Middle America. Whereas entertainment elites are sealed off *physically* by means of limos and velvet ropes, cultural elites like Susan Sontag and Norman Mailer insulate themselves *intellectually* from the masses.

Cultural elites are nastily derisive about their fellow Americans, especially their alleged lack of intellectual capacity and inability to comprehend the deep thoughts of our self-appointed geniuses. Quite a few would prefer to live abroad. "My America is called Europe. It is my place of dreams," Sontag gushed after declaiming upon the awfulness of America's consumer culture. "Most of the things I like are in Europe."[2]

Even as they're dredging up the usual complaints about dumb Americans who shop at Wal-Mart, our cultural elites tend to ignore the unpleasant reality that Europeans are just as consumeristic as Americans, if not more so, but also poorer in terms of standard of living. But the real reason they hate America and love Europe is that over there (especially in France, where Sontag lived for some years), cultural elites are celebrated, not derided as pretentious buffoons. Over here, whenever they say something particularly obtuse or stupid (or both, as is usually the case), someone like me will call them on it.

Americans' alleged "lack of intellectual capacity" also serves as a convenient excuse to explain why their books don't sell. The truth is, of course, that they don't sell because they're turgid, unreadable, and crammed with pseudo-intellectual jargon. Well-written books on medieval and military history, the Greek and Roman classics, literary fiction, and volumes on politics and philosophy—even when they present liberal views—are regularly huge sellers in Borders, Barnes & Noble, Books-a-Million, and on Internet sites like Amazon.com. If Americans are too philistine to read, why did they invent these outlets?

The condescension of people like Sontag and her friends to their "intellectual inferiors" in America is a pose that goes back to at least the beginning of the twentieth century, when middle-class liberal intellectuals first began to notice that "the proletariat masses" were becoming increasingly influential, educated, and literate. Horrified at the thought of the lower orders *enjoying* art, intellectuals tried hard to make their endeavors way too complex for the likes of you and me to understand. Only those initiated into

# Elitespeak alert!

Elites love to talk about Middle America. What they mean by Middle America, however, is that it is the "Middle of Nowhere." It reminds them of those maps of Africa used by nineteenth-century explorers that were blank in the middle—to signify "Terra Incognita," the Unknown Land. The explorers thought cannibals lived there; the elites, on the other hand, believe a mysterious tribe known as *Redneckus Americanus* occupies these strange lands. These fierce natives are conceived to be armed with fire-throwing "guns" and worship an idol named "God." Whenever an elite is forced to visit Middle America (Boise), he will always make sure he carries three things to ward off danger: a copy of the *Village Voice*, complete with listings of all off-off-Broadway productions; a battery-operated radio, tuned to NPR; and an emergency number for Tom Daschle. ∎

"the Club" (i.e., those blessed with properly respectable opinions) could make heads or tails of the new, ultra-highbrow, obscure "modernism" suddenly appearing in art galleries, in poetry collections, and on the stage. Contemptuous of the masses' conservative tastes and their beliefs in religion and morality, the literary class built an unbridgeable moat around itself. Today, the baleful effects can be seen in the artistic community's pretentious, offensive garbage on canvas and the unreadable, jargon-laden books pumped out by academics. As a consequence of their snobbery, liberal intellectuals viciously turned against the "lower classes"—even as they proclaimed about how much they loved them and hated the evil capitalistic system that allegedly exploited them.

For example, Virginia Woolf, the darling of university English departments, whose work is the basis of the movie *The Hours*, is currently the queen of Hollywood. What did she think of her social inferiors? In her diary, she wrote about "a self-taught working-class man," noting "we all know how distressing they are." Women she encountered in a public lavatory were nothing to her but "common little tarts." Witnessing some middle-class women eating cakes in a restaurant, the great novelist mused that they were "scented, shoddy, parasitic," and queried, "Where does the money come [from] to feed these fat white slugs?"

And let's not forget D. H. Lawrence, who despite his apparently Fascist sympathies is also beloved by our liberal elites for his "sensitive" (that is, sex-obsessed) novels like *Lady Chatterley's Lover*. This is the same man who proposed that "all schools be closed at once. The great mass of humanity should never learn to read and write." Our modern elite hasn't actually been able to close the schools, of course. But thanks to the teaching methods they have imposed on a skeptical public, they've ensured that thousands of poor American children will never learn to read and write.

Among some members of the cultural elite, hatred of the lower classes (which includes both the working class and the middle class) grew so consuming that it became murderous and anti-democratic. Many leftist intellectuals, such as Aldous Huxley (author of *Brave New World*), became obsessed with destroying popular democracy and replacing it with a socialist central government run by people like himself (who, presumably, "knew best"). After all, Huxley believed that "about 99.5 percent of the entire population of the planet are stupid and philistine." Since nothing could be done about their "appalling imbecility," it was crucial that the remaining 0.5 percent (which included himself and his buddies) "dominate the rest." Then there's H. G. Wells, author of such classics as *The Time Machine* and *The War of the Worlds*, who felt popular patriotism and religious belief "caused" war and thus agitated for an atheist world government. Not surprisingly, both men loathed Christianity, and Wells was asked by no less a personage than Eleanor Roosevelt to leave the United States during the 1930s on account of his burning anti-Semitism.

How was Wells's proposed world government "domination" to be achieved? As early as 1901, decades before Hitler's genocide, Wells was writing that the mentally and physically unfit must be exterminated. The "swarms of black, and brown, and dirty-white, and yellow people" in Africa and Asia will "have to go." In Europe, the "vicious, helpless and pauper masses," "the weak and silly and pointless" and "the lumpish, unteachable, unimaginative people" must be annihilated in a "merciful obliteration" through disease, starvation, and execution. The playwright George Bernard Shaw agreed with his colleague that "extermination must be put on a scientific basis if it is ever to be carried out humanely and apologetically as well as thoroughly.... If we desire a certain type of civilization and culture, we must exterminate the sort of people who do not fit into it."

Now, it also goes without saying that today's liberal intellectuals don't often use the wild-eyed eugenic rhetoric employed by Wells and Shaw—though they are just as willing to stand up for euthanasia and abortion—but we can still pick out several general strains of their thought that have miraculously survived to the present day.

Note the continuing contempt for regular people and the way they wish to live their lives, the same antireligious ideology, the faith in an imposed "world government," and the distrust of democracy.

**BUSINESS ELITES.** As I said, being an elite is not necessarily about being a liberal and/or a Democrat. There are plenty of capitalist elites atop some of America's greatest corporations who advance their company's financial interests by sacrificing American ones. Indeed, the *Wall Street Journal*, a fine newspaper in many ways, has an editorial board obsessed with "open borders" and making immigration standards even looser than they already are. On a broader level, since September 11 the gulf between elite and public views of immigration have widened considerably. Most Americans instinctively recognize that unrestricted immigration benefits wealthy Americans at the expense of the rest of us, because a significant increase in the labor supply will inevitably drive down the price of that labor. But the elites—who rarely have to worry about losing *their* jobs, or about any economic problem more serious than which offshore island represents the best tax haven—benefit from the cheaper labor provided by illegal immigrants, and so they aren't really moved by such concerns.

It was not so long ago that the *Wall Street Journal* had a tradition of printing an editorial each Independence Day calling for a five-word constitutional amendment: "There shall be open borders." There was even a rumor that the opinion pages had an unwritten ban on publishing freelance op-eds contradicting the official policy of allowing virtually unrestricted immigration, "legalizing" illegal entry, and authorizing an amnesty for undocumented workers.[3] Needless to say, since September 11, the *Journal* has toned down the "Hey, party at our place!" rhetoric owing to the risk that budding Islamist terrorists might take advantage of such largesse. Even so, the *Journal* occasionally reverts to form, as it did when it editorialized in favor of extending the Section 245(i) program that allows certain foreign applicants to pay $1,000 to accelerate processing of their forms to achieve permanent residency status. Otherwise, applicants had to return to their native countries and await a lengthy scrutiny of their backgrounds, which might turn up a criminal record. Though getting dewy-eyed at the thought of hardworking undocumented workers being reunited with their families thanks to Section 245(i), the *Journal* inaccurately claimed that the program applied only to immigrants who had entered the country legally and to those whose visas had expired or were about to. Actually, Section 245(i) also covered those who entered the United States illegally, had worked here illegally, or had failed to keep their legal status continuously—categories that included several of the September 11 hijackers, the plotters behind the first World Trade Center bombing in 1993, and the New York subway bombing conspirators.[4]

The most strikingly elitist aspect of the *Wall Street Journal's* editorial stance is not that it favors essentially unrestricted immigration to help its friends in the business community, but how arrogantly it dismisses those who disagree with its proposals as nativist, closed-minded, and anti–free market. This type of elitism is a far cry from the virulent *anti*-Americanism of the left; if anything, it is a touchy-feely *post*-Americanism of the right. The obsession of the *Journal* and some of its "globalized" corporate advertisers with eradicating American borders with NAFTA countries, allowing the free movement of peoples back and forth, and eroding our sovereign power to choose who enters this country signals their willingness to dilute American-ness for the sake of internationalism. President Vicente Fox of Mexico—the *Journal's* amigo magnifico—summed up the post-American elitist mentality when he declared that "by building up walls, by putting up armies, by dedicating billions of dollars like every border state is doing to avoid migration, is not the way to go."

The tough question we need to ask is: Why is it not the way to go? I can see the advantages of such a deal from Fox's angle: he can divert Mexico's excess labor force northwards to work in such minimum-wage jobs as looking after the elites' children, painting elites' houses, mowing the elites' lawns, and cleaning elites' homes. But from *our* point of view, the power of the independent nation-state to ensure its own citizens' best interests is the cornerstone of its existence. That's the whole point of spending billions on training our military and maintaining our borders. If that power is surrendered or compromised, then the nation-state is finished. Let's not let that happen to America.

There is an unpleasant whiff of elitist post-Americanism emanating from other parts of our business community. Mark Krikorian of the Center for Immigration Studies has noted that several high-ranking executives have renounced their American citizenship to exploit tax advantages. For example, John Dorrance III, a billionaire Campbell Soup heir, became an Irish citizen, while Michael Dingman, a director of Ford Motor Company, became a proud Bahamian citizen. In 1993 alone, 306 well-heeled Americans became "voluntary expatriates," as the euphemism goes, thanks to clever lawyers. Yes, U.S. estate taxes are way too high (they are zero in the Bahamas) and the tax code ridiculously Byzantine, but surely buying another country's citizenship to save some money is not something to be applauded.

Some American corporations are lured into the similar temptation of setting up tax shelters in Bermuda by establishing brass-plate "headquarters" abroad to avoid taxes. Republican Senator Charles E. Grassley of Iowa, who with Democrat Senator Max Baucus of Montana introduced bills in 2002 to end the practice, noted that "during a war on terrorism, coming out of a recession, everyone ought to be pulling together. If companies don't have their hearts in America, they ought to get out."[5]

The tax scam is a minor problem compared with the greater moral issue of corporations forsaking their American-ness by embracing "globalist culture." There is nothing wrong with globalization; in fact, I'm all for it, but globalization should be about free trade bringing mutual economic benefits, not erasing every hint of national identity. Ralph Nader (for all his faults, Mr. Nader is genuinely non-elitist) caught these companies with their pants down back in 1996. He wrote to the CEOs of America's hundred biggest corporations asking them to recite the Pledge of Allegiance (including the phrase, "one nation under God") before their annual stockholder meetings on behalf of the *corporation*.

About sixty CEOs responded. All—apart from one, Federated Department Stores (which operates Bloomingdale's and Macy's)— either rejected the idea, promised to "review" it, or were noncommittal. Ford Motor Company secretary John Rintamaki went so far as to state, "We do not believe that the concept of 'corporate allegiance' is possible." Other respondents thought the scheme too "political and nationalistic" for such global citizens as themselves. August Busch III of Anheuser-Busch replied that "while our company headquarters remains in St. Louis, we are a global company." Really? That's not how your ads market you. Same with Kodak, which felt that the company must "maintain a global perspective to compete effectively in a global economy." Granted, Kodak needs to compete effectively in the global economy, but how does that preclude its chairman opening up its annual meeting with a pledge to the very country that has allowed it to prosper? Others thought asking for a pledge was tantamount to totalitarianism. "Demanding recitations of allegiance—in language that may not reflect the beliefs of all persons present—is actually contrary to the principles on which our democracy was founded," said Aetna's Dick Huber. Unlike Huber, Caterpillar, Inc. didn't get on its political soapbox, concluding simply that "a symbolic once-a-year gesture would not be a productive use of our time at our stockholders meeting." How long does reciting the Pledge of Allegiance take? Twenty seconds, maybe?[6] Now, Nader's gambit could be interpreted as a publicity stunt to elicit "loyalty oaths," but nevertheless the point was made: A core business elite exists whose ethos is that what's good for *it* doesn't have to be good for America.

**WORLD CITIZEN ELITES.** Hang out for any length of time at an "anti-war" protest in the United States and you're sure to hear some of the scruffy speakers inciting "citizens of the world" to action. They don't identify themselves as American citizens because these global elites consider the concept of national identity pernicious—except when used to declare personal victimization. They're embarrassed to be Americans.

These citizens of the world often work, when they do feel like working, for nongovernmental organizations (NGOs) that have become increasingly powerful since the end of the Cold War. These international nonprofit groups work hand in glove with the UN to help execute its multilateralist agenda.

On the one hand, NGOs do a great deal of good and so does the UN. NGO staffs volunteer for risky tasks in war zones and provide aid for those in deprived countries. The UN provides a diplomatic forum for every country in the world to have its say.

On the other hand, NGOs and the UN pose a special sort of danger to Middle America. They are committed to "globalism" (as opposed to economic "globalization"), which is fundamentally anti-American. Globalism seeks to demolish American sovereignty, erode our independence of action, interfere in our domestic affairs, and denigrate our values and traditions.

Those employed by the big international NGOs and the UN can be suspected of having a conflict of interest: Are they loyal to their country of origin or to the cause of globalism? By their very nature, NGOs are, well, nongovernmental, which means they cannot be identified with the policies of any government. Neither are they accountable to any government, let alone answerable to a democratic electorate. In fact, NGOs owe their allegiance to no one but themselves. Just because NGOs are nongovernmental doesn't mean they're nonpolitical. Nearly all of them, and certainly the larger ones, are profoundly left-wing—though they would never admit it. NGOs have their own agendas, in other words. Amnesty International, Greenpeace, and Human Rights Watch are biased political organizations masquerading as "nonpartisan" watchdogs for the cause of globalism. Their vaunted "independence" is only a moralistic cover for their anti-American activities. This assumption that they are too high-minded for any democratic supervision whatsoever is elitism at its most abhorrent.

No wonder they cozy up to the UN. Sometimes it seems like there's a mutual UN-NGO support group *against* nation-states.

As for the UN, it is turning into the nucleus of an elitist, globalized government run by NGOs in which we are "global citizens" living happily under "global law." Jimmy Carter, our former president who did such a fantastic job messing up everything that he almost lost to Ted Kennedy, of all people, enunciated globalistic aims in his Nobel Peace Prize speech. First he made clear that he was "not here as a public official, but as a citizen of a troubled world." Not as an American, Jimmy? Then he cheered on the UN by saying that under its auspices, the "international community" has "struggled to negotiate global agreements."[7]

Carter was being a bit sneaky about the Great Global Gameplan. The former president's globalism leads him perilously close to favoring unelected bureaucrats and full-time activists from the "international community" over a democratic government presiding over the richest, most powerful, and freest country in world history.

These are the elites. They have big plans for us. Are you ready?

# 2

# When It All Started to Go South

How did we get into this mess? How did we get to a point where a significant percentage of the American population wants America to be torn down, tradition by tradition? How did we come to feel defensive about who we are and what we stand for? How did doing things the "American way" become something so many Americans find revolting? How did so many come to have a greater affinity for the views of anti-Americans abroad than they do for their fellow citizens?

The answer is that we created this monster elite class.

The elites didn't wake up one morning, realize George W. Bush was in the White House, and go berserk. There wasn't one event that triggered this wave of elite anger and self-loathing. It has been building, morphing, and spreading for a very long time. Most would think it all began in the 1960s, but surprisingly enough, today's poisonous elites have their roots in the antebellum South.

## SWEET HOME MANHATTAN

To our modern elites, the South is the font of all evil. It's a place where racist rednecks rule and the *Jerry Springer Show* trawls trailer parks for fat, stupid inbreds. The elites who don't hesitate to slip into (bad) Southern drawls to ridicule Southerners are, of course, the first ones to scream "Racist!" when someone dares criticize a black radical, or "Sexist!" whenever NOW is called to the mat. These are the same people who always scream "Intolerance!" but to them, slurs against the "redneck South" are not just tolerated, they are encouraged. Mocking the pickup truck–driving, tobacco-chewing, shotgun-owning South is one of the elite rites of passage.

But remember, to the elites, you don't have to live in the South to be a stupid redneck. It's all about your state of mind. To them, we are all Southerners now.

To the elites, the South, even decades after the last of the Jim Crow laws were abandoned, still represents everything that is wrong with life in America. It's teeming with Jerry Falwell clones who are a bunch of mindlessly patriotic, instinctively racist, NRA fanatics. They couldn't possibly understand the nuances of life in a complex, multicultural, multi-ethnic world. If you are living out-side the New York–Washington, D.C.–Los Angeles–San Francisco orbit, then you are living in *Deliverance* country. If elites don't come to the rescue, then homicidal, incestuous hillbillies and weird-looking kids who play the banjo will soon populate the entire country.

To elites, the South, like the Midwest or anywhere in Middle America, is as distant as the moon. William Faulkner captured this attitude perfectly in *Absalom, Absalom!* (which was published in 1936 but is set mostly in the nineteenth century), when Canadian Shreve McCannon quizzes his Mississippian roommate about Southern life. "Tell about the South. What's it like there," he asks. "What do they do there. Why do they live there. Why do they live at all." As I said, this stereotyping of the South goes back a long way.

But wait a minute! You might be thinking: What about Clinton and Gore? What about Jimmy Carter? What about Bill Moyers and Dan Rather and Howell Raines (ousted editor of the *New York Times*), for gosh sakes? Aren't they Southerners? Aren't they

# **Elite**speak **alert!**

Bill Moyers, Dan Rather, and Howell Raines: The acceptable faces of the South, primarily because they periodically apologize for being from there. They are the token Southerners among the elite, which prides itself on its exclusive inclusiveness. Everyone else regards them as bores. ■

beloved by elites? Of course they are—the elites will always make room for self-hating Southerners who mouth the elite message with a twang. What elites won't tolerate—what they can't tolerate—are people with attitudes that are truly *popular* in the South. They can stand Gore because Tennessee wouldn't vote for him in 2000. They can stand Jimmy Carter because he's constantly feuding with Southern Baptists.

This was even true for Bill Clinton, whom elites liked to think of as a smarter, more liberal version of Elvis. One of the most amazing facts about Clinton is that the more you had in common with him, the less likely you were to vote for him. If you were a Manhattan socialite, a Hollywood lefty, a Silicon Valley mogul type, or an African-American professor, you were a Clintonite. But if you were a middle-aged white Baptist from the South married to your first wife, which is a description of Clinton himself, you almost certainly despised the man. Think about how strange that is. Imagine if African-Americans from Chicago didn't support Jesse Jackson, or Irish-Americans from Boston didn't support the Kennedys. In American politics, your base is almost always the people *who are the most like you*. But this rule didn't apply to Clinton. Ambitious Southerners have to decide between the elites and their hometowns. If they're popular at home—like Trent Lott or Phil Gramm—they're despised on the coasts. If they're the toast of New York—like Clinton and Gore—they're seen as traitors at home.

Ironically, Southerners themselves invited many of the stereo-types the modern elites use to mock the South. In the antebellum South, the white elite "plantation class" looked down its nose at both its black slaves and the landless whites later known as "white trash." The belief was that these whites were descended primarily from the lower classes of the British Isles, where they had resided either in the poorhouses or in prison. The Southern elite view at the time depicted these poor whites as shambling, lazy, hunched, misshapen creatures with rotten teeth.

Not welcome in the established churches, many poor whites turned to fire-and-brimstone evangelical preachers for spiritual nourishment. And so the stereotype evolved of malformed, illiter-ate, racist, violent, gun-toting, genetically inbred hillbillies (many of these whites fled to the hills where land was cheaper) with a fanatical passion for Bible-beating, intolerant Christianity. After the Civil War, this once purely Southern stereotype traveled to the North, where the ancestors of our modern-day elites picked it up.

So the next time you hear some p.c. "intellectual" making cracks about trailer parks, tell him he's drawing on stereotypes popularized by slaveholders! He's ridiculing people for being poor, as if it's some sort of crime. How does that jibe with his so-called compassion?

The constant sneering condescension, that poor Southern whites are forced to endure, is exacerbated by their insistence on maintaining their traditional religious beliefs. Somehow, they didn't get the memo stating that the twentieth century was sup-posed to represent the end of fervent religious belief. A recent poll of Southern attitudes found that 75 percent said "religious faith is extremely or very important in my life" (the figure was 63 percent for non-Southerners).[1]

The larger issue of the elites' religious bias will be discussed in a later chapter, but before we get much further it is critical to understand that the fear of religion—especially the Judeo-Christ-ian tradition—is a driving force behind the elite agenda. The elites want people to rely on *their* infinite wisdom—not some guy who doesn't even read the *New Yorker*. When they say, with bumper sticker originality, "separation of church and state," what they really mean is the elimination of church, and the expansion of state. (The state as run by them, of course.)

## MENCKEN AND THE MONKEY BUSINESS

It was that Southern religiosity that led to one of the most vicious literary assaults on any single group in American history. H. L. Mencken became a hero to generations of elites through his newspaper reporting on the "Scopes Monkey Trial." Uninterested in the subtleties of the debate over evolution—completely indifferent to the concerns of those who felt their traditional religious teachings to be in danger from teachers who despised them and their culture—Mencken gleefully seized upon the case to mock and ridicule everything he could find in the South. We owe the popularization of the phrase "white trash" to Mencken. He also coined the phrase "Bible Belt" to describe the "bigoted" South. In true elite fashion, Mencken approved of the elitist antebellum South of the slaveholders but couldn't stand the postwar South, where power had devolved to the despised white trash.

The 1925 "Monkey Trial" was ostensibly about the battle between teaching creationism versus the theory of evolution in Tennessee schools. When the schools banned the teaching of evolution, the ACLU kicked into action. It advertised for volunteers to get themselves arrested for teaching evolution, and then offered to pay for their defense. John Scopes, a math teacher turned biologist, accordingly violated the statute, and the ACLU sent Clarence Darrow to represent him. The prosecutor was William Jennings Bryan, a devout Presbyterian and three-time Democrat presidential nominee. Bryan was sometimes known as the Great Commoner for his outspoken defense of populist ideas against the elites of his time, and spent most of his career crusading for many causes we think of as liberal. He spoke out against the distribution of wealth resulting from laissez-faire capitalism. He pleaded with Americans not to use their power to bully smaller countries. His pacifism was so strong that he resigned as secretary of state for President Wilson because he feared Wilson would lead the country into World War I. But Mencken, who despised the poor people Bryan fought for, saw him as nothing more than a cartoon figure.

**Elite**speak **alert!**

The ACLU: dauntless fighter for freedom... well, at least the elites' freedom to dominate the rest of us. ∎

To Mencken, the trial was a clear-cut case of tolerance, progress, urban sophistication, and secularism (Darrow) versus country backwardness, religion, tradition, and conservatism (Bryan). Mencken's "reporting" from Dayton, Tennessee, reeked of prejudice and elitism:

- About Bryan: "[H]e has been oozing around the country since his first day here, addressing this organization and that, presenting the indubitable Word of God in his caressing, ingratiating way."

- More on Bryan: "He has these hillbillies locked up in his pen and he knows it.... They understand his peculiar imbecilities. His nonsense is their ideal of sense."

- He referred to the "the so-called minds of these fundamentalists of upland Tennessee," and at other times, dismissed the townspeople as "morons," "yokels," and "Neanderthals."

Reading these quotes, you have to wonder whether Mencken—and the elites who laughed over his insults—was motivated by love of science or love of snobbery. Speaking of evolution, why is it that the elites haven't evolved much in their own stale thinking? Any one of Mencken's insults from 1925 would work perfectly in a cocktail party conversation among the elites today. They repeat the same snickering about religion, the same slurs about stupidity, and the same lies about bigotry. So much for having a monopoly on tolerance.

## BLACK DOVE DOWN

Yet overt elitism of the Mencken sort took a breather during the Depression and World War II. The ravages of war and poverty brought the nation together—and God was more important than ever. East Coast millionaires didn't seem so smart after the stock market collapsed in 1929, and elites of any stripe no doubt found it awkward to mock the common men who were dying for their country by the thousands in places like Guadalcanal and Italy. Men from Savannah and New York fought side by side in the Pacific. Their boots hit the same beaches in Normandy. There was little room in the national conversation for elite mockery.

Nevertheless, the end of "the Good War" brought new tensions between the elites and Middle America. In the late 1940s, most Americans were horrified to learn that high-ranking members of our government had been active members of the Communist Party, and there was widespread interest when Congress began investigating Communist influence in American life. But the elites—many of whom had dabbled in communism (or at least socialism) during the hard years of the 1930s—were appalled to find people like themselves called on the carpet for their political beliefs. They immediately spun the story in their own way, seizing upon the extreme actions of Senator Joseph McCarthy to paint Middle America's fear of Communism as a demonic witch hunt. The "common man"—so celebrated in the 1930s and 1940s by FDR, Carl Sandberg, John Steinbeck, and countless WPA paintings—once more became the dangerous boob attacked by Mencken.

Later, tensions between the elites and Middle America grew during Vietnam and the civil rights movement. By the time the baby boom generation began to come of age in the late 1960s, the patriotism of their parents was suddenly passé. From their perches of relative comfort, many in this new generation decided to protest against an America they believed reflected the values of Archie Bunker. This was the birth of a new elite that snubbed the country for which their fathers had fought and died.

The liberal journalist James Fallows once wrote that in Harvard's Class of 1941, thirty-five men died in World War II, among the hundreds in active duty. But by 1970 (Fallows's class), things had changed dramatically. Military service was by then something that "other people" did. Few served their country, and a very small percentage reported having *any* contact with the military.

Because the elites refused to participate, the burden of military service was increasingly shoved onto the shoulders of low-income whites, lower-class blacks, poor Southerners, and Hispanic immigrants. The elites, meanwhile, anxious to avoid the draft, headed off to graduate school. They would go on to become trial lawyers, public interest "advocates," journalists, or college professors. Many of the elites dodged a bullet (literally) and took the easy way out: denigrating those who did fight as "baby-killers," "genocidal," and "racists." Republican elites who didn't serve at least waved American—rather than Vietcong—flags.

## SQUEAL LIKE AN ELITE, BOY!

The 1960s radicals equated American traditions and reviled the South. To leftist agitators, law-abiding, churchgoing, quiet, ordinary Americans were now square, out-of-touch, closet bigots who needed reeducating. (Remember the slogan: "If you're not part of the solution, you're part of the problem!") Ungrateful undergrads at the best universities thought it was cool to call working-class policemen "pigs."

The bumper sticker "Question Authority" became the mantra of a new generation that believed our elected leaders were not merely wrong or mistaken but fundamentally evil. To them, American actions at home and around the world were tainted, corrupt, patriarchal, racist, and illegitimate. America was a hellhole compared with the wonderful Soviet Union and Mao's paradise in China during the Cultural Revolution. College students were no longer content to engage in civilized debate; they supported a full-blown revolution.

Yet for all their bluster and the lavish media coverage they received, the views of the 1960s radicals, even in their heyday, represented little more than a fringe movement. Only 10 percent of Americans supported withdrawal from Vietnam as late as November 1967, while just 5 percent of the population had tried marijuana. The closest thing America ever had to a vote on the radical agenda was the 1972 election between evil warmongering Republican Richard Nixon and hippie favorite George McGovern. It wasn't close. Nixon carried forty-nine states—including McGovern's home state of South Dakota—and garnered 520 electoral college votes, compared with his rival's seventeen. Even then, the elites convinced themselves that somehow Nixon had cheated. There was no way a golden boy like McGovern could be beaten by a lower-class nobody like Tricky Dicky! Pauline Kael, the *New Yorker's* film critic, famously wondered how on earth Nixon had won, since absolutely *no one* she knew had voted for him. Of course many ordinary Americans knew nobody who had voted for McGovern.

While the country is divided politically today, the elites who cut their teeth at the antiwar rallies thirty years ago still haven't made much headway in persuading the nation that American power is inherently dangerous, and that American intentions are inherently suspect. When Operation Iraqi Freedom finally began, polls showed at least 77 percent of Americans supporting it, while in March 2003 a record 58 percent said the UN was doing a "poor job." (And despite all the elite attempts to smear the justification for the war, most Americans believe we did the right thing.)

But if they aren't numerous, how did the elites manage to entrench themselves so deeply into American culture? The answer lies in the rise of a "professional class" since 1945. After World War II, young professionals flocked to comfortable civil servant positions and corporate jobs. Their children went to good colleges, where they dabbled in the new protest culture. After graduation, they took jobs as consultants, analysts, journalists, activists, producers, art directors, publicists, professors, entrepreneurs, advertising executives, authors, and foundation heads. Their 1960s experience formed their adult political outlooks.

By the 1990s, their messiah had finally come! "One of them" was finally running the show. Bill Clinton was in the White House and they couldn't "stop thinking about tomorrow," a tomorrow that brought back the glory and idealism of their youth. Money for nothing and the chicks for free! Much of the harsh rhetoric was gone, but one thing wasn't—their unflinching belief in their own intellectual and moral superiority. As early as 1974, Fallows detected an arrogance forming among the new elite, which "constantly fret[ted] about how to make the public overcome white backlash, support the UN, and conserve energy by obeying the fifty-five-mile-per-hour speed limit."

More than twenty-five years later, and after eight years of their boy Clinton using the nation's bully pulpit, the elites are still "fretting" about anemic support for the UN and the imaginary specter of endemic white "racism" against minorities. (Their man from Hope didn't deliver them to the political promised land after all, and we can even drive sixty-five miles an hour these days.) Today their list of grievances goes way beyond America's "illegitimate" wars. The elites of today want to regulate everything from what we eat to where we pray. Those who challenge this continuing attempt to remake American society into a socialist paradise are branded "out of the mainstream" or "intolerant." We the American Electorate are a major inconvenience to the elites, because we still believe that Americans shouldn't be ashamed of who they are and where they came from. We the American Electorate are the only thing standing in the way of their Brave New World, where America leaves behind its cowboy past, and becomes a compliant member of the global village.

As wonderful as winning elections would be, America's elite knows that they have other ways to have enormous influence over pesky voters. Many of their gains since the 1960s have been achieved nondemocratically. By inserting themselves into unaccountable but pivotal positions (in the media, universities, Hollywood, nongovernmental organizations, and the courts), the elites exercise anti-American cultural, political, legal, and social influence far out of proportion to their numbers.

## OUR GRASS IS DEFINITELY GREENER

The poor dears. One understands the elites' zealous commitment to dominate the legal, entertainment, and educational arenas when one sees just how badly their message fares in the heartland. The elites seethe as we, the people, hold the majority. While they continue to exert a stranglehold on the media and the universities and elsewhere, they are losing ground—geographically and electorally.

Of course the elites will always deny this. They put forward a confident, optimistic attitude. Before the 2002 midterm elections, liberal commentators John Judis and Ruy Teixeira predicted resounding success for the elites. In their book, *The Emerging Democratic Majority*, they predicted that Americans living in "ideopolises" (their word for large metropolitan areas) would swamp the GOP in coming years. These ideopolis inhabitants are educated professionals with "progressive centrist" politics that "reflect the outlook of the social movements that first arose during the '60s." These are the elites who work in the high-tech industry (or what's left of it), universities, social services, and the government.[2]

"Ideopolis" is just a fancy word for "Blue America," the phrase popularized by writer David Brooks (among others) for the areas that voted Gore in 2000. "Red America," on the other hand, is Bush Country.[3] (I always thought the colors should be switched—red for the coastal elites, blue for the rest of the country.)

"Democrats have made their greatest gains in the nation's very largest metropolitan areas," wrote political sage Michael Barone. These places are filled with "sophisticated, cynical, secular voters" living in the largest U.S. cities—New York, Los Angeles, Chicago, San Francisco, Philadelphia, Boston, and Detroit. These elite havens also happen to be places where abortion rights and gun control are regarded as the gifts of God (not that She exists, of course).[4]

Lavish incomes are the norm, too. Even as they rail against evil corporations and wealth inequality, the ideopolis elites are thriving financially. These include the "super-rich," individuals like Ted Turner and Bill Gates, who at times seem to be tormented by their own success. Turner's left-wing political and environmental views are well known—who can forget the $1 billion pledge he made to the United Nations? (Hard to know which is a worse investment—AOL Time Warner or the UN.) Gates is not as flamboyant as Turner, but his politics are just as liberal. He opposed the Washington State ballot initiative 602 (which proposed an immediate tax rollback); he supported Initiative 676 (gun control); and he has given millions to support Planned Parenthood and "reproductive health and family planning" (which used to be known as "population control").[5] His dad also helped lead the fight to preserve the estate tax.

So the elites have many of the super-rich on their side, and they own the big cities, but that still has not given them the political power they crave. Crucially, notes Barone, the "major metro areas are *casting a declining share of the nation's votes* (italics mine), while fast-growing counties beyond metro-edge cities, with family-size subdivisions and megachurches, are heavily Republican."[6] At this rate, the elites' influence will be limited almost entirely to the big cities. In elite lingo, they will be "effectively contained."

Let's take a closer look at the land of big churches and family-friendly subdivisions. Termed "Sprinkler Cities" by David Brooks, they are suburbs of suburbs experiencing astounding growth as Americans move there to escape high taxes, bad schools, and the ludicrous house prices caused by an influx of bankers and lawyers. In about a year, the population of Douglas County, Colorado, jumped by 13.6 percent, while Irving, Texas, has exploded by 7,211 percent since the 1950s. Towns like Mesa, Arizona, have tripled in population in less than a decade—Mesa is now home to 400,000 people, making it larger than Minneapolis, St. Louis, or Cincinnati.

There is no way on earth the elites can keep up with this massive shift. By definition, elites can never outnumber common folk, and increasingly, the common folk are escaping those metropolitan areas in which the elites are concentrated. In the Sprinkler Cities outside of the major cities, Republican registrations easily outnumber Democrat ones, sometimes by as much as a factor of four times. During the 1990s, downtown Atlanta grew by 23,000, but its suburbs welcomed no fewer than 1.1 million people. In fact, the combined population of the ideopolises constitutes only 28 percent of Americans, with another half—repeat, *half*—living in suburbs, and the rest in the (already heavily Republican) rural areas. Imagine Atlanta happening on a national scale. It would be an elite nightmare.

The suburbs of America are also where you can actually find true multiculturalism. Today's suburbs contain more "nonfamily households" (e.g., young singles, empty nesters, and retired couples) than traditional two-parent, two-kids-and-a-dog families. You wouldn't know it from reading the *New York Times* or watching Peter Jennings, but most Asian-Americans, half of the Hispanic population, and 40 percent of American blacks live in the suburbs.[7]

Just as remarkably, the growth of the suburbs has obscured the massive numbers of young blacks reversing the twentieth century's Great Migration to the North. Every year, tens of thousands return to the South their parents and grandparents left. Only it's not the Old South but the New South. Between 1915 and 1960, more than 6 million blacks departed for northern cities like Chicago, Detroit, Pittsburgh, and Cleveland. But their descendants are finding that northern cities are actually far more (unofficially) segregated than almost anywhere down south. Between 1995 and 2000 alone, more than 210,000 blacks moved to southern states, according to University of Michigan demographer William Frey. "These are new hubs of places creating new jobs, [and] these are areas that have a growing black middle class," Frey says. Atlanta, Memphis, Dallas, and Orlando are all experiencing a boom in black migration.[8] For comparison's sake, check out Milwaukee. There, "you can basically take a marker and map out the white boundaries and the black boundaries," said Genyne Edwards, twenty-nine, an African-American lawyer living there.[9]

## THEY COULDA BEEN CONTENDERS

In the run-up to the November 2002 midterm elections, Democrat strategists mistakenly believed that Bush's presidential victory was a fluke impossible to repeat. *This* time, they said, we've got him. *This* time Democrats would gain seats in the U.S. House and Senate and push the White House onto the defensive. On the surface, their expectations looked realistic. After all, the stock market was plummeting, the economy was spluttering along, an Iraqi war was in the offing, and even Bush's sky-high popularity rating was taking hits.

The Dems took heart, comparing polls conducted in January/February 2002 and September/October 2002. At the beginning of the year, no fewer than *46 percent* of voters in the swing "weak Gore" states (i.e., those in which Al narrowly won in 2000) wanted the GOP to gain control of Congress, compared with just 39 percent favoring the Democrats. As for the president, even in the "weak Gore" states he was bagging 71 percent job-approval ratings. By the fall, however, these same voters were coming home: now 50 percent of "weak Gore" voters wanted the Democrats running Congress, while GOP support had slipped to 40 percent. If the trend continued into November, predicted Dems, Bush would be heading for a very nasty upset.[10]

Of course it was Daschle and Gephardt who were left stunned by the midterm results. Since the Civil War, only two presidents have won additional House and Senate seats in their first term—FDR in 1934 and Bush in 2002. Bush's feat is more impressive. FDR not only had crushed presidential nominee Herbert Hoover in 1932, but also already had enormous Democrat majorities in the House and Senate. Bush, on the other hand, came back from a controversial presidential election (remember all those "Bush is not my president" and "Re-elect Gore" bumper stickers?), had to limp along with just a small majority in the House, and was forced to contend with a Democrat-controlled Senate, thanks to Jumpin' Jim Jeffords of Vermont.[11]

Once again, Democrat hopes were dashed. While the GOP's victory seems narrow, it actually represents a devastating defeat for Democrats. For decades, one of the most consistent rules of American politics has been the importance of economic issues. Conventional wisdom suggests that enough swing voters will vote on economic concerns that such issues will usually trump everything else. And for two elections in a row, the economic issues seemed to help the Democrats. In 2000, they could run on a strong record of prosperity. In 2002, they could blame Bush for economic problems. *But both times they lost.* There's a term for a political movement that can't win even when the economy is on its side—it's called a "loser."

More evidence of this fact can be seen in polling data showing that even in "weak Bush" states, the president's support hadn't slipped at all. In fact, it had risen by a few points. And in "Bush country," the Dems didn't have a chance. "Virtually all of the culturally conservative areas of the country" were locked down for the GOP in those midterms, Ronald Brownstein of the *Los Angeles Times* observed. Middle America simply would not vote for the Democrats, even during times of economic difficulty. Even in the affluent, socially liberal elite strongholds, the Democrats only held on by their fingernails.

What happened in Georgia in 2002 demonstrates the Democrats' dilemma. For more than a century, Georgia had not elected a Republican governor. Sonny Perdue surprised everyone by upsetting the Democrat incumbent. Perdue garnered 248,000 more votes this time than did his GOP predecessor in 1998. "Perdue gained some ground in rural and small-town counties," Brownstein noted. "But mostly he benefited from doubled or even quadrupled margins in the exurban counties surrounding Atlanta—rapidly growing and culturally conservative communities on the crab-grass frontier between the countryside and the most distant suburbs." That's the wave of the future, the tsunami that threatens an electoral wipeout of the elites.

There were similar tales in Minnesota and even California. Walter Mondale brought in Minneapolis and St. Paul but really got hammered in the ring of exurban counties outside the Twin Cities. Republican Norm Coleman picked up a tidal wave of votes in counties previously sympathetic to Gore. And how about California? "Democrat Governor Gray Davis was routed in the more culturally conservative inland—from Sacramento and Fresno to San Bernardino and Riverside—and was left clinging to a thin sliver of socially liberal coastal counties, like a man hanging on a ledge."[12] Of course the elites couldn't keep up the charade for long as California citizens organized a historic effort to recall Davis.

So the elites' grip on that ledge is getting weaker and weaker. But it's on the less-reported local level that GOP dominance is particularly marked: Republicans gained more than 120 seats in state legislatures, and now hold a majority of *all* seats nationwide. In twenty-two states, Republicans control both state houses, compared with the Democrats' seventeen and another ten divided between the parties. (Nebraska's unicameral legislature is officially nonpartisan, but is under de facto GOP control.) Sooner or later, those ten divided state legislatures are going to tip to the Republicans and the Dems will be pushed into smaller and smaller playpens.

In short, the Dems have already paid a big political price for the 1960s radicalization that turned them against Middle America. The New Deal coalition that governed this country for almost forty years after 1932 rested on a celebration of the common man. FDR and Truman were master populists, and even John F. Kennedy was careful not to offend the sensibilities of Middle America. Their Democratic Party was proudly—even boisterously—patriotic. Their Democratic Party didn't feel a need to lecture Americans about sexual mores. Their Democratic Party welcomed voters who owned guns, were devoutly religious, and liked to wave the flag.

But that Democratic Party—to which Ronald Reagan himself had once belonged—died in the 1960s, and the last forty years have seen a slow but steady stream of disillusioned former Democrats becoming Republicans. In the 1980s, the Southerners and blue-collar voters who abandoned Jimmy Carter's party were called "Reagan Democrats," reflecting the optimistic hope of many in the press that though these folks voted for Reagan, they were still Democrats at heart. But twenty-three years later, the evidence is clear that many of these voters left the Democratic Party for good.

This all spells political trouble for the elites. Since most of them are Democrats, they rely primarily on Democrat politicians to push their far-reaching agenda. Yet they see their political influence (which was never particularly strong in the first place) eroding, slowly but surely. Even when the Democrats do manage to chalk up political victories, elite goals still go unachieved. Even an extraordinary politician like Clinton could do little to promote liberal ideas, and his one major effort to push a liberal agenda (see nationalized health care) resulted in one of the most thorough electoral defeats (remember 1994?) in recent American history. We still have at least 65 million gun owners out there. The SUV is still a national status symbol. We're glad we're the world's sole "superpower."

The debate for the hearts and minds of Americans is over, and the elites have lost. Defeated in election after election, winning only when they can obscure their ideals (as Carter and Clinton did) by posing as Bible-toting Southerners, it is clear that they certainly cannot claim the mandate of "the people" for their cause. But the elites won't let the American voters get in the way. This game is not over. Not by a long stretch. The elites are desperate to win. So since they can't win with these rules, they're going to start trying to change the rules. The next stage in the elite campaign will be an attack on the foundations of our democracy—on our "American-ness."

# 3

# The Elite Agenda

hat is America? It is a country founded upon unique political and cultural principles. It is a country inhabited by a people united in their allegiance to these principles. If we abandon our principles, we lose *our* America. Because the stakes are so high, the danger posed by the elite agenda must be taken seriously. We must understand their goals and recognize their tactics.

If they are not stopped, then we can be sure that internationalist bureaucrats will continue to gain power, and our domestic democracy will be stifled. Abraham Lincoln's famous reference to government "of the people, by the people, and for the people" will become meaningless. Elite rule will rob us of the freedoms we have fought so many battles to uphold. Acquiescing to elite rule is a betrayal of America.

Four critical principles have made America the greatest liberal democracy in history. Every single one of these is under furious attack by the elites:[1]

Majority rule
Individual rights

Equality of opportunity
Limited government

We all accept the importance of these American values without thinking much about their true meanings. Elites take advantage of this. They invoke these concepts but use these terms in very different ways from the ways most Americans use them. To elites, for instance, "democratic values" have nothing to do with voting for your representative or expressing the will of the people—rather, they are used in name only to establish elite rule over us.

## THE COMMON MAN CAN'T WIN

Let's start with majority rule. Though our system of government acknowledges that the minority has certain critical rights, it rests on the assumption—an assumption that always makes elites uncomfortable—that the majority has rights, too. In fact, collectively speaking, majority rights outweigh those of the minority. As long as the restrictions in the Constitution are respected, the majority and its representatives are free—and indeed entitled—to turn their political beliefs into law and public policy.

Now this was, and is, an exciting idea. After all, in most of the countries that have ever existed, the majority could *not* rule. Instead, almost all of the people who have ever lived on earth have been forced to live under elite rule. Oh, the elites didn't always agree with one another, and they didn't always call themselves by the same term. Sometimes they claimed the title of "king." Sometimes they were known as "samurai." Sometimes they were called "Brahmins." But in every time and in every country, the outcome was basically the same: A few people made all the rules that everyone else had to live under.

And that's what made America so extraordinary. That's what de Tocqueville came to see. That's what Lincoln was so determined to preserve. Have we always had a perfect democracy? No. For too long many people—particularly blacks—were excluded from their proper role in the political process. But we've always held on to the ideal of government of, by, and for the people. To this day, the idea of majority rule is far more exciting—and far more revolutionary—than any of the goofy slogans you'll see coming out of Ivy League political science departments.

"But Laura," I hear some of you saying, "what about a tyrannical majority? Weren't the founders concerned about that, too?" Of course they were. And they put in place rules to protect the minority. For example, if you don't like what the majority is doing, you can exercise your freedom of speech and freedom of the press to create a new majority that will agree with you. In 1964, Ronald Reagan went on national television to urge Americans to vote for Barry Goldwater. They refused, for the most part, and Goldwater was crushed. But conservatives continued to work for their beliefs, and sixteen years later Ronald Reagan was overwhelmingly elected president. That's how democracy works.

In their generosity, the American people recognize numerous protections for the minority. Even minorities that are despised by most Americans—such as the Ku Klux Klan—enjoy such protections. But our modern elites, unhappy with the prospect of majority rule, have sought to take advantage of this generosity and to paralyze democracy by subjecting it to unreasonable demands and sensitivities of political minorities. Typically, even one individual can frustrate democratic choices by heading to court—a favorite haven of the elites. And in those courts, the rights extended to individuals are far more extensive than the rights the founders intended to give them—or the rights most Americans believe they should have. (More on that later.)

Because they're so concerned with the rights of minorities (including themselves), the elites always ignore the fact that the *majority has rights*, too. In fact, thanks to the principle of majority rule, the majority's rights outweigh the minority's.

Every time we yield to a militant atheist's demand that the reference to God be dropped from the Pledge of Allegiance because it "offends" him, the rights of millions of believers are trampled. In these cases, the minority should grin and bear it, just as sometimes you have to laugh at your boss's jokes to keep him happy. Or to put it another way, the minority should grant the majority common courtesy.

It's maddening how often elites proclaim that minority rights trump those of everyone else. Terrified of the thought of all those yahoos actually using their votes to determine the government of

**One of my listeners, D.L. (USN Ret.), of Anchorage, Alaska, poignantly captured the way many Americans feel about the elite attack on majority rule:**

"I'm an American, I can't pray in school, because it may be offensive to someone. I can't fly my flag, because it may be offensive to someone. I have to tolerate when someone desecrates our flag, a shrine, or symbol that holds significant meaning to the country I defended for twenty years and still today. I have to worry about the feelings of Muslims, Hindus, Buddhists, Marxists, Leninists, Communists, homosexuals, and everyone else. Yet they can oppress me, squash my beliefs, deny my rights to freedom of speech, disgrace my flag, defecate on our Constitution and country. Yet it's okay for them to be intolerant of Americans in our own country and tell us what we can and can't do. This is America, learn our language and use it, learn our culture and enjoy it, live our way and be free.

"America is like my house. You come into my house you respect me and my rules. You don't like my rules you can leave on your own. Argue my rules in my house and you may leave head first with the rest following. They choose not to leave freely, now it's time for them to leave my way, and for the bleeding hearts, Wah!, that's all the concern they get and they can leave, too!" ■

the country, the elites constantly denigrate majority rule. They tell us that the rights of the many *oppress* the few, who *struggle for liberation* from the dictatorship of majority rule. To elites, the majority's views are never above suspicion. In fact, such views must be suspicious simply because they represent the majority. The elites see majority rule—which most Americans regard as the cornerstone of a nation living together harmoniously—as a monstrously bad thing. In their framework, the minority is always a victim. The majority is always an oppressor.

So we end up in this crazy situation of elites using the courts to order the majority to kowtow to political minorities in the name of "equality." Think of all the major victories the elites have chalked up through this strategy. God is banished from schools. Colleges and universities use "affirmative action" to admit less-qualified applicants. Even in states where abortion is widely seen as murder, the people can do nothing to stop this grisly practice.

## CONSTITUTIONAL TIMEOUT

Now at this point, some of you reading this are wondering about the electoral college that we use to elect the president, and the fact that in the Senate, each state (regardless of its population) has the same number of senators. Some of you might even recall that as the Constitution was originally written, senators were chosen by state legislators, not by popular vote. Don't these facts, you ask knowingly, *prove* that the founders didn't believe in majority rule?

No, it doesn't. Obviously, just like Americans today, the founders disagreed over major political issues, and some of them trusted the people more than others. But the Constitution plainly states that only the House of Representatives—which has always been directly elected by the people and reflects the population of the states—may initiate new tax laws. In other words, the founders put the "power of the purse" squarely in the hands of the people.

And Americans quickly ensured that the electoral college and the Senate would not block majority rule in any way. When the Electoral College did not reflect the popular vote in 1800, the Constitution was immediately amended to weaken its importance. In the early twentieth century, when Americans grew concerned that the Senate did not sufficiently reflect the popular will, they took the power to choose senators away from state legislators and gave it to themselves. These actions show that for most Americans, the framework of the Constitution is fully consistent with majority rule.

While the fact that each state has an equal vote in the Senate certainly gives a large advantage to sparsely populated states like Wyoming and Vermont at the expense of majority rule, the whole point of this rule is *not* to give more power to elites, but to prevent elites from dominating the system. The founders wisely recognized that elites would generally be concentrated in states with the most people, and that other Americans would need to be protected from the enormous power that can be wielded by large cities. And they were right. After all, no one really believes that powerful elites in places like Kansas and Montana are somehow holding down the oppressed masses of Wall Street and Hollywood.

It should come as no surprise that many of the elites want to scrap the Electoral College since the majority of the voters in states like South Carolina and Idaho don't have much tolerance for the elite agenda. In one of her first legislative proposals as a senator, Hillary Clinton proposed abolishing the Electoral College. (She owes her election to urban voters.)

## TOLERATE THIS!

As we have seen, the elites regularly use American respect for individual rights to try to block majority rule. But it turns out that not all individuals are created equal in the eyes of the elites. Compare two different protests against "offensive" art.

When Catholics (and others) objected to the government-funded Brooklyn Museum of Art's "Sensation" exhibit that featured blasphemous, repulsive, and pornographic "art," the New York *Daily News* immediately denounced them as "cranks" and "bigots," while Norman Lear's People for the American Way ranted about conservatives trampling over the right to "free expression."

The elites argue that if you complained about the painting in "Sensation" of a black Virgin Mary smeared in elephant dung and festooned with photos from porn magazines, then you must be closed-minded and stupid. When former New York City mayor Rudy Giuliani threatened to pull the city's funding from the museum, the elites went into spin-overdrive. "You don't have a right to government subsidy for desecrating somebody else's religion," he sensibly pointed out. For the elites, Giuliani became the devil himself; a *Village Voice* cover depicted him dressed as Satan hiding behind the Madonna. Predictably, the ACLU charged onto the scene, as did Susan Sarandon, the editorial boards of most national newspapers, and Floyd Abrams, the famous First Amendment lawyer. Christians, Giuliani, and anyone who dared to protest against the filth being shown at the Brooklyn Museum were pilloried. Cries of "censorship" were heard from the art houses of Manhattan to the coffee shops of San Francisco. In the end, thanks to all the publicity, "Sensation" made a fortune, as East Coast intellectuals, pseudo-intellectuals, and wannabe intellectuals, lined up and paid $9.75 (plus $29 for the catalogue) to demonstrate their hipness.

# Elitespeak alert!

Be afraid, be *very* afraid, when elites use the phrase "free expression." It is actually invoked to shut you up. To the elites, "free expression" is *their* right to offend, insult, and abuse you and your values as much as they like. But when *you* criticize them, this is known as "censorship." ■

Let me clarify that. "Sensation" *did* make a fortune, but *not* for the museum. All the real money flowed to Charles Saatchi, the London-based advertising magnate who owned the "artworks" on display. *He* had been the one who organized the exhibition, not the Brooklyn Museum. Saatchi is an art speculator, and it turns out all those elitists who ranted about "free expression" got sucker-punched by someone a heck of a lot more clever than themselves. Saatchi *used* them to drum up interest in the show, raise the market value of the "artists" on display, and fattened his bank account.[2] Smooth move, buddy.

It's great to see the elites falling flat on their faces, but what I want to know is: Would the ACLU have so vigorously defended "Sensation" on First Amendment grounds if the Virgin had been traditionally portrayed—no dung, no porn allusions—in a Christmas Nativity scene out in front of the Brooklyn Museum? Unlikely. That certainly would have been an unconstitutional establishment of religion, right? (Well, not really, but that's what they would have said.) Their outrage over Giuliani's threat to cut the museum's funding had less to do with concerns about free expression than it did with the desire to bait average Americans, especially all those close-minded Christians out there. I mean, what's a little dung among friends?

Yet invariably, where there is elite outrage, there is usually an elite double standard. When the Cincinnati Playhouse in the Park (the city's main theater) decided to produce a fifty-minute play for high school students called *Paradise*, it could have used some help from the ACLU. The play was inspired by the story of Ayat al-Akhras, an eighteen-year-old Palestinian suicide bomber who blew herself up in Jerusalem, and one of her victims, Rachel Levy, a seventeen-year-old American-Israeli high school senior. During the drafting process, the play was scrupulously tested for objectivity at an invitation-only reading for religious leaders, academics, and local parents. One parent, Majed Dabdoub, decided to bring ten uninvited friends (mostly Muslims) to the reading, and afterward confronted the playwright, Glyn O'Malley. According to people at the meeting:

- "You could see the level of hate in the room."
- "[Several] people in the room refused to recognize this was a work in progress, nor did they acknowledge the efforts the playwright had made to be balanced. They spoke with extreme disrespect and misinformation."
- There were numerous anti-Semitic comments expressed, including "veiled" suggestions about the play's source of funding and the religious background of the Playhouse's artistic leadership. (Actually, the funding came from the Lazarus Fund, which is a nonpolitical charitable foundation run by Federated Department Stores. Ed Stern, the theater's Artistic Director, is Lutheran, not Jewish.)
- One Muslim ranted that suicide bombing was the equivalent of Patrick Henry's "Give me liberty or give me death." Dabdoub complained to local schools that the play was "not appropriate, not educational . . . has a narrow political agenda and is racist in nature."

What happened? A tiny minority of Muslims succeeded in stopping the play from being performed in schools. Production of the play was temporarily suspended. As for O'Malley, in an e-mail sent to many of his colleagues he commented, "If playwrights are going to have productions of their work stopped, their civil liberties violated, First Amendment rights quashed by libelous slander campaigns based on works in development; if theaters are going to be bullied into halting the development of new works because of smear campaigns and terror tactics by extreme special interest groups, then this isn't the U.S. I want to live in."[3]

While the facts of the Cincinnati incident are not perfectly parallel to those of the "Sensation" exhibit (there was no government threat to cease funding in Cincinnati), the playwright was clearly under fire because of the content of his expression. Needless to say, when the Cincinnati story broke, Susan Sarandon, Floyd Abrams, and the ACLU were nowhere to be found. That should not come as a surprise though, since Ohio is just another fly-over state (not as fun to rally in cities where you can't get a decent facial!). More important, the Cincinnati Playhouse wasn't insulting Christianity, showcasing pornography, or mocking American traditions. Message to Christians: If you're offended, get over it—artistic expression must be protected. Message to Muslims: We feel your pain, and we'll make you feel better—artistic expression be damned.

## WHAT'S TRUTH GOT TO DO WITH IT?

The elites take for granted that the majority is always wrong and the minority is always right. But in a country so devoted to majority rule, how do they go about ensuring that "justice" prevails? Many of them believe that the best way to do this is to enforce a system of *proportionalism*. For example, if women are 50 percent of the population, then they should be 50 percent of all lawmakers. Anything less is "institutional sexism." When the elites say they want "equal opportunity," what they really want is a guarantee of equal *results*.

This outcome-based approach to employment, education, or government benefits perverts the principles of nondiscrimination and individual rights. It is a fraudulent concept, an elite front for introducing quotas under the guise of establishing "fairness" and "justice."

Look what has happened to Title IX, the federal mandate that has been interpreted to enforce strict proportionality for male and female college athletes. It is a beast that has killed off many men's baseball, wrestling, and swimming teams in the name of "equality" in athletics for women. Now, I played two intercollegiate sports, but the fact is, women aren't as interested in participating in sports

as men are. Even at all-female colleges, only 16 percent of women take part in sports, according to the Independent Women's Forum, and that is before factoring in the rising number of older, married women and mothers attending college who have no time for team sports. Moreover, activities where there has traditionally been a high level of female interest—like dance, cheerleading, and drill team—are conveniently excluded from the proportionality test.

Title IX was originally intended to foster equality of opportunity and end sex discrimination, but its meaning has been twisted by the elites. They now use it to destroy equality of opportunity and institutionalize discrimination—*against* men. In years to come, we can expect to see the elites try to place Title IX-style diktats over every facet of our lives for the sake of their notion of "justice." The Bush administration took initial steps to reexamine Title IX in 2002, with the goal of reforming its proportionality tests. Elites organized a massive counteroffensive with the help of their celebrity and journalist friends. Not surprisingly, the administration's Title IX task force backed down.

Is the way Title IX has been administered for college sports so very different from a law requiring that companies institute proportional hiring for women, blacks, Hispanics, Native Americans, Muslims, the disabled, and the obese? And why stop there? How about the military's Special Forces? Fire and police departments? Never forget that the Constitution is no impediment to the elite agenda, since elites think most of its provisions are archaic and outdated. The rest of us know that the proportionalist approach violates traditional notions of "equal protection" enshrined in the Constitution. The elites treat the Equal Protection Clause like Silly Putty, stretching its meaning at will to achieve their political goals.

Another depressing example of proportionalism in action was provided by the furor over the famous photo of the three white New York City firefighters raising the flag amid the ruins of the World Trade Center. This photo, which is our generation's equivalent of the immortal World War II shot of the six Marines raising the flag over Iwo Jima, became an elite obsession the second it was announced that the Fire Department wished to cast a bronze statue commemorating the image. Despite the fact that there were three whites in the photo, advocacy groups pressured the Fire Department into agreeing that since minorities were "underrepresented" in it, two of the white guys would be airbrushed out to make way for one Hispanic and one African-American.

In their misguided pursuit of "fairness," elites ignored the real issue. For most of us, what was important was not the skin color of firemen in a photo—it was the courage and resilience captured by the camera—an indomitable spirit that defines America.

Over the last few decades the entire history of America has come under covert attack by elites in academia. Traditionally, and properly, our history classes used to teach that this country embraced all cultures while assimilating them into a genuine American civilization that attracted intense loyalty from her inhabitants.

America *is* diversity in action. In 1942, for example, a Japanese-American leader distributed this statement so that his followers could swear loyalty to, and fight for, their adopted country. "I believe in [America's] institutions, ideals and traditions; I glory in her heritage; I boast of her history; I trust in her future. Because I believe in America, and I trust she believes in me, and because I have received innumerable benefits from her, I pledge myself to do honor to her at all times and in all places."[4]

Can you imagine a similar statement being issued nowadays when the educrats teach that America represents nothing more than a shameful tale of exploitation, hatred, oppression, and imperialism perpetrated by a ruling class of Dead White European Males? Dream on. The elites tell immigrants to resist assimilation to ensure that our sense of unity and loyalty to America fade away.

## THE BLAH-BLAH SISTERHOOD

Proportionalism is also the bread-and-butter of groups like Emily's List, a political action network that raises cash for Democrat, pro–abortion rights women candidates. "Six of seven members of Congress are men, and women hold a tiny fraction of leadership positions," says Ellen Malcolm, president of the organization. "As long as gender parity remains a distant goal, Emily's List will help women run and sometimes defeat 'good' men in primaries."[5] Recently, Emily's List began branching out into fundraising for "women of color," asserting that they too are "underrepresented" in politics. (Hey, Emily, what about giving a push for more female conservatives in politics?) Of course, Emily's List is only interested in promoting certain types of women—those who have accepted the elites' orthodoxy. This is elitism in its purest, most noxious form, for it implicitly tells women how they must think in order to be authentically women. Show me a "proportionalist" and I'll show you an elite in disguise.

Now, it would be nice if there were more Republican women around Capitol Hill and fewer Democratic windbags like Robert Byrd and Ted Kennedy, but that won't happen in Emily's world. The female candidates *they* foist on voters are never Republican, gun-owning, pro-life women like me, but Democrat fembots mindlessly spouting San Fran Nan-isms (of the sort we hear from Representative Nancy Pelosi of California). You didn't hear Emily's List cheering Condi Rice and Karen Hughes for landing high-profile jobs in the Bush administration. Indeed, when the Republican National Committee launched a campaign to persuade more women to vote for the GOP (as opposed to introducing quotas), Emily's List president Ellen Malcolm nastily lampooned the committee's cochairman Ann Wagner for running "a pretty road show" and making a "meaningless gesture."[6] Sisterhood, shmisterhood.

Elite groups like Emily's List have a vested interest in perpet-uating the myth that minorities are oppressed in our liberal democracy. And the list of aggrieved "minorities" grows ever longer. Women, of course, plus every racial and ethnic group on the planet, along with gays, lesbians, bisexuals, the "trans-gen-dered," "prisoners of the state" (i.e., violent felons like Leonard Peltier), illegal aliens, every indigenous people, those confined to insane asylums, and the poor (except those who also happen to be members of the U.S. Armed Forces). And let's not forget, vic-timhood isn't limited to our shores. Third World countries, in the elite mindset, have been exploited and neglected by America. These places are thus filled with victims who need to be protected by America's elites. (Elites blatantly ignore America's colossal food and aid donations, our financial bailouts, and most recently the billions pledged by President George W. Bush to fight AIDS in Africa.) Elites have grand ideas about how to protect these vic-tims, which inevitably means that America gets handed not only the blame but also the tab. That's how it always is when the elites run the show.

## WE ARE ALL INDIVIDUALS!

Even as liberals exhort us "to do our own thing," elitists hate indi-vidualism because individuals think for themselves. What they really mean by "Do your own thing" is "Do what we tell you to do and be like us." They assert *group* rights over individual rights and the ability of people to make their own decisions. Just as Ford cus-tomers used to be able to choose any color they liked for their new Model T so long as it was black, in the elite world you can be as "individualistic" as you like, so long as you pay tribute to the right group.

For instance, thanks to the propaganda pumped out by the race-relations mafia, blacks are expected to "act like blacks" and get behind the Jackson-Sharpton-NAACP agenda. If any African-

American dares to step out of line and suggest, say, that school vouchers might be a good idea to help inner-city kids, he or she gets slammed down as some sort of race traitor. Such is the despicable treatment meted out to any black conservative. When "Banana Boat" crooner Harry Belafonte branded Colin Powell a "house slave" merely for supporting the decisions of the Republican president he serves, Belafonte skated with virtually no criticism from his fellow entertainers. Appearing on *Larry King Live*, Belafonte couldn't disguise his scorn and disdain for Powell, our nation's first black secretary of state. Powell, you see, wasn't thinking or acting "black enough" for Belafonte—another stark example of the elite mentality, disguised as concern for minorities.

The elites hate real individualism because it threatens their theory that liberal democracy is illegitimate and repressive. As usual, they miss the point. Living in a free-market liberal democracy *is* tough. Nobody should doubt that. It is left to individuals to forge their own way in life, develop their natural talents, work hard, and be responsible for their own decisions. That's freedom—freedom fettered only by laws guaranteeing civil behavior. And throughout American history, this remarkable sanction for freedom has given millions of lower-income people the incentive to use their own initiative and enterprise to improve their well-being instead of being recipients of redistributed wealth. In the process, Americans have created the most successful economy in the history of the world.

As the depressing experience of 1960s social programs in the inner cities shows, however, ill-conceived do-goodism in the form of massive government intervention does not create successful and happy citizens. Instead, it traps people in a permanent underclass addicted to welfare in crime-ridden neighborhoods. In the elite world, the only people "moving on up to the East Side to deluxe apartments in the sky" are the elites themselves. The rest of us are supposed to wallow around at the bottom of the heap, fighting for the scraps they deign to give us.

Elites claim they are just protecting us from the consequences of untrammeled selfishness, but we already have better institutions for that. To ease the hardship and soften the impact of individualism, men and women (married or single) band together in voluntary associations in their communities, churches, and clubs that inculcate common values and offer support. These associations can adapt to the needs of small groups and are available to all, regardless of race, sex, or national origin. Because Americans have such faith in these voluntary communities, they have felt free to give the *individual* extraordinary political freedom. Over a century ago, Justice Harlan's dissent in *Plessy* v. *Ferguson* got it exactly right: "The Constitution is color-blind, and neither knows nor tolerates classes among citizens."

But the elites don't get this. For them, the key units of society are not individuals or the little platoons comprised of families and communities, but the "group" you are born into and from which you can never escape. The elites don't just tolerate "classes among citizens"—they create them. As usual, Hillary Clinton (Democrat, United Nations), perfectly summed up elite group-think when she addressed a Martin Luther King Jr., holiday get-together. While a person "of course" should be judged by the content of his character rather than the color of his skin, she asked, "But what is character? The sum total of who you are. The color of your skin and how you deal with it is part of your character." So much for the pursuit of a color-blind society—for Hillary and her acolytes it's more like "color-blind when convenient."

If it's not your skin color that defines you, it is probably some other imagined class of victimhood that does. If you are an ethnic minority, if you are "transgendered," if you are vertically challenged, if you are plus-sized, if you are double-jointed, if you are...well, you get the point. Elites see the formation of new victim groups as essential for fulfilling the elite agenda. If you are just another American citizen working to support your family, going to church regularly, and paying your bills on time, then why would you need help from the elites?

Elite-think dictates that government-supervised "social justice" for these and other "oppressed" groups is more important than individual freedom and the right to make your own choices. To our elites, it would be so much easier if we all lived in a kind of paradise where we are cared for by Wise Elite Government, and where Bad Guys like Middle Americans, Christians, Southerners, and Republicans are forced to pay slavery reparations, suffer race and sex quotas, and endure "speech codes" that censor alleged "hate speech."

## TAKE THIS CAR AND SUV IT!

Elites of course are excluded from the rules laid down by the Wise Elite Government, just as Soviet Communist Party apparatchiks enjoyed benefits (like private car lanes) denied to the laboring masses. The elites always make sure they're taken care of, even as they want to dictate how the rest of us live our lives.

A funny example of elite hypocrisy at work was turned up by the *New York Post* after my old friend Arianna Huffington kicked off an ad campaign claiming that Americans who drove SUVs "supported terrorism." The *Post* noticed that the very same celebrities blowing air kisses at Arianna "consume huge quantities of fossil fuels in their stretch limos, Gulfstream jets and oversized Beverly Hills mansions." Norman Lear, for instance, the producer of *All in the Family* and the anti-SUV campaign's guiding hand, built a parking garage for no fewer than twenty-one cars. The forty-five-foot high structure, according to the *Los Angeles Times* (citing Lear's neighbors), "was built in violation of city height restrictions [and] has ruined the aesthetics of the wooded canyon."

Barbra Streisand and hubby James Brolin, who are supporters of Lear's Environmental Media Association, both drive SUVs, as do no-longer-amusing comic Chevy Chase and his wife. "They keep it in the back and it's very rarely used," said Chase's spokesman. "They only use it when they have to attach the horse trailer or when they're carrying a lot of kids."[7] Right. So it's okay when Chevy Chase needs to tool around Westchester with his offspring (and horses, presumably), but when *you* need to ferry the kids to school in your town, you're practically running an al Qaeda training camp.

The same elite hypocrisy extends to other issues as well.

Gun control is a pet issue for the elites. They want you and me to disarm, as they have multimillion-dollar compounds with high-tech security systems, panic rooms, and armed guards. Former talk show host Rosie O'Donnell set the standard for antigun hypocrisy when she railed against NRA member and actor Tom Selleck during his guest spot on her show. It was later learned that her bodyguard packs heat and that she was herself profiting from gun sales as a celebrity spokeswoman for Kmart—one of the nation's biggest gun retailers. And let's not forget peace-loving actor Sean Penn. When his automobile was stolen off the streets of Berkeley, California, in April 2003, he had to admit that a 9mm Glock and a .38-caliber Smith & Wesson were among the contents inside. And one of the guns was loaded.

The elites exempt themselves from the burdens they place on us. The elites are determined to keep choice out of education, nixing the voucher movement every step of the way. Yet they happily send their kids to private schools. Michael Moore, who has made millions by holding himself out as a champion of the little guy, lives in a $1.27 million pad in Manhattan and sends his daughter to a private school. The elites bemoan the fact that the "system" funnels too many young men into prison. But many of the elites live in gated neighborhoods with their own security details, or so far away from bad areas that crime isn't a threat. The elites' concern for the rights of panhandlers (begging is just another form of free expression) and the homeless (give them a check instead of coupons for shelter and food) have created a costly mess on the streets of elite cities like San Francisco and Santa Monica.

## THE GROUP HUGGERS

To elites, the lifeblood of American democratic politics—the clash of opposing views in an adversarial system—is biased against "underrepresented" groups because there must be a winner and a loser. Elites don't like games where there's a possibility of losing. That's why they cheat so often.

We must ditch the cut-and-thrust of debate, say the elites, and stop those talk radio attacks that make us look like idiots. We need to end competitiveness between individuals and parties and replace it with "consensus" and "power sharing" between groups. This is like replacing NFL teams fighting for a Super Bowl slot with an amateur touch football league to make sure everybody gets to play.

Yes, it's all "It Takes A Village" and touchy-feely, but the effect of introducing "consensus politics" into America will be to snuff out majority rule in favor of "shifting coalitions of minorities."[8] James Banks, a leading author of "multicultural educational" textbooks, made the elitist case explicitly when he wrote that in order "to create an authentic democratic Unum with moral authority and perceived legitimacy the pluribus (diverse peoples) must negotiate and share power."

In other words, Banks—a guy whose books your children's teachers read for pointers—does not even believe that America is an "authentic" democracy with "moral authority" and "legitimacy."[9] This is shameful.

Now, it is tempting to write off Mr. Banks as a nut—certainly we've long since grown accustomed to having our textbooks written by people with anti-American views, but he's hardly alone. Justice William Brennan—one of the most venerated of all liberal heroes, the man who devoted his career to expanding the powers of the Supreme Court at the expense of the elected branches of government—also announced that the "majoritarian process has appeal under some circumstances, but I think ultimately it will not do." In other words, Brennan believed it was appropriate to supplant the vision of the Founding Fathers and American democracy with his *own*. "Faith in democracy is one thing, blind faith quite another," he intoned. Justice Brennan, by all accounts, was a lovely man, but this is a warped view of what the role of the Court should be.

When our own leaders and educators don't believe in America's virtues, how are our system of government and way of life going to survive? Remember what happened to the Roman Empire after its elites no longer believed it was worth defending against the onslaughts of barbarians. We have more than enough modern barbarians attacking us today. What we don't need are fifth columnists undermining our will to resist. Let's get this straight once and for all: Judges—even liberal heroes like Justice Brennan—are *supposed* to have "blind faith" in democracy. Believing in democracy is not some sort of *option*. It's not up to a judge to determine whether we should enjoy "the majoritarian process." In America, that power belongs to the people.

All this talk of the problems with "the majoritarian process" is nothing more than a smokescreen to justify taking power away from the majority and giving it to a minority—an elite minority. Under majority rule, everyone can have his say, but the elites want to ensure that only they get to talk while everybody else listens. By shutting down debate and silencing their critics, the elites want to keep you out of power.

In Argentina, a law has already been passed banning political parties that do not contain a proportional percentage of women as candidates. France has a similar rule. Which means that if your chosen party is not politically correct enough to satisfy the ruling elites, then your vote has just been terminated. This is what the elites would like to happen in America. They already effectively did this with the abortion issue—by going to the courts to manufacture a "privacy right" from which the alleged right to abort emanates, thus striking down abortion laws in every state and removing the subject from effective political debate. One Supreme

Court decision swept away our nation's long tradition of protecting the right to life.

Fierce and passionate debate in the public square and the press,
and especially in the grandest forum of all, Congress, is vital to the
healthy functioning of the body politic. Though a lot of people
make a fetish of "bipartisan" solutions and judge a congressman
by how often he can strike deals with the opposition, we desperately need *partisan* conflict—except when the nation is in dire
peril.

The whole point of the party system is that it divides people
into yes and no, or pro and anti, camps. It forces them to choose
where they stand. And by forcing them to choose, it allows us to
know what sort of people we have voted for. Voters can then identify which party best represents their heartfelt beliefs. But in a system of "shifting coalitions," there are no clear-cut decisions
reflecting the people's will, only messy compromises reflecting the
elites' views.

For the elites, local, state, and national legislatures are a
sideshow to the main attraction—using the courts to change
America to mirror their own beliefs because they can't win demo-
cratically. Thirty years ago, the Supreme Court legalized abortion
in *Roe* v. *Wade*, but the protests continue. If anything, the rancor
over "choice" has become more bitter as time goes on. This is
because millions of Americans believe that the Supreme Court has
usurped their right to a legislative voice on the legality of abortion.
An activist Supreme Court made law without reference to the Constitution. It imposed legalized abortion on us as a diktat. On such
a great moral issue, elected legislatures should have debated and
decided. In the end, the regulations surrounding abortion—if
abortion were permitted at all—would have reflected the majority's views. That is what happened in this country before *Roe*.

As I was finishing this book, we got yet another example of
how much the elites feel free to trample on the values of most
Americans. Five people—count 'em, five out of 280 million—uni-

laterally decided that homosexual sodomy is protected by the Constitution. Now you might not buy this as it is inconceivable that sodomy is one of the things that Americans have fought and died for since 1776—but, you see, our views don't matter. Because those five people happen to be Supreme Court justices and—as the elites constantly remind us—whatever they say goes.

We hear from the elites that there is a "sea change in public opinion" on gay issues, so it was right for the court to reflect that in the Texas sodomy case, *Lawrence v. Texas.* One little problem: "Reflecting public opinion" is not the proper role of the Supreme Court—but rather is the job of the popularly elected legislatures. Many state legislatures had already repealed sodomy bans from their statute books, but the court stepped in, proving itself, in the words of dissenting Justice Antonin Scalia, "impatient of democratic change." On issues from affirmative action to abortion to school prayer, the Supreme Court has firmly aligned itself with the elites in the culture war, and against the voters. These critical social issues can no longer be entrusted to the democratic process—in other words, the people—because the people can no longer be trusted to come to the right conclusions. Therefore these decisions must be made by unelected, unaccountable, life-tenured elites who impose their will on the American people. Instead of protecting the democratic process, and respecting and enforcing its outcome, elite judges shut it down, cast aside its results, and enforce their own "enlightened" worldview without regard to rule of law.

And if you don't like being governed by five liberal lawyers, or if you're worried that the court might next decide to legalize gay marriages, or even if you just want the president to appoint justices who would act with a bit more restraint, then you are a "bigot" (Barney Frank's pejorative of choice) or are being "divisive" or "intolerant." You can expect to be treated with the same kindness that the elites meted out to Robert Bork and Clarence Thomas.

Elites manipulate the law to get their way because it shuts out democracy. It wasn't so long ago that voters at the state and local level made decisions about education, welfare, taxation, and other issues that affected their lives. Politicians who did not respond to voter concerns were given the boot. In the last fifty years, however, the elites have hijacked democracy. Already, we have federal courts telling school boards what to teach, banning our children from praying in public places, and ordering tax increases to pay for the pet obsessions of our liberal judiciary.

The situation is only going to get worse. If the academic elite at our law schools has its way, the Voting Rights Act will be applied to require that only ethnic minorities can represent ethnic minorities. In the future, instead of our representatives being elected by the people freely choosing between candidates in their district and state, these representatives will be sent to Washington on behalf of whichever minority group they claim to lead. They won't be representing Americans to the best of their abilities, they'll be fighting for their *group* at the expense of other Americans, and so elite rule will be perpetuated.

We need to be especially vigilant about elite manipulation of the courts for the purposes of liberal activism. Elites want to use the courts to achieve what they cannot achieve through democratic means—to legalize gay marriage, to expand the "rights" of illegal aliens, to limit the president's options in foreign affairs, and the list goes on. With the elites, it never ends.

## DIVIDE AND CONQUER

Given the elite obsession with control, it's naïve to hope that maybe, just maybe, they will stop interfering with our lives. Since the goal of Wise Elite Government is to guarantee *equality of results*, there must be interference. Interference means two things: big government; and the erosion of the private sphere. Every facet of life must be subordinated to elite rule, which claims to be based on "fairness," "diversity," and "democratic values" but which is really unfair, nondiverse, and undemocratic.

The impact of this slow transformation of American life is going to be immense. I cannot emphasize this enough. "If long-term trends continue and serious opposition to group rights and 'diversity' fails, it is likely that liberal democracy will steadily evolve into a new form of regime," warns John Fonte of the Hudson Institute.[10] The America that has survived since the War of Independence and emerged triumphant from the titanic struggles against Nazism, Communism, and totalitarianism in the twentieth century will ebb away, just as in Europe the aristocrats lost out to popular democracy. True, aspects of aristocracy still exist across the Atlantic—the Queen remains England's head of state, for instance—but the monarchy is a shell of its former self. In the America of the future, the same thing will happen to Congress if elites win.

"Rule by a self-governing people," another fundamental principle of this Republic, will be the major casualty of the elite's drive for domination. The elites firmly believe that the time of the independent nation-state is over. After all, they don't even believe in the notion of American citizenship. We are hyphenated Americans and citizens of the world, so why should they promote independence for it?

But if we will not be running the show, who will be? Supranational governmental and judicial organizations, that's who. Sounds like science fiction, but not quite. Anthony Giddens, a leading theorist of the elite movement, says, "I'm in favor of pioneering some quasi-utopian transnational form of democracy."[11] Wow.

The key word here is "transnational." It is code for abolishing our borders and sovereignty in order to live under UN mandate. No, this isn't some wild theory cooked up by the vast right-wing conspiracy over a few beers. Among the elites, it's spoken of openly. As hardcore an elitist as Strobe "the Globe" Talbott, the deputy secretary of state for former President Clinton, says that by the end of the twenty-first century, "nationhood as we know it will be obsolete: all states will recognize a single global authority." Well, not to worry, since Talbott assures us, "No matter how permanent and even sacred they may seem at any one time, in fact [countries] are all artificial and temporary." That's news to me. Tell that to the French. In any case, Talbott thinks we should shift sovereignty "upward towards supranational bodies" because it's a "basically positive phenomenon." Right. So handing over the keys of the kingdom to the UN is a "basically positive phenomenon?" Maybe for him and the elites, but certainly not for us.

When America disappears, the elites will have won. We can't let that happen.


## WHY DO THE ELITES HATE AMERICA?

As any Columbo wannabe will tell you, cracking the crime and finding the culprit depend on revealing his motive. In this case, we know that the elites want to murder America, but why?

After September 11, the media was full of anguished articles with headlines like "Why Do They Hate Us?" The elites couldn't understand the terrorists' "motivation." (Imagine the Jews, the Poles, and the French in 1939 sitting around pondering Hitler's motivation.) To the elites, it obviously had to somehow be our fault. So what did they do?

Some elites assumed that the terrorists—otherwise known as Islamofascists—were angry with us because a racist, imperialist America had "colonized" their countries. What "colonization?" In fact, it would be more accurate to say that we had liberated them, by helping them develop their oil industry, providing them with markets, and ensuring their security from aggressive dictators like the former strongman Saddam Hussein. You can just imagine what the elites would have said during World War II: "The reason why the Nazis are attacking us in 1945 is because we colonized France after the 1944 D-Day landings." That's how stupid they sound when they whine about America taking over the Middle East. Ignore what the elites have to say. America has fought to protect Muslims all over the world, most recently in Iraq, Afghanistan (where we freed

Muslims from extremist tyranny), Bosnia, Kosovo, Somalia, and also—lest we forget—Kuwait, in the first Gulf War. The elites have a very selective memory. But that's never stopped them from imposing their views on us, especially when it comes to history.

Other elites believed that "poverty"—caused by American capitalism, obviously—had driven the hijackers to murder thousands (despite the fact that the terrorists themselves were mostly from middle- or upper-middle-class families). As Susan Sachs of the *New York Times* declared, "Predictably, the disappointed youth of Egypt and Saudi Arabia turn to religion for comfort." Of course, Bill Clinton couldn't resist chiming in, claiming that "these forces of reaction feed on disillusionment, poverty and despair."

The poorest, most desperate, and most disillusioned countries in the world are places like Nepal, Ethiopia, Madagascar, Cambodia, and Turkmenistan, but are these hotbeds of terrorism? No. Instead, modern terrorism stems from one area, the Middle East, parts of which are very poor and brutalized, but it is also home to some of the world's wealthiest people.

Geraldine Brooks, an experienced American journalist, recently interviewed Islamists throughout the Middle East and concluded that those "hearing the Islamic call included the students with the most options. . . . They were the elites of the next decade."[12] Just as the radical leftist groups operating on American campuses in the 1960s were packed with well-off college kids who looked down their noses at working-class cops, it is their Muslim counterparts who have launched a full-scale war against America. Judging by the profiles of the September 11 hijackers, if you wanted to be chosen by Osama bin Laden (a multimillionaire) for suicide missions, you had to be wealthy, privileged, and educated at the Middle East's best private schools.

These killers were obsessed with America. They hated everything about it, even as they enjoyed living here. But those who argued that the terrorists were jealous of American achievements were wrong.

At first blush the envy factor seems plausible. After all, since the time of the Greek and Roman empires, every powerful nation has attracted resentment because of its riches and advantages. That's only natural, and in any case, who cares if the French get envious? What are they going to do, bore us to death with their overwrought movies? Stop Champagne exports? Ask for the Statue of Liberty back?

James Burnham, the conservative Cold War commentator, once summed up our situation this way: "Americans have not yet learned the tragic lesson that the most powerful cannot be loved— hated, envied, feared, obeyed, respected, even honored perhaps, but not loved." So let's learn to live with the fact that not everybody is going to think we're terrific. Then again, that's their problem, not ours. Wanting everyone to like us is another unfortunate legacy of the baby boomers. Bill Clinton suffers from this affliction to this day. It baffles him that a hefty percentage of the American public doesn't love him, doesn't think he's a political sage, doesn't think his "good intentions" override his bad behavior. This obsession with being liked has bad consequences for everything from how we raise children to how we conduct foreign affairs.

Another alarming facet of the "they're just jealous" rationale is that it blinds us to the truth. Terrorists, and their facilitators and friends, aren't jealous at all. Like our own self-hating elites, they *genuinely* detest democracy and the principles enshrined in the Constitution. They are revolted by our freedoms and our power and our independence. And that's why they want to destroy them. As Hussein Massawi, the former leader of the terrorist outfit Hezbollah, bluntly admits, "We are not fighting so that you will offer us something. We are fighting to eliminate you." Well, the feeling's mutual, Hussein.

It should come as little surprise that our internationalist elites frequently make excuses for terrorism. In a disgusting e-mail by Darios Fo, the 1997 Nobel Laureate for Literature, written just after September 11, he spuriously claimed that "the great speculators

[American businessmen] wallow in an economy that every year kills tens of millions of people with poverty [in the Third World]—so what is 20,000 dead in New York? Regardless of who carried out the massacre, this violence is the legitimate daughter of the culture of violence, hunger and inhumane exploitation."

**A listener who identified himself only as JP wrote:**

"There is a fever pitch of Anti-Americanism going on right now. . . . I don't like what I see [but] I fear nothing, I am an American. Still, I worry that some people are completely unaware of what lies ahead." ∎

With attitudes like this, elites make the world safer for terrorism. Whether in politics, universities, the entertainment industry, or international institutions, elites work (sometimes) quietly *within* our system to undermine and weaken it. Long-term, this is a poison in our national bloodstream, weakening the America we love. Elites can't seem to shake their "blame America" mindset. They are fundamentally anti-American. While it is their right to speak out, it is our right to point out that these views run contrary to the basic principles of what it is to be an American.

But what's their motive? Why do they hate America so intensely? They believe that America became great by oppressing others—that we got rich by making everyone else poor. Actually, the introduction of socialism into the Third World by Soviet- and Chinese-backed dictators made them poor, as well as dead. Up to a hundred million people have been murdered by radical left-wing regimes in the past century, but the apologists in our elite universities never talk about it.

They'd rather blame it all on America.

# 4

# Shut Up and Entertain Us

▶ The Entertainment Elites

L ike most suburban kids my age growing up in the late 1970s, I pestered my mother to drive my friends and me to the movies on the weekends. I liked to stay all afternoon, sometimes watching the same movie twice. On Sunday mornings, I would sit curled up in front of the little black-and-white television set in my bedroom, watching the station that ran old movies at 7 o'clock—films like *Casablanca, Mutiny on the Bounty, A Christmas Carol, Mr. Smith Goes to Washington, His Girl Friday.*

Today I'm still a movie nut. I try to see a movie a week—and when I don't because of work or other obligations, I feel weird and anxious. Directing legend Sidney Pollack explained the love of film better than I can: "I know the truth. I want something better."

As for music, I really started to get into it in college. The Police, the Stones, and '80s bands that no one remembers anymore. I am still mesmerized by the lyrics of Bob Dylan, and moved by the haunting vocals of Bono. And when I block out the lyrics, I admit that I can really get into Dr. Dre.

So you see, I am not a conservative who believes that we live in a cultural wasteland. I marvel at the talent of young writer/directors like M. Night Shyamalan, Spike Jonze, and the Coen brothers. At

**75**

any given time my CD player is loaded with Coldplay, Counting Crows, Ryan Adams, U2, Bonnie Raitt, and Steve Earle. I own every Springsteen album. Susan Sarandon and Tim Robbins rarely fail to amaze me on screen.

## Elitespeak alert!

George W. Bush: the most stupid man who has ever lived. It must be true. Everyone in Hollywood says so. If only Fidel were our leader (sigh). ∎

But then actors and musicians started to ruin it for me. They started speaking. Shouting. Ranting. Not about acting, not about music, but about politics.

"In the name of fear and fighting terror, we are giving the reins of power to oilmen looking for distraction from their disastrous economic performance."

**—SUSAN SARANDON**, at an antiwar rally, Winter 2003

Susan and her life-partner, Timmy Robbins, are the leading stars of today's entertainment elites.

Hold it right there. "Laura, there are no elites here anymore! That era is long since past," said my director/actor/writer pal Paul Mazursky, who lives in Los Angeles.

Of course when I use the term "elite," I mean elite in their own minds. Because they have hit the big time in music, on screen, on stage, or on the page, they think this entitles their political views to special attention and respect.

Since George W. Bush won the presidency (or as the left says, he was "selected, not elected!"), various actors, directors, writers, and singers in the entertainment industry have been privately and publicly seething. This artistic clique, like the entire Dem-elite establishment, thinks President Bush is a dopey, knee-jerk conservative cowboy from Texas. They still can't believe he pulled it off—that he's actually president. How infuriating! Al Gore is so much smarter! And so are we!

Their symptoms include a bitter, endless rage. Their underlying condition is an anti-Bush addiction. It should be treated at Betty Ford. ("My name's Barbra, and I'm a Bush-hater.")

Celebrities get their fixes by making some of the more moronic and simplistic political pronouncements ever uttered. Here's a sampling:

"The [Bush Administration] is run exactly like *The Sopranos*."
—**GEORGE CLOONEY**, January 2003

"Yes, he [Bush] is a racist. We all knew that but the world is only finding it out now."
—**DANNY GLOVER**, to a reporter in Brazil, February 2003

"George W. Bush is like a bad comic working the crowd, a moron, if you'll pardon the expression."
—**MARTIN SHEEN**, in an interview in *Radio Times,* February 2002

"Just to let you know, we're ashamed the president of the United States is from Texas."
— **NATALIE MAINES**, Dixie Chicks lead singer, on stage before her London concert, March 10, 2003

"I believe that the administration has taken the events of 9/11 and has manipulated the grief of the country, and I think that's reprehensible."
—**DUSTIN HOFFMAN**, February 2003

"We have a president for whom English is a second language. He's like, 'We have to get rid of dictators,' but he's pretty much one himself."
—**ROBIN WILLIAMS**, March 2003

"Bush is a f—cking idiot."
—**JENNIFER ANISTON**, *Rolling Stone* interview, September 2001

"Coyote? The group of 'em, a pack of coyotes—tricky, cunning, making sure to take care of themselves but doing it in a wily way, making sure they never get caught."

—**ROBERT REDFORD**, in an interview with the *New York Times Magazine,* December 8, 2002

"I hate Bush. I despise him and his entire administration. It makes me feel ashamed to come from the United States—it is humiliating."

— **JESSICA LANGE**, accepting an award at Spain's San Sebastian film festival, October 2002

"Has everyone lost their f—king minds?...I don't like Bush. I don't trust him. He's stupid; he's lazy." —**CHER**, October 2000

Breathtaking, coming from a group as intellectually distinguished as this. George W. Bush ran an energy company, a major league baseball team, and the state of Texas, and has more formal education than most of the Bush bashers combined. (Unless, as *Investor's Business Daily* wryly noted, "you count the 10 years Alec Baldwin took to get his B.A. in drama from New York University.") "Oh, he was only able to do all that because Daddy helped him," goes the familiar Hollywood elite response. This from an industry that thrives on nepotism—or are all the Baldwin brothers really that talented, and I'm just not getting it?

But buckle your seat belt. It gets even better when Hollywood drops the Bush-bashing for "serious" political analysis.

"When you see the reality of war, you see how atrocious it is. And I think the American public would turn on the dime against war if they saw some of the pictures of the children's heads blown off."

—**TIM ROBBINS**, April 2003

"I have a feeling something hidden is at work here that will someday see the light of day. I keep asking myself where all this personal enmity

between George Bush and Saddam Hussein comes from. It's like the story of Captain Ahab and the great white whale from *Moby Dick*."
    —**RICHARD GERE**, at the Berlin Film Festival, February 2003

"Once we do this unprecedented thing of having a war on speck [*sic*], a pre-emptive strike. I mean, it's against the whole—everything this country is supposed to be about."
    —**SUSAN SARANDON**, on CBS's *The Early Show*, February 2003

"Republican comes in the dictionary just after reptile and just above repugnant. . . . I looked up Democrat. It's of the people, by the people, for the people."     —**JULIA ROBERTS**, 2000

"I know that's a harsh thing to say, perhaps, but I believe that what happened in 2000 did as much damage to the pillars of democracy as terrorists did to the pillars of commerce in New York City."
    —**ALEC BALDWIN**, March 2002

But even if they hate Bush, and are political simpletons, they support the troops and love America, right? You decide.

"Have we gone to war yet? We f—ing deserve to get bombed. Bring it on. . . . I hope the Muslims win!"
    —**CHRISSIE HYNDE** of the Pretenders,
    during a San Francisco concert, March 2003

"America's in a really volatile place right now, and there's a lot of really confused people. And I'm not interested in being a target of a lynch mob mentality."     —**MADONNA**, on *Dateline NBC*, May 2003

Never mind all that. At least they have really profound ideas about how to keep American safe in the post–September 11 world.

"Stop bullying the world! Stop saying, 'Do it our way or no way counts!' That is not civil!"

—**HARRY BELAFONTE**, on CNN's *Larry King Live*, October 15, 2002

But of all the stupid statements made by the entertainment elites, my favorite was Barbra Streisand's quoting...ahem... Shakespeare during her speech at a Democratic fundraiser in Los Angeles: "Beware the leader who bangs the drums of war in order to whip the citizenry into a patriotic fervor, for patriotism is indeed a double-edged sword."

Funny Girl! The passage Babs attributed to the Bard was actually an e-mail hoax that one of her interns, minions, or writers had picked up off the Internet. She has been an actress for thirty years but couldn't tell that a hackneyed line like that couldn't possibly have come from a writer with Shakespeare's sense of rhythm and lyricism. It turns out that Streisand, who fancies herself a serious actress (*Yentl*) can't even distinguish between seventeenth-century English and soap opera dialogue.

Methinks the entertainment elite doth protest too much. The list of their insipid quotes about Bush, war, and the U.S. role in the world could fill this entire book. Yet it isn't just the sheer volume of the entertainment elites' left-wing comments that have so many Americans saying, "Shut up and sing! Shut up and act! Shut up

# Elitespeak alert!

Www.barbrastreisand.com: the Hollywood elite's online one-stop shop for perceptive, cutting-edge commentary on the burning issues of the day. While you're there, you can also find creative new spelling tips ("Dear Congressman 'Gebhardt'") and brush up on your Shakespeare ("Beware the leader who bangs the drums of war...") ∎

and entertain us!" It is also their tone—unfailingly arrogant, invariably patronizing. They believe they have cornered the market on wisdom and experience, not just in the entertainment world but in the *entire* world.

## AIR TIME FOR AIRHEADS

Whenever a top entertainer has a political bone to pick, he or she has an instant platform. Both network and cable television love nothing more than to bestow air time on an indignant, self-righteous celebrity. (Unless, of course the celebrity is pro-life and wants to publicize the horrors of partial-birth abortion.) So for the months leading up to the war in Iraq, it was Susan, Tim, Martin, Janeane (Garofalo), and Mike (Farrell), in an ensemble anti-Bush performance. The media gobbled it up. They were everywhere. Susan at an antiwar rally in D.C., Mike in Los Angeles debating Sean Hannity, Michael Moore on any show that would flash the cover of his book. They are given the platform because they are celebrities. Period.

If the Hollywood elite wants to be taken seriously as policy-wonk wannabes, what better outlet than the Sunday morning shows? All three networks scrambled to get the antiwar celebs booked. Sarandon and Farrell were the invited guests challenging *National Review*'s editor Rich Lowry on CBS's *Face the Nation* on February 23, 2003. Veteran host Bob Schieffer said to Sarandon: "Well, let me just ask you—you say [Saddam] is a grave threat and we should disarm him. But how do you do that?" Bob, I love ya, but you're asking an actress about disarmament! Or do we want to end up like Thelma and Louise, at the bottom of a ravine in a fireball?

Farrell then appeared on NBC's *Meet the Press* the next week with former actor Fred Thompson. Thompson's qualifications? A former U.S. senator who headed sensitive investigations as chairman of the Senate Governmental Affairs Committee. Farrell's? Two decades ago he played the role of B. J. Hunnicut in *M\*A\*S\*H*, and then fifteen years later he followed it up by producing the over-looked classic *Patch Adams*. No word on when *Patch Adams Returns* will start production. Never would be best. Now with some time on his hands, he is cochair of Artists United to Win Without War. Farrell united behind this logic: "[I]t is not necessary for [Saddam Hussein] to cooperate for us to get the satisfactory results of the inspections." And of the Hussein threat, Farrell unequivo-cally stated, "He can do no harm to anyone." Tell that to the thou-sands of blindfolded skeletons in the mass graves. Tell that to the gassed Kurds. Tell that to the women who survived the rape rooms.

Hollywood's human rights crusaders strike again.

CNN's Larry King gave celebrated actor Sean Penn the full hour on January 11, 2003—but not to talk about the state of the film industry or a new project. Instead, Penn wore his foreign policy hat and discussed his recent three-day "fact-finding" trip to Bagh-dad. He went beyond merely advocating a principled opposition to a war. He tried to dazzle us with his Zen-like analysis: "I believe that this administration is, in good intentions, inadvertently teach-ing a master class in the manifestation of rage into hatred."

Hey, Spicoli, you're no Spinoza.

The underlying message is that you and I are too stupid, too ordinary to "get it." Penn explained that he took an interest in Iraq because as a successful actor, he had "an added responsibility," being that most Americans "don't have the time to attack their own ignorance on issues beyond popular media." Let's try to follow this line of logic: Because we have "regular" jobs and responsibilities, we cannot possibly hope to be as informed as someone who plays make-believe and gets paid millions for it? (And yes, I think Penn is supremely talented on camera.) Because we pick up our own groceries, do our own yard work, and may even watch—gasp!—the Fox News Channel, we can't make rational decisions about our political leaders?

"I don't know of a country where the people are so ignorant of reality and of history, if you can call that a free world."

—**JANE FONDA**, talking about America
at a lecture in Vancouver, April 2003

This is what Fonda, Penn, and the rest of the celebrity bleeding hearts believe deep down. And they want us regular people to give them a standing ovation for sharing their political enlightenment.

But of course most of us do not give a tree monkey's toenail about their views.

When people like Penn hear Americans reacting in disgust to their political comments, they are dumbstruck. "You mean not everyone loves me?" These people are so used to being sucked up to, so continually surrounded by packs of acolytes, toadies, and hangers-on, they have lost all sense of what life is like in real America. Small wonder our Hollywood elites come across like pampered aristocrats on the eve of the French Revolution.

Penn was reportedly shocked when, after his three-day visit in Iraq in December 2002, the Iraqi News Service reported that Penn had "confirmed that Iraq is completely clear of weapons of mass destruction."

## HERE COME THE DRAMA QUEENS!

"There's a chill wind blowing in America," warned actor Tim Robbins in April 2003. He breathlessly spoke of a new thought police that was working to enforce political conformity on the entertainment community since September 11. The best part of this is that Robbins was the invited speaker at the prestigious National Press Club in Washington, and his (endless) remarks were aired in their entirety by C-SPAN. With all the media face time Robbins and Sarandon get, you can forget a chill wind. A Category 5 tornado wouldn't shut them up.

"Susan and I have been listed as traitors, as supporters of Saddam, and various other epithets," he bawled. Hey Tim, loved you in *Shawshank Redemption*, but here's a hint: Don't say things that give aid and comfort to dictators and maybe people won't think you're supporting dictators. And when you step into the political fray with as little understanding as you have about foreign or military affairs, be prepared to be treated just as any other clod would be.

By the way, the staggering price that Robbins and Sarandon had to pay for their antiwar views was a canceled anniversary party for *Bull Durham* at the Baseball Hall of Fame and Sarandon's being disinvited to speak at a Florida United Way event. Oh, the horror!

The music industry has its share of drama queens, too. Front and center among them is Natalie Maines, lead singer of the ditsy Dixie Chicks. (And before you ask, yes, I love their music.) When the Chicks realized Natalie's moronic (and cowardly) anti-Bush comments in England might actually hurt their careers here in America, they agreed to an ABC interview with Diane Sawyer. In a cozy living room set, Maines laughed, cried, and waxed superficial. "If you don't like who I am, I really can't do anything about that. I am not going to change for anybody because I know who I am. [Crying] . . . And I like who I am. [Weeping]."

Get me to a vomitorium!

Maines then offered a classic nonapology apology for her statement that the Dixie Chicks were embarrassed that President Bush was from Texas: "It was the wrong wording with genuine emotion and questions and concern behind it." Perhaps the most hilarious part of the interview was when she said, "Am I sorry that I asked questions and that I just don't follow? No." Of course "following" is precisely what Maines was doing—following the uninformed, rabidly anti-Bush lemming mentality of the entertainment elite.

And yes, like Penn, she actually believes that Americans are inherently too stupid to know the difference between the real deal and a phony. She told *Entertainment Weekly*, "I feel patriotic and strong. We will continue to be who we are."

I'm sure the troops felt the love.

The anti-Chick heat got so hot for a while that people were having "melting parties" with Chicks CDs. Country stations tossed their songs out of the rotation, and I tossed their *Fly* CD out of a Toyota at sixty miles an hour. Irrational exuberance? Yes, but it made me happy—and isn't that what the elites believe? If it feels good, do it!

## HYPOCRISY, STAGE LEFT

The Dixie Chicks' feathers were singed so badly that even music legend Bruce Springsteen felt the need to come to the rescue. "They're terrific American artists expressing American values by using their American right to free speech," he said in a statement on his website. "The pressure coming from the government and big business to enforce conformity of thought concerning the war and politics goes against everything that this country is about— namely, freedom."

Janeane Garofalo, petite actress and member of Artists United to Win Without War, echoed Springsteen in an interview with the *LA Weekly*: "There are boycotts and guys driving tractors over their CDs—that's Nazi stuff."

Janeane Garofalo may have been funny once or twice in her life, and Springsteen might be born to run, but both of them need to read the Constitution before they make fools of themselves again. Only in the warped minds of entertainment elites can individuals organizing boycotts amount to "pressure coming from the government," or people throwing away CDs be equated with "Nazi stuff."

Indeed, the antiwar movement used the word "Nazi" almost as frequently as the word "like" in the days and weeks leading up to the start of Operation Iraqi Freedom. The slogans on placards, T-shirts, and buttons were so catchy, so fresh: "Bush is Hitler!" "Cheney is Hitler!" "Rumsfeld is Hitler!" As Dennis Miller pointed out on *The Tonight Show* one night on one of his many anti-antiwar rants that everyone is Hitler to them "... except the short guy with a mustache over there sticking people into wood chippers."

Plus, the last time I saw the words "artists," "united," and "against" together in an organization title, the artists were *leading* a boycott. The year was 1985, and there was a great debate in this country about how best to effect political change in South Africa. Some thought it was right to engage the country economically, while others thought it was right to shut down all ties. The divestment movement was relentless on college campuses and fully embraced by the entertainment elite.

In the music world, the divestment effort was led by a group called Artists United Against Apartheid. The man in charge was Steve Van Zandt of Bruce Springsteen's E Street Band (and more popularly known as Silvio in HBO's *The Sopranos*.) He pushed for a boycott not only of Sun City (the South African resort that paid top dollar to entertainers who performed there), but of the entire country. Springsteen, Bono, Jackson Browne, and Bonnie Raitt all sang in the chorus of the song (Ain't Gonna Play) "Sun City" that became an anthem for the anti-apartheid movement.

But if the music industry was enlightened and ahead of its time to boycott Sun City, why are fans and DJs who boycotted the Dixie Chicks Neanderthals? When artists get together to use their economic clout to express their opinion, it's a morally pure boycott. When conservatives do the same, it's a blacklist. Ain't gonna play Sun City is good, ain't gonna play the Dixie Chicks is "Nazi stuff."

It pains me to write this. I had the chance to meet Steve Van Zandt at the 2003 Grammys, and he was the coolest—very kind and unassuming—because he was being Steve the entertainer, decked out in his black bandanna, snakeskin boots, and rock-and-roll jewelry. The problem is, most musicians don't stop to realize how silly they can sound when they get beyond what they do best—entertain. Imagine a political talk show hostess with no musical background going on Larry King to lecture The Boss on musical arrangements. "Dude, you needed more bass in 'The Rising'!"

But our celebrities won't be deterred. In an interview with Melbourne's *Sunday Herald Sun* in February 2003, Van Zandt delved into the Iraq situation. "I have long supported Kurdish independence in Iraq and have not been a fan of Saddam Hussein's for a long time now," he said.

Not *a fan*?

"I think we should have got rid [sic] of him last time and finished the job off," he added. "Having said that, though, I know from my reading that he is an independent and paranoid kind of character who would be reluctant to work with Osama bin Laden."

Stop, Stevie! Stop! I'll never watch you on *The Sopranos* the same way again. Or hear you the same in the chorus of "If I Should Fall Behind." The "fan" line will keep popping into my head.

And to think Van Zandt is among the least objectionable of the entertainment crowd. He has nothing on Jessica, Barbra, Janeane, Danny, Natalie, Martin, Sean, Tim, and Susan. They are on an anti-Bush mission and proud of it.

Of course this is where the left will say, "Wait, what about conservatives Arnold Schwarzenegger, Bruce Willis, Mel Gibson, Clint Eastwood, Kelsey Grammer, Fred Thompson (former Tennessee senator), and Charlton Heston? And in rock and roll there's Ted Nugent and Kid Rock!" Sure, and country music is loaded with right-leaning talent: Toby Keith, Darryl Worley, the Warren Brothers, Charlie Daniels, Hank Williams Jr., and others. But it is a simple fact that in Hollywood and in the arts community of New York, it's *de rigueur* to be left-wing. And if you're not left-wing, then odds are you'll keep quiet about your politics. (Mega-stars like Gibson, Eastwood, and Schwarzenegger are no longer intimidated.) But even a high-wattage celebrity like Kelsey Grammer acknowledges the stigma. He was one of the few celebs to attend the 2000 Bush inaugural—and he knew it was a risky move. Before he took the stage, he joked nervously, "After tonight, I may never work in Hollywood again!"

But you don't get the sense that any of the Republicans in Hollywood wake up in the morning obsessed with how much they hate Tom Daschle and Nancy Pelosi. They rarely talk about politics on television. They rarely headline at conservative political rallies. Even when Bill Clinton was president, the few Republicans in Hollywood kept pretty quiet.

With people like Martin Sheen, Barbra Streisand, Michael Moore, Susan Sarandon, and Mike Farrell, being anti-Bush is a way of life. Everything this man stands for—God, family, country—makes their skin crawl. Why? For one simple reason. Because George Bush is an effective communicator of the conservative agenda and has the power to implement it. Plus, he succeeded their hero Bill Clinton—the darling of Beverly Hills, Brentwood, Bel Air, Santa Monica, Malibu, and the Hollywood Hills. Plus he beat Al Gore, the heir apparent. This makes George W. Bush the most dangerous man on the planet, certainly more dangerous than Osama bin Laden.

Hollywood, of course, wants us "regular people" to believe that their concern here is a principled one. They care about "the people." (Not American people, just "the people.") Consider this gem from Sheryl Crow: "I think war is based in greed and there are huge karmic retributions that will follow. I think war is never the answer to solving any problems. The best way to solve problems is not to have enemies."

Could I buy a vowel here? I do not recall her crowing about Bill Clinton's use of our military might in the mid-1990s in Bosnia. Why? She was too busy entertaining the troops at the invitation of the Clinton administration to worry about the karmic retribution. When pressed about why her antiwar pals in the entertainment biz didn't wail when Clinton used unilateral military force in Iraq, Janeane Garofalo, appearing on Fox News, revealed that "it wasn't very hip." What is hip is pig-piling George W. Bush or America whenever a Republican sets foot in the White House.

Others like Sarandon and Sheen jumped to impart the worst possible motives on the Bush administration, especially its "new policy" of preemptive military action. They repeat what they hear other left-wingers say on television or what they read in *The Nation*. Military force is never a good option, it's a failure in diplomacy, blah, blah, blah. So where was all this righteous harrumphing when Clinton forced a regime change in Haiti? When he ordered a cruise missile strike against a pharmaceutical factory in Sudan? When he authorized three days of air strikes against Iraq in December 1998? When he bombed Bosnia? When he drove Slobodan Milosevic from power after eleven weeks of air strikes in Yugoslavia? Remember, Milosevic posed no threat to us. But not a peep from Susan Sarandon & Co. Where was Artists United to Win Without War back then? MoveOn.org?

They could tolerate our military as long as Clinton was in charge (Hollywood loved all those Clinton-era military cutbacks), but most would rather that the American military not exist at all. They'd prefer a UN military, or a Global Military for Justice. As much as they dislike the military, the real piñata for the entertainment elites today is Bush. They have developed an unthinking, instinctive hatred for everything he stands for. To think he is almost the same age as Clinton, went to a liberal Ivy League School, but he's—ick—a Republican.

## IS IT THE DNA?

"We're actors—we're the opposite of people!" says one of the characters in Tom Stoppard's 1967 play *Rosencrantz and Guildenstern Are Dead*. Stoppard was on to something.

Most of the entertainers I've gotten to know over the years are knee-jerk lefties—a writer for *Roseanne* and *Spin City*, one of the most famous music producers of all time, a Grammy-winning singer-songwriter. And most of their friends are liberals who (again) think George W. Bush is a dolt, that Bill Clinton is a deity, that we need to "work with the UN more."

What is going on here? How did these entertainers become so out of touch with the views and values of the public that makes their livelihood possible? With a country that supports their lavish lifestyle? Do the arts (acting, singing, and writing and all the others) turn reasonable people into liberals, or are liberals drawn to the arts? Why do entertainers today feel such visceral hatred for President Bush?

Think of the aspiring actors you knew in high school. (The analysis that follows applies to musicians, too.) The students who join the drama club tend to be the kids who don't exactly fit into the mainstream of high school. Outsiders in their own hometowns, or just shy and introverted, they seem to come to life on the stage. Like so many extracurricular activities in school, acting is an outlet for them to express themselves, make like-minded friends.

When they graduate from high school, most young actors just continue on with their lives. Get regular jobs, go to college, and possibly act in a local theater group as a hobby. But some take the chance and follow their dreams. They try to take their acting to a higher level.

Some take the safe route and go to college to study drama. But most know that a college degree is not required. American singers and actors—from Streisand to Brando to Pacino—are usually not college types. They also know that talent agents don't make it to Fort Wayne or Fort Worth, Cheyenne, or Charlotte.

So the young actor piles up his few belongings, convinces a couple of friends to tag along, and moves to Los Angeles or Manhattan—and usually he's not very homesick.

Jessica Lange was born in Cloquet, Minnesota, and after a brief stint in college and some time in Paris studying to become a mime, she found herself in SoHo, waiting tables and doing part-time modeling. Susan Sarandon grew up in suburban New Jersey, studied drama at Catholic University, and ended up in New York City. Julia Roberts left her home in Smyrna, Georgia after graduating from high school to take a stab at acting in the Big Apple.

Young actors like Sarandon or Lange or Roberts flood into New York and Los Angeles every year, and soon find out that the unemployment rate in the acting world hovers around 100 percent, if you count the 130,000 actors with Screen Actors Guild cards, and the thousands upon thousands waiting to get them, all frantically chasing the same dream and the few available parts.

But these odds don't deter the young actors and actresses, who share cramped living quarters, sleep on couches, and wait tables between cattle-call auditions. Weeks, months, and years go by and that big break rarely comes. But many actors keep slogging on, in a state of semi-adolescence, even as the rest of us have long since gone on to working in "regular" jobs, getting married, and starting families.

The actor's world over time becomes more isolated, as friendships tend to involve mostly other actors and other countercultural types who are trying against all odds to make it in the strange world of entertainment. It becomes a life that's hard to leave, because it is all the actor knows. "One more year" is the mantra, because the big break is always just around the corner. A friend once told me that "acting is like playing the lottery, only with your life." He wasn't kidding.

And then there's the obvious. Think for a moment about what actors actually do for a living. "The actor creates with his flesh and blood all those things which all the arts in some way wish to describe," said the legendary acting coach Lee Strasberg. In short, actors play make-believe. A very sophisticated variety, no doubt. But make-believe nonetheless. At acting classes, they are asked—required—not so much to think but to feel. To emote. To empathize. To suspend judgment. To understand the people they are to play. How would they dress? How would they speak? How would they feel? How would their characters see the world? It's a gift, that kind of empathic power, and the great actors have it.

When Hollywood types speak about issues, they almost always start with the words, "I feel." It's what they do. They get paid to feel, not to think. This is not to say that actors, especially great ones, are not smart. Most are quite smart. Watching *Inside the*

*Actor's Studio* on Bravo, one cannot help but admire the actors' dedication to their craft—Tom Cruise, Dustin Hoffman, Meryl Streep, Kevin Spacey. Host James Lipton tosses out the questions about the nuances of acting, and I'm almost always mesmerized.

But invariably their intelligence relates to one line of work—acting. Their experience is in the world of entertainment, interpreting their roles on stage and screen. Unless they have had other important professional experience (in business or politics), their artistic know-how does not make them well suited to address, let's say, universal health care.

Indeed, their training and entire life's work leads them inexorably to a liberal position. No one would benefit more from socialized medicine than the mostly out-of-work acting community. Unemployment benefits enable many actors to follow their dream longer than most otherwise could. They think, in a country as rich and free as ours, why *not* have free medical care for everyone? Why *not* raise taxes on the rich? Remember, to underemployed actors, everyone seems rich. In 2001, nearly 75 percent of Screen Actors Guild members did not make more than $7,500, the amount they needed to earn to qualify for pension benefits.

Of course there is that one person in ten thousand who hits the acting lottery. She gets that part on a sitcom, or a supporting role in one film that leads to another that leads to the big time. And wham! The actor goes from rags to riches almost overnight. Scripts and party invitations roll in. Clothing designers line up to give her clothes. She suddenly has an agent, manager, accountant, lawyer, publicist, personal assistant, and personal trainer. They all tell her how wonderful she is. They provide insulation from the outside world. From picking up her dry-cleaning to negotiating a new contract, they have it covered.

With such an arbitrary system of enrichment, it's no wonder that actors lose sight of how the rest of the American workforce operates. Most Americans work their way up to middle management, with their prime motivation being to support their families;

# The Elites' Favorite Movies

**AMERICAN BEAUTY** (1999)—Twisted story of suburban dad in midlife crisis who rebels against it all by obsessing about teen daughter's best friend. The elite stereotype of our service members is embodied in the repressed, homophobic, wife-beating, Nazi-memorabilia-collecting Marine who lives next door.

**DEAD MAN WALKING** (1995)—Directed by elite poster boy Tim Robbins. Elite fave Susan Sarandon plays a nun who empathizes with condemned killer played by elite bad boy Sean Penn. Message: the death penalty is cruel and unusual punishment.

**PLATOON** (1986)—Directed by Oliver "Grassy Knoll" Stone. Highlight: Tom Berenger plays a vile thuggish sergeant who terrorizes a Vietnamese family. Americans portrayed as essentially boorish, unfeeling louts who throw their weight around. Elites rewarded Stone with Oscars for Best Director and Best Picture. Message: We were the bad guys in this one.

**ABOUT SCHMIDT** (2002)—A veiled elite lampoon of Middle America. Nebraskan retiree played by Jack Nicholson struggles with life after his wife's death. It's all so unfulfilling. So why did the filmmaker change the plot line from that of the original book, in which the main character was a retired Manhattan attorney with a house in Bridgehampton, Long Island?

**BOWLING FOR COLUMBINE** (2002)—Michael Moore versus the gun industry. A documentary with more smoke and mirrors than Harry Potter. Message: Guns and gun people are scary and stupid. ∎

there's a very clear connection of effort, reward, and purpose. But in acting there is no middle management. You either make it or you don't. Writer Dinesh D'Souza explains it this way: "People who make a lot of money for a little work start to feel that the whole system of wealth creation is just a matter of luck." If people do not succeed, it's because "they are just victims of bad luck, so the government has an obligation to help them."

In addition to their lack of appreciation for the capitalist system that has made them zillionaires, there remains the simple issue of geography. Actors live in cities that are among the most liberal in America. A musician friend in New York told me that before September 11, he rarely heard an actor or musician say a good word about former Mayor Rudy Giuliani. Words like "fascist" or "racist" tripped off their tongues while they sat in their Che Guevara T-shirts sipping triple espressos. They are now using the same adjectives to describe George W. Bush. The Republicans might change, but the "-ists" never do.

## WHY HOLLYWOOD'S POLITICAL MONOLITH MATTERS

So Hollywood and the entire entertainment culture is liberal, out of touch with the rest of us, and narcissistic. Who cares? What real influence do they have anyway? After all as a political movement, liberalism is on life support.

Nice try, but it's not so simple.

Remember that "chill wind" that Tim Robbins was wailing about during the Iraq War, when he felt that artists were being cowed by the patriotic fervor whipped up by the Bush administration? Tim didn't get it quite right. The real chill wind today that blows through the entertainment world isn't coming from the government, it's coming from the entertainment world itself. The reigning liberal orthodoxy—anticapitalist and antireligious—affects what we see and hear as entertainment consumers. More important, it affects what we *don't* see and hear.

There are many great movies about the Nazis and stories about the Holocaust. *Schindler's List* was riveting. But where is the movie *Stalin's List*? Why is it that Communists in Hollywood movies are depicted as complicated, sensitive souls and victims of the Hollywood blacklist while Nazis (i.e., Republicans) are invariably one-dimensional, thuggish, and stupid?

There are innumerable movies and plays bashing capitalism. Arthur Miller's *Death of a Salesman* is an American classic. But where is the play *Death of an Apparatchik*? Oliver Stone's *Wall Street* was great. But where is the movie *Tiananmen Square*?

Don't hold your breath waiting for films with such antiliberal themes, because the liberal monopoly on the arts has a stultifying effect. It's why Hollywood is one of the leading incubators of "political correctness," which is just another way of saying "no conservative opinions allowed." And it's why elites who hate America can love one of America's greatest industries, the entertainment industry—because it spins the wonderful fables they want to believe about America. Not the classics of the Golden Age of Hollywood, made before the elitists took over the business.

## HOLLYWOOD'S LOVE SCENE WITH FIDEL: A DICTATOR FOR ALL SEASONS

In 1996, American roots musician and musicologist Ry Cooder gathered together some of Cuba's greatest musicians of the 1930s, '40s, and '50s to collaborate on the record *Buena Vista Social Club*. It was a smash hit and a Grammy Award winner, and in 1998, director Wim Wenders traveled to Havana to chronicle the camaraderie between Cooder and his new Cuban musician friends, as well as their remarkable concerts in Amsterdam and New York's Carnegie Hall.

"In Cuba, the music flows like a river," said Wenders. "I want to make a film that'll just float on this river—not interfering with it, just drifting along."

Of course, what doesn't flow like a river in Cuba is freedom. Or free expression. And regrettably, what movies like *Buena Vista Social Club* do is glamorize Castro's reign of terror and give the entertainment and academic elite ammunition to continue their love affair with communism and socialism. Of course there is that inconvenient little issue of Fidel Castro's executing, imprisoning, and abusing tens of thousands who simply did not believe in the communist utopia, but hey, Cuba has a great music scene! Millions have died and suffered around the world because of communist dictatorships, but Hollywood still cannot seem to shake the attraction, so busy is it shaking to the groove.

The entertainment elites are dedicated to human rights—except when human rights become inconvenient to their broader left-wing political agenda.

I'm still waiting for a song like "Ain't Gonna Play Havana." Or musicians calling for worldwide economic sanctions against the tyranny of Castro. If Wim Wenders had made a film about the music scene in apartheid-era South Africa, wouldn't we have heard something about racism? How come when the subject is Cuba, we don't hear about . . . communism?

"Oh, Laura, that's so simplistic! The situations are totally different. South Africa was a racist regime. Cuba is just . . . well . . . just different."

It must be fun to be an artist. You get to make up your own moral universe. And then you can change it whenever it suits you.

If divestment from South Africa was one of the pet causes of the entertainment industry in the 1980s, somehow, the very same entertainers see the U.S. embargo against Cuba as counterproductive. Worse, they even fall over themselves to make excuses for Castro.

In the late spring of 2003, after Castro rounded up seventy-five dissidents—writers, economists, poets—and in sham, secret trials sentenced them to prison terms of up to twenty-eight years, where were the human rights crusaders in Hollywood? A few like Danny

Glover and Harry Belafonte reacted not by condemning Castro but by condemning the United States. More than 160 artists and so-called intellectuals signed a "declaration of support" for Cuba, which sounded as if it had been written by Castro himself. The group warned that Washington's "harassment against Cuba could serve as a pretext for an invasion." Yes, I'm sure the first thing on President Bush's agenda is "Invade Cuba today."

The following exchange on MSNBC's *Buchanan & Press* (May 7, 2003), with Pat Buchanan squaring off with the former Screen Actors Guild president, actor Ed Asner, reveals volumes about Hollywood's blind spot for Fidel:

**BUCHANAN**: What is it about Harry Belafonte, frankly, and Danny Glover that they can attack the American government and defend a guy who would basically put them in prison for doing what they do here in the United States?

**ASNER**: Well, they may well be put in prison here for those—for the support they are giving to Castro, the way things are going in this country. I am opposed to capital punishment by any country, by any person, so I disapprove of Mr. Castro's executing. I understand that the trial was very fair, that the death penalty is exercised in Cuba. And, therefore, by Cuban standards, the trial was fair and judicious, even though I abhor the death penalty.

**BUCHANAN**: I want you to name individuals in this country who have made political statements criticizing President Bush who have been put into a penitentiary for five, ten, or twenty-five years, like these dissidents who criticized Castro were put into prison. And is this not a real slander on your own country, to suggest that it behaves in the same manner as Fidel Castro?

**ASNER**: My country is much more fortunate. So it doesn't have to afford the excesses that Fidel Castro has to resort to by constantly being embargoed by the United States.

**BUCHANAN**: Why does he have to do this? Why does he have to do it?

**ASNER**: Why does he have to do it? Because he feels the imminent threat of the Bush administration. I don't regard the Bush administration as being representative of my country.

**PRESS:** Do you really believe this, I think, idiocy coming from Castro that the Bush administration has a plot to invade Cuba and topple Fidel Castro? That's what he's telling his people and that's what he's basing this on, Ed.

**ASNER**: Once again, the Bush administration is beginning to lower the crunch on Castro. They just canceled student scholastic trips and museum trips to Cuba, which will once again lower the flow of about 600,000 people in these types of visas that have been traveling to Cuba. So that has been stopped.

**BUCHANAN**: He has persecuted his own people. He has denied them free elections for forty years. He is an unelected dictator who puts people in prison on his own. What is the infatuation...

**ASNER**: We didn't have a free election in 2002.

Asner and his acolytes hate Bush and never give him the benefit of the doubt. They love Fidel and always give him the benefit of the doubt. So to them, our system is corrupt. Fidel's is "complex."

Friendly visits from industry heavyweights like Steven Spielberg, Oliver Stone, Ted Turner, Yoko Ono, Matt Dillon, Leonardo DiCaprio, and Jack Nicholson give Castro the cultural cover he needs. Castro opens his presidential palace to Hollywood's top tier, which feeds the hungry ego of the writers, actors, and directors who make the Castro Connection. They return to the United States after being given star treatment by official "guides," raving about the experience. Castro is so charming! So cosmopolitan! He loves literature and good music! He gave me a box of his private stash of cigars! Supermodels Naomi Campbell and Kate Moss met Castro after a Havana fashion shoot in 1999 and compared him to Nelson Mandela: "He said seeing us in person was very spiritual."

The more dinners Castro hosts for Hollywood moguls (and the same goes for business, political, and intellectual figures), the more legitimacy he brings with him onto the international stage. In April

2001, Kevin Costner (rumored to vote Republican, at least in the past) flew to Havana for dinner and a movie with Fidel. The movie was Costner's new project *Thirteen Days*—about the Cuban missile crisis!

What looks like Castro's genuine openness to artistic expression is really his clever way of maintaining his steel grip on power—the kind of power that orders sham, secret trials of "enemies of the state," then sentences them to languish in state prisons for decades. Stalin practiced the same trick, as did Saddam. Artists and poets who praised the regime to the skies were rewarded with gifts, fine houses, and all the perks. Those who didn't, well, we don't know what happened to them. They simply disappeared, never to be seen again.

But our Hollywood human rights champions always look the other way.

As sickening a spectacle as this is, many in Hollywood have fallen hard for Castro's overtures. Castro is a master at stroking the ego of attention-addicted entertainment types. To them he is a romantic, idealistic figure, who has defied all odds by surviving the collapse of the Soviet Union and outlasting nine American presidents. How cool is that? And plus, if America is an "imperialist" aggressor, as many in Hollywood's antiwar movement believe, who better to cozy up to than the man who beat back the American imperialists thirty-five years ago?

They see him as "the ultimate visionary, a Robin Hood who understood long before anyone else that battling the U.S. 'will be my true destiny,'" writes Damien Cave in the *Washington Monthly*. "Celebrities essentially become children when it comes to Cuba," he writes. And there's no better example of this than Oliver Stone, who has described Castro as "one of the Earth's wisest people."

Stone spent thirty hours hanging with Fidel in Feburary 2002, and from those magical moments he put together *Comandante*, a ninety-five-minute "documentary" for HBO. The big premiere was supposed to happen in May 2003, but HBO temporarily put the brakes on shortly after the dictator's springtime crackdown. Some editing and refilming might be in order, HBO said. Imagine how pro-Castro the film must be for HBO to pull it!

I was actually disappointed. Stone painted such a loony, ominous picture of America in *JFK* and *Nixon*—it would be a comic delight to see him getting weak in the knees for the anti-American dictator who keeps on ticking. And think of what a challenge filming a movie in Cuba would be—every time you announce the time of the next "shoot" to the local camera crews, they run and hide!

## ENTERTAIN THIS!

Of course, celebrities are people, too. Just because they have a SAG card doesn't mean they lose their First Amendment rights. But thankfully most entertainers spare us the constant political lectures. We rarely hear from Al Pacino, Robert De Niro, Robert Duvall, or Gene Hackman, or even from the younger actors like Johnny Depp or Tobey Maguire. It may be because they know it's bad business, or that no one cares what they think, or maybe they are just not all that political. They may know that when we see them as political animals, they lose some of their on-screen magic.

Entertainers, especially those who have made it, have so much to offer our needy world, and many donate their time and money to worthy charities. Bravo! Who can forget the smash song "We Are the World" produced by Quincy Jones, Lionel Richie, and Michael Jackson? They got the biggest names in music to perform together, raising millions for starving Africans. Today Quincy Jones is still at it—music and philanthropy. He's now spearheading a massive campaign to bring primary care medicine to poor children around the world.

And there are a few entertainers out there who are liberal, and yet, unusually, have the credibility to back up their views. Bono (the front man for the band U2) spent years learning about AIDS prevention and Third World debt relief. The merits of his views aside, at least he is intelligent and informed and has some firsthand experience with these matters. I interviewed him in the summer of 2001 and was thoroughly impressed. This makes some conservatives wince. So be it.

But the vast majority of the celebrities today who feel the need to lash out are mindlessly anti-Bush, antimilitary, anti-Cheney, anti-Ashcroft, anti-SUV (as they fly off in their G-5's), and antisuperpower (at least as long as we're the superpower).

"They should keep their mouths shut," said Robert Duvall of the celebrity Bush-bashers in April 2003. Even liberal actor Ron Silver, who appeared with me at a pro-troops rally in Washington, said he was embarrassed for some of his colleagues, and that they should think before they speak.

That won't happen anytime soon, though. The popularity and successes of the Bush administration will not shame the entertainment elites in silence. While some are taking a breather from their anti-Bush blather, others vow to keep their traps flapping.

"They [Bush and his supporters] are going to do the thing they're going to do, but we'll be heard from when it's appropriate, and in the manner that is appropriate," vowed Mike Farrell in the days following Operation Iraqi Freedom.

## STUPID WHITE MAN

"We live in fictitious times. We live in the time when we have fictitious election results that elect a fictitious president. We live in a time where we have a man sending us to war for fictitious reasons."
—**MICHAEL MOORE**, accepting his Oscar for Best Documentary
(March 27, 2003)

It was Oscar night. And it was all about Michael: "Shame on you, Mr. Bush. Shame on you. And any time that you have the pope and the Dixie Chicks against you, your time is up." (Since when did the Hollywood elite care about the views of the pope?) His anti-Bush rant in front of a worldwide audience served his interests—an uptick in book and movie sales. He's one big, hulking, sweating, self-promoting machine.

Michael Moore deserves his own section in this book because he is in a league, a very big league, of his own. He captures the essence of what the Hollywood elite is all about. He says what they all *want* to say. His latest book is Babs's bible and he is the darling of the international media.

My one encounter with Moore was in a face-off on the Independent Television Network in Britain, shortly after the Republican sweep in the 2002 midterm elections. He was in the studio with the (liberal) anchor in London, I was in Washington participating via satellite. Speaking as if the election hadn't just happened, Moore railed against Bush. He seemed unwilling to confront the reasons for the Democrats' big flop with the voters. I suggested that perhaps it had something to do with the fact that so many on the left (like Michael) think Americans are stupid. At the end of the segment, in double boxes with me on screen, Moore's final rebuttal was: "This is why they always win. They're better looking than we are."

Unfunny and unsubstantive. Typical Michael Moore.

He has gotten rich by assailing the rich. He is a champion of the everyman even as he sends his daughter to a fancy Manhattan private school. He has vilified corporate America but corporate America bankrolls his books and documentaries.

What a guy.

Moore made his mark in 1989 with his critically acclaimed documentary *Roger and Me*. The overweight everyman with the worn-out baseball cap, Moore spent two years unsuccessfully trying to get an interview with General Motors CEO Roger Smith. Smith ordered the closing of a number of GM factories, one of which was in Flint, Michigan, where most of Moore's documentary is set.

# **Elite**speak **alert!**

Stupid White Men: Not, as you might expect, an autobiography by Michael "Two Dinners" Moore, but a stinging, insightful critique about, like, how BAD and DUMB AmeriKKKa is!!!!! Move over, Toqueville. The book's huge sales are testament to just how many stupid white men there are in this country. Michael is currently working on his next project, *Clever Fat Man*, the story of a liar who makes a manipulative "documentary" and earns millions of lovely greenbacks. I can't wait. ■

What Tom Wolfe and Hunter S. Thompson did for nonfiction, Moore did for documentaries. *Roger and Me* was immensely entertaining, even if it was an utter travesty of the truth.

But we soon learned that Moore had no range. He is a one-note Mikey. His mid-1994 TV series *TV Nation* and his 1996 book *Downsize This* rehashed the same themes we saw in *Roger and Me*. Corporations are bad. The average working stiff doesn't have a chance.

Moore saw himself as the Mike Wallace for the six-pack crowd, a puffed-up terminator of the tax shelter set. But in the 1990s he had a hard time drumming up sales or success. There was no Republican president to blame, the economy was booming, and Moore, who makes has bucks off of other people's adversities, needed a new target.

He found one in George W. Bush and in the sort of America Moore thinks Bush represents—moronic, gun-owning Republicans. *Stupid White Men* was a *New York Times* bestseller for more than a year, and *Bowling for Columbine*, his latest documentary, is now the bestselling documentary in history.

*Stupid White Men* captures the essence of what the Hollywood elite is all about. To them Moore seems positively brilliant, with insights like this: "There is no recession, my friends. No downturn. No hard times. The rich are wallowing in the loot they've accumulated in the past two decades, and now they want to make sure you don't come a-lookin' for your piece of the pie." Don't come a-lookin'? Michael also thinks it's a mark of literary sophistication TO WRITE IN CAPITAL LETTERS WITH LOTS OF EXCLAMATION MARKS!!!!!!

To call the book sophomoric would be an insult to sophomores in high school and college. Don't come a-lookin' for a piece of the pie around Michael. He ate it all.

Which brings me to his documentary *Bowling for Columbine* (or as Dennis Miller called it, *Trolling for Concubines*), Moore's look at America's alleged obsession with guns and violence. Again the theme: America has it all wrong, and places like Canada and Switzerland have it right.

When it was first screened at the Cannes Film Festival in the late spring of 2002, the European audience loved it. According to Chris Kaltenbach of the *Baltimore Sun*, who was reporting from Cannes, "(the screening) was followed by a thirteen-minute standing ovation, the longest anyone could remember." "[Moore's] movie," he reported, "was the only one that everybody was talking about.... Clearly, the French couldn't get enough of this unshaven, overweight, self-described schlub from Flint, Michigan." A group of French educators, the Jury Education Nationale, awarded him their grand prize, and yet another prolonged standing ovation, according to Kaltenbach.

"I want this movie to act as a warning to this country and to other countries," Moore told the adoring audience. "If you as a society allow this sort of violence, if you allow your government to beat up on those who have little or nothing, you will end up like us." Moore left Cannes with the affection of the Europeans, awards from the French, and a distribution deal from United Artists.

No one was surprised that he won the Oscar for Best Documentary. It was a lock from the beginning. How could it not be, what with its NRA bashing and coarse, snide mockery of Middle America. (No, Mike, you don't inoculate yourself from scrutiny when you say that you're a life-long NRA member.) The problem is, *Bowling* is not a documentary, which the Academy defines as a nonfiction production. *Bowling* is a lie, an elaborate deception. There's more truth in a mockumentary like *This Is Spinal Tap* than in *Bowling for Columbine.*

The Academy was not concerned about the fact that Moore had, according to a *Forbes* investigation, misrepresented a key scene in the film where he targets a bank in Traverse City, Michigan. As a long-standing promotional event, the bank offered customers opening new accounts a rifle instead of paying interest on a certificate of deposit. (This is more reprehensible to the Hollywood left than Saddam's gassing his own people.) According to the movie, "I put $1,000 in a long-term account, they did the background check, and, within an hour, I walked out with my new Weatherby." Shocking stuff. But it's not real. The bank employee who opened the account for Moore, Jan Jacobson, says that Moore's film company worked for a month on staging the scene. In reality, new account holders have to pick the gun up at a dealer in another city after a week-to-ten-day waiting period. Nobody just walks out of the bank holding a rifle. "He just portrayed us as backward hicks," complained Ms. Jacobson. Ah, there's nothing like a true-blue (as opposed to blue-collar) elitist like Michael "Man of the People" Moore humiliating the very folks he claims to be protecting.

Here's what the *Times* of London said about Michael Moore: "Richard Schickel, arguably America's most distinguished observer of the cinema, was rather more forthcoming about Moore's general approach: 'I despise our gun laws in the States, too. But Moore's tactics, I think, give aid and comfort to the enemy. In short, he's careless with his facts, hysterical in debate and, most basically, a guy trying to make a star out of himself. He's a self-aggrandiser and, perhaps, the very definition of the current literary term, "the unreliable narrator." This guy either can't or won't stick to the point, build a logical case for his arguments. It's all hysteria—but, I think, calculated hysteria.'"

That one misrepresentation was bad enough. But there are many, many others. What about the cartoon sequence equating the NRA with the KKK and claiming the two are connected? It's garbage, of course. In fact, the Unionist founders of the NRA were diametrically opposed to the Confederate founders of the KKK. Or how about Moore's claim that our government gave $245 million to the Taliban in 2000 and 2001 to prop up the regime? Again, not true. The money was not given to the government but distributed through American and international humanitarian agencies to stave off famine and clear land mines. Or what about Moore's claim that he bought several boxes of ammunition at a Wal-Mart in Canada without a question being asked or showing any identification? Yet again, Canadian firearms officials have raised questions about Moore's veracity.

So blinded is he by anti-American self-loathing that his ideology gets in the way even of reporting simple facts. Moore asserts that a Lockheed Martin factory in Littleton, Colorado (home of Columbine), trucks missiles with "Pentagon payloads" through town "in the middle of the night while the children are asleep." He speculates that knowledge of these nearby weapons of "mass destruction" might have inspired the Columbine boys to go on their shooting spree. "What's the difference between that mass destruction and the mass destruction over at Columbine High School?" Leaving aside the bizarre assertion that these missiles had anything to do with the massacre (I mean, I live near the Pentagon and Andrews Air Force Base but I've never had any inclination to become a mass murderer), Moore gets it completely wrong. That Lockheed Martin factory manufactures rockets, but rockets *for launching television satellites*, the kinds of satellites that air the shows that interview Moore.

Here's another example. David Hardy, a former Interior Department lawyer who has assiduously dissected Moore's film, observed that in *Bowling*, Mike films a B-52 on display at the Air Force Academy and Moore claims the plane has a plaque under it that "proudly proclaims that the plane killed Vietnamese people on Christmas Eve of 1972." Um, no, it doesn't. The plaque in question reads: "B-52D Stratofortress. 'Diamond Lil.' Dedicated to the men and women of the Strategic Air Command who flew and maintained the B-52D throughout its 26-year history in the command. Aircraft 55-003, with over 15,000 flying hours, is one of two B-52Ds credited with a confirmed MIG kill during the Vietnam Conflict. Flying out of U-Tapao Royal Thai Naval Airfield in southeastern Thailand, the crew of 'Diamond Lil' shot down a MIG northeast of Hanoi during 'Linebacker II' action on Christmas Eve, 1972." That's a little different from Moore's spin. But Mikey never lets facts get in the way of his agenda.

Perhaps worst of all is Moore's depiction of former NRA president Charlton Heston, which was truly despicable. Moore wanted to portray Heston as a heartless gun nut in the aftermath of Columbine. To do this, he showed footage of a Denver NRA meeting that took place ten days after the shootings—including clips of Charlton's Heston's famous "cold dead hands" speech where he raises a gun above his head. But Heston didn't even say these words at that Denver meeting. Moore grabbed that footage from a meeting a year later in Charlotte, North Carolina, where Heston had received an antique musket as a present. Moore spliced and cut and edited and deleted to create a travesty of the truth. Referring to the Heston "speech," David Hardy points out that "Moore has actually taken audio of seven sentences, from five different parts of the speech, and a section given in a different speech entirely, and spliced them together. Each edit is cleverly covered by inserting a still or video footage for a few seconds." In intent and method, there is nothing different between Moore's propaganda and the techniques used by Stalin's professional liars.

Fictitious presidency? Fictitious election? Guess it takes a fictitious "documentary" maker to know.

The smoke and mirrors have worked well for Mike. Thanks to the success of *Columbine*, Miramax (which is owned by a big bad corporation, Disney) has agreed to cover production costs of Moore's next project, *Fahrenheit 911*. "The primary thrust of the new film is what has happened to the country since 9/11, and how the Bush administration used this tragic event to push its agenda," said Moore, a man obsessed.

Someday soon Michael may get a taste of his own medicine. An enterprising director named Michael Wilson is making a film called *Michael Moore Hates America*, which he says will both expose Moore's lies and present inspiring stories about the America Moore doesn't celebrate. If I were making a documentary about Michael Moore, I'd call it *Michael and Me*. I would spend two years running around trying to snag an interview with Moore as he hops from limo to limo, or wait to ambush him with questions outside his posh Upper West Side Manhattan apartment.

I would return to Flint, Michigan, and talk to the locals about Michael. The world would find, as Matt Labash pointed out in a brilliant vivisection of Moore's career in *The Weekly Standard* back in 1998, that Michael isn't really from Flint, as he has implied over and over again. He is from a nearby white middle-class suburb. I would talk to Donald Prieh, Moore's high school teacher, who once told the *Flint Journal*, "Moore has always used Flint."

In *Michael and Me*, the world would learn that Moore played fast and loose with the facts in *Roger and Me*. "His much touted 30,000 GM layoffs came not in 1986 as Moore implied, but over the course of a decade, and in several different states," wrote Labash. "He showed people getting evicted who'd never been GM workers, and as the press began detailing discrepancies, Moore accused various journalists of lying or being GM tools."

Wouldn't it be fun to interview those fake GM evictees? And the journalists whom Moore tried to smear?

I would also love to interview some of the people who worked with Michael Moore. Someone like Haskell Wexler, one of the world's greatest cinematographers. In Labash's article, Wexler says of Moore, "He's not unlike a lot of people I used to know in the left-wing movement. They love humanity and hate people."

"It was striking how many former associates—all predisposed to side with Moore—bitterly revile him," wrote Labash. "Randy Cohen, a former Letterman writer and coexecutive producer of *TV Nation* who was fired by Moore, offers a typical compliment: "I despise Mike and regard him as a vile and dishonorable man, but I think *Roger and Me* was terrific.""

Last, I would love to interview Ben Hamper, the man who was Moore's sole link to a real-life assembly line. Hamper worked for GM, and also wrote the very funny *Rivethead: Tales from an Assembly Line.* (Hamper paints a very different picture of life at GM from the one Moore paints, describing in detail not only the mind-numbing monotony of the work, but the many benefits and raises that earned GM the nickname "Generous Motors" among the workers. But what would Hamper know—he only worked there!)

When Moore finally paid a visit to Hamper's GM plant to "hit rivets, act manly, and bid adieu to the life he'd never known," wrote Labash, he showed up in a Honda. I guess Mike's on the side of the workers, but only the ones employed by Honda.

In *Michael and Me*, I would save the very best scenes for the end. The showstoppers would be these two exchanges between Moore and Bob Costas on Costas's HBO show *On the Record* in late spring 2003. Both would show the world just what a kook, what a nut, and what a megalomaniacal narcissist Moore really is.

**MOORE:** What happened to the search for Osama bin Laden?

**COSTAS:** Obviously they're pursuing Osama bin Laden as we speak.

**MOORE:** Really, you believe that?

**COSTAS:** Yes.

**MOORE:** You do believe that?

**COSTAS:** Sure. And if they could find him, and perhaps they eventually will, they'd be gratified by that.

**MOORE:** You don't think they know where he is?

**COSTAS:** You think they know where Osama bin Laden is and it's hands off?

**MOORE:** Absolutely, absolutely.

**COSTAS:** Why?

**MOORE:** Because he's funded by their friends in Saudi Arabia! He's back living with his sponsors, his benefactors. Do you think that Osama bin Laden planned 9/11 from a cave in Afghanistan? I can't get a cell signal from here to Queens, all right? I mean, come on. Let's get real about this. The guy has been on dialysis for two years. He's got failing kidneys. He wasn't in a cave in Afghanistan playing...

**COSTAS:** You think he's in Saudi Arabia, not Afghanistan, not Pakistan.

**MOORE:** Well, could be Pakistan, but he's under watch of those who have said put a stop to this because...

**COSTAS:** Including, at least by extension, the United States, he's under the protective watch of the United States?

**MOORE:** I think the United States, I think our government knows where he is and I don't think we're going to be capturing him or killing him any time soon.

When Bob Costas dares to criticize Moore, and tells him that statements like that about Osama bin Laden hurt his credibility, and possibly cost him readers and viewers, this is Moore's response. "I'm the biggest-selling author in America, I've got the biggest-selling documentary of all time [laughing], I get twenty million hits a day on my website, how many more people do I need to convince [laughing maniacally]."

*Michael and Me* would be one terrific documentary, and I wouldn't have to stage a single scene. But I won't hold my breath waiting for a distribution deal from Harvey Weinstein, buddy of the Clintons. And if it ever did make it to the screen, I sure as heck won't get any standing ovations over there in Cannes, or any Oscars. But I know my documentary would knock 'em dead in the red states, and the fly-overs. Exposing a disgusting documentary filmmaker who poses as a down-to-earth everyman who's for the Middle American working guy but is really a nasty, egomaniacal hypocrite who makes his fortune from the very fat cats he purports to despise, and then goes and lives with them in the Big City, is a story almost anyone would love.

Even Michael Moore.

## STILL SEETHING, STILL BREATHING

During and after our brilliant military campaign in Iraq, I actually started to feel sorry for those on the left. The country rallied behind our military heroes. Our national pride once again shone brightly. The flag was everywhere. In other words—a nightmare scenario for people like Susan Sarandon and Tim Robbins. (Oh, but wait, that's right . . . they support the troops!) Many of the entertainment elites are regrouping, taking their seething behind closed doors, as they wait for their next opportunity to showcase their political acumen.

Every day that we didn't find WMD in Iraq, the anti-Bush clique in Hollywood became a bit more gleeful. (Hey, has anyone considered sending Hans Blix and his team to Malibu? These people seem a little too happy!) Babs fired up her website again. Sean Penn wrote a postwar manifesto that ran as a full-page ad in the May 30 *New York Times*. And you thought the Unabomber was a windbag! Penn's rambling screed was part Maya Angelou, part Workers World Party. But more than anything it was all about Sean; like so much in Hollywood, it was a glorification of the self. "In Iraq and in the United States, *I* want to see who's the boss. *I* want to see who's [*sic*] the people. *I* want to see who are the sheep, and *I* want to know the lions." (Read: Americans, you sheep, you! You still support Bush? Wake up! I am Sean! Hear me roar. I am a lion. Meow.) "I have consulted over 100 experts in our Middle Eastern affairs. . . . *I* spoke at length with wary [weary?] war correspondents," he wrote, in a transparent attempt to make us realize how informed he is, dammit! In Sean's world, we are "on the verge of losing our flag," and that "that same flag that took *me* so long to love, respect, and protect, threatens to become a haunting banner of murder, greed and treason." In one paragraph, Penn, pleads for civility in discourse, in the next he personally attacks President Bush, denigrating not only his service in the Texas Air National Guard during the Vietnam War, but his entire being: "This young man of privilege, who never had the curiosity to set foot outside our country before becoming president." With such searing insight, who could resist the Penn prescription for what ails us?

As I was finishing this book, the entertainment elite was energized by accusations of bad U.S. pre-war intelligence, and is back at the blame-Bush game. It's so easy to play. It's the only game they know. Susan, Barbra, Sean, and the gang are gearing up for the presidential election. Howard Dean is collecting a lot of cash from Hollywood, and John Kerry isn't far behind. Penn, Bonnie Raitt, and Robin Williams were expected to join Democrat presidential hopeful Dennis Kucinich on the campaign trail in northern California. Man of the people Kucinich and the crew were set to shuttle around in a Greyhound bus fueled by recycled vegetable oil. Maybe that explains Penn's ungrammatical, circuitous, and hyperbolic manifesto—broccoli fumes.

You think it's bad now. Just wait until George W. Bush wins reelection in 2004—these elites will be beside themselves, so demoralized they might actually go back to entertaining us again.

5

# God, You're Fired

lites are God-fearing people. But not in the sense most of us mean. They are "theophobic." They have an abiding fear—often expressed as an intense hostility and dismissive mockery—of all things religious. Any mention of the Almighty risks setting them off into one of their tirades against "organized religion." One thing is for sure: *they are obsessed with religion.* And their obsession is undeterred by reason, truth, history, or the "collateral damage" their obsession inflicts. As G. K. Chesterton said, "For the enemies of religion cannot leave it alone. They laboriously attempt to smash religion. They cannot smash religion; but they do smash everything else."

Nothing threatens the elites so much as true faith. They recoil like vampires at the sight of a cross. They charge into court at any mention of God in the classroom. And public prayers are sure to land you before a judge.

Of course the elites will fall all over themselves to deny that they are antireligious. They think religion is tolerable—as long as it's kept private and doesn't interfere with your public life or public opinions. Take the grilling that the Democrats on the Senate Judiciary Committee gave Bush appellate court nominee William

**113**

Pryor in June 2003. In the eyes of the elites on the Judiciary Committee (Chuck Schumer, Diane Feinstein, Pat Leahy, and Ted Kennedy), Pryor already had one strike against him—he's from Alabama. Worse, though, than Pryor's being a Southerner was the fact that he is a devout Catholic. In questioning, Pryor stated that yes, he was pro-life and pro–traditional family. This of course put him on a collision course with the Dem-elite agenda.

The Democrats' evidence that Pryor is a religious extremist is that he once called *Roe* v. *Wade* an "abomination" and also rescheduled a personal family vacation to Disney World when he discovered that it would coincide with the theme park's gay pride day. Pryor cited his religious beliefs to explain both views. So, like clockwork, the antireligious zealots got to work. The ACLU and People for the American Way trashed him, and other liberal advocacy groups joined in, too. In his questioning of Pryor, Schumer made it clear, without explicitly saying so, that people who take their religion seriously are immediately suspect. "[Pryor's] beliefs

# The Big Lie

" 'm spiritual but not religious" is the mantra of the antireligion elites. They feel that by saying that, they somehow have covered their bases and yet still sound cool to all the "right" people. Take Madonna, who made millions from songs such as "Like a Virgin," "Like a Prayer," and "Papa Don't Preach." She regards her Catholic roots as something to "evolve" away from. Consider her comments: "Catholicism is a very masochistic religion . . . . There is a certain darkness within it . . . . It's not a very loving religion . . . . It's not very flexible. It doesn't make room for human error." (Apparently, she skipped the repentance part of catechism.) In another breath, she claims, "I don't make fun of Catholicism. I respect it. Deeply." ■

are so deeply held that it's very difficult to believe those views won't influence how he follows the law," Schumer sniped. "When you believe abortion is murder, how can you convince the public that you are capable of being fair?"

Pryor repeatedly told the committee that if confirmed he would follow the *Roe* v. *Wade* precedent—but that wasn't good enough. The truth is, if the Left had its way, there would be a religious litmus test preventing any devout Christian from becoming a federal appeals court judge. Toward the end of the hearing, when Orrin Hatch asked Pryor about his religious affiliation (presumably to drive home the litmus-test point), liberal Patrick Leahy vehemently objected. "It's irrelevant if you are Catholic. I hope this isn't a question we're going to ask in the future.... We will all regret it if we do."

## THE GREAT ELITE UNIFIER

There can be no doubt that the central prejudice that unifies all elites is their hostility to religion—at least real religion. They can't stand the idea that there is someone greater, someone more important, someone more powerful than themselves. That God exists, that He created the universe, that He should be obeyed are ideas that run smack against the elite dogma. The truths that God created us, that He is our loving father, that He is our merciful savior are not good news received joyfully and accepted by elites. Instead, these messages are viewed as if they were personal insults. And that's because to the elite mind they are insults—they represent an affront to the supremacy of the individual. To their minds, the belief that God created the world was debunked during the Scopes monkey trial. This is a fairy tale that is not even worthy of discussion.

Elites believe that they are the sole judges of what is right and wrong. They implicitly (and often explicitly) establish themselves as their own gods. According to Madonna: "I think that all of us have God in us, and that we have godlike qualities, the ability to be like God." Madonna professes that she doesn't have a "religion" because "I don't like that word, 'religion.'" Instead, she says, "I'm spiritual." Hey, you, get off my cloud.

The muddleheaded delusions of the elites obviously cannot coexist with real belief in God; the elites' beliefs are founded on arguments about power. Elites believe in the supreme power of each individual to decide all things, unconstrained by objective morality, obligation, responsibilities, or truth. And the power-mad do not react well to the Higher Power.

The elite "spirituality" leads to a sort of theological "downsizing." Elites are convinced that they don't need God, so they have fired Him. They feel that they can best fulfill that role themselves, and they are eager to enforce conformity to their view. Elites first attempt to eliminate religion from their own lives, and then they set about eliminating it from public life. "Separation of church and state" is insufficient. *Now there must be separation of Church and life.* If religion is to be tolerated at all, it must be so *strictly* private that the elites don't have to see it or even come in contact with it. Keep your rosaries off my ovaries.

Indeed, the elites' hostility to religion is so deep that it is the great divider between elites and average Americans.

## AMERICAN BELIEFS AND ELITE PREJUDICES

Americans are, and always have been, a deeply religious people. Survey after survey has confirmed this conclusion. For example, a recent international survey conducted by the Pew Research Center for People and the Press found that more Americans are committed to their faith than people in any other industrialized nation. In the United States, 59 percent of those surveyed said that religion was "very important" in their lives, as compared with 33 percent in Great Britain, 21 percent in Germany, and 12 percent in Japan, for example. A Gallup poll found that 60 percent of Americans say that their religious beliefs affect all aspects of their lives; and

46 percent of Americans describe themselves as "born-again" or evangelical Christians. Large percentages of Americans regularly attend churches, synagogues, and mosques. They read the Bible, the Torah, and the Koran. They pray. They believe in sin, forgiveness, and redemption. They belong to faith-based organizations. They believe that America and her people have been richly blessed by God. They believe the Constitution didn't create rights but recognized rights and liberties that are endowed by God. They know that for our rights and liberties to be truly secure, we must never forget the true source of these rights and liberties. They know that faith in God is a virtue, not a vice. They view religion as a bulwark of democracy, part of America's life and history, and consistent with good citizenship.

Elites reject all of these things as superstitious folkways of the uneducated masses that have no place in the postmodern and post-Christian world. The elites have their own catechism:

**BELIEF IN GOD IS IRRATIONAL.** Faith and reason are mutually exclusive. Religious people suspend rational thought and are driven by emotional fervor, an active fantasy life, or psychological weakness. Because religion is irrational, religious people are a bit unstable, odd, weird. They are to be mocked, feared, or—perhaps—pitied. They are, after all, only a product of their environment. (This is the elites' version of the denial of free will, a sort of secular Calvinism.)

**BECAUSE IT IS IRRATIONAL, RELIGION IS IN OPPOSITION TO SCIENCE, LEARNING, AND PROGRESS.** It is a vestige of the "Dark Ages." Its adherents, according to a now-infamous *Washington Post* article, tend to be "poor, uneducated, and easy to command." Elites still believe that religion is the opiate of the masses, the self-delusion of uneducated rubes who don't know any better. They believe that religion is a condition that retards social development, but that may be cured by education, assuming it is caught and treated early enough in the young. According to elites, educated people can be delivered from the irrational grip of religion, from the folktales, from the misguided and dangerous superstitions, from the pitchforks and torches. And once they are released, they must "liberate" others, through a coercive, and often oppressive, secular proselytizing.

**RELIGIOUS PEOPLE ARE JUDGMENTAL AND UNFORGIVING.** They are "hate-mongers." They are all like the "Church Lady" on *Saturday Night Live*—gleefully condemning others to eternal punishment. They are holier-than-thou hypocrites who don't practice what they preach. Yet they are always willing to "impose their beliefs" on others. Elites—especially those in the media—like nothing more than exposing what they perceive to be hypocrisy among religious people. Religion causes prejudice, bigotry, and "closed-mindedness." Religious people discriminate against women, they bash gays, they enslave the human spirit, and they are vaguely responsible for a host of other troubling social conditions.

**RELIGION IS OPPOSED NOT ONLY TO LEARNING, BUT TO LIBERTY.** Religion seeks to enslave people to superstitions and to enforce all sorts of rules that are aimed only at promoting human misery. Why all the rules? The commandments? The "thou shalt not this" and "thou shalt not that?" It's all so negative. And it causes the most irrational of human emotions: guilt. Millions of dollars are spent on psychiatrists and psychologists to liberate the victims of religion from this irrational guilt. To the elite mind, guilt is always irrational because it is based on the premise that the one who suffers from it has done something "wrong." But the masses need to get over this antiquated notion. There is no "wrong" (except for the "intolerance" generally exhibited by religious people). Because there is no wrong there is no sin. So who needs forgiveness? And redemption? Forget about it. I'm okay, you're okay.

**RELIGION DAMAGES PEOPLE AND IT DAMAGES SOCIETIES.** Individuals must be liberated from religion, and religion must be driven out of our public life. It should not be allowed to continue damaging our country. It should not be "imposed" on people through public prayers, public discussion, or even traditional ceremonial recognition of God. The ACLU, Americans United for Separation of Church and State, People for the American Way, and numerous other similar organizations have long successfully used lawsuits and threats of lawsuits to drive religion out of the public square. According to one pamphlet aimed at the eradication of religion in public life, adherents of this philosophy must "infiltrate the schools. . . . Do not allow students to carry any religious goods or propaganda materials."[1] Sounds like an ACLU publication, doesn't it? Actually, it's a document published in 1997 by the Donglai Township Committee of the Chinese Communist Party that counsels how to stop the "illegal activities of an underground Catholic Church." The fact that you can't tell the difference between the ACLU and the Communist Party shows just how far the elites have come in their hostility to religion.

**RELIGIOUS PEOPLE ARE SUSPECT GENERALLY, NOT JUST IN THEIR RELIGIOUS BELIEFS.** Acceptance of the irrationality of religion reveals a fundamental character flaw and weakness of the intellect. Therefore, all opinions held by religious people should be rejected. Indeed, that very argument is all you need. You don't need to discuss merits, facts, or engage in rational debate. Simply say, "That position is based on your religious beliefs," and nothing further is needed. Abortion is the prime example of this. No need to discuss the constitutional, biological, psychological, or any other arguments, because people who oppose abortion purportedly do so for religious (that is, irrational, bigoted) reasons. The abortion debate is just one example of how religion is divisive and harmful to public life.

For the elites, the sacred has become the profane. When it comes to public life, you should check your religion at the door.

They view religion like that sweater that Mr. Rogers used to put on when he got home—comforting, but meant only for use in private. Should we expect any less from the culture that proclaimed "God is dead" on the cover of *Time* magazine?

The common characteristic of these elite prejudices is, of course, that they are false. Actually, these elite criticisms of religion and religious people apply instead to elites themselves. They harbor an intense bigotry against people of faith. It is openly and unapologetically present in every elite stronghold, including the media and the universities. Religious people are routinely censored precisely because of the content of their speech—and such censorship is justified by elites in the name of freedom, the right to "freedom from religion." The elites impose the secularist agenda mercilessly on others; they do not brook dissent. Elites preach freedom and practice censorship. It is the elites who are the hypocrites. It is the elites who conduct modern-day witch hunts and inquisitions to detect and eradicate religious expression. It is the elites who are irrational and superstitious, rejecting Aquinas and Augustine in favor of mood rings, crystals, and magic eight balls. It is the elites—not religious Americans—who threaten our country and its freedom.

## THE ELITE CAMPAIGN AGAINST RELIGION

Discrimination against believers—particularly against Christians—is practiced with unabashed virulence throughout the elite secular culture. For example, Ted Turner recently proclaimed that "Christianity is a religion for losers" and joked that the pope should step on a land mine. When Ted saw CNN employees wearing ashes on Ash Wednesday, he asked them "What are you? A bunch of Jesus freaks? You ought to be working for Fox." None of this provoked media outrage or calls for his resignation. In fact, Turner even divorced Jane Fonda reportedly in part because of Fonda's conversion to Christianity. "She just came home and said, 'I've become a

Christian.' Before that, she was not a religious person. That's a pretty big change for your wife of many years to tell you. That's a shock." Adultery? Irreconcilable differences? Not really. But if you pray, you're gone. As the *New York Post* reported: "The 62-year old billionaire founder of CNN revealed in an interview last month that Fonda's decision to turn Christian turned his stomach—and helped turn his marriage sour." So much for freedom of conscience.

Jesse "The Body" Ventura, when governor of Minnesota, held forth in *Playboy* magazine: "Organized religion is a sham and a crutch for weak-minded people who need strength in numbers." Although Ventura went on to discuss his own apparent belief in reincarnation when he stated, "I would like to come back as a 38 double-D bra." Go figure. At least his IQ can stay the same.

Bill Maher, formerly host of *Politically Incorrect* and now host of his own HBO show, regularly spouts the elite dogma about religion: "Religion is extremist. It is extreme to believe in things that your rational mind knows are not true." Religion, then, requires its adherents to reject what their reason tells them and accept something they know to be false. On *Politically Incorrect* Maher said, people believe "a lot of stupid Muslim tricks and stupid Christian tricks, okay? They believe a lot of things, and it's such a fundamental belief that if the other guy doesn't agree with you, he's got to go, and we're guilty of the same thing." In other words, all religious people are the same: extremist, irrational, unthinking, unblinking idiots who are ultimately dangerous because they are incapable of logical argument and often resort to violence. When Maher was asked directly by CNN's Larry King whether he thought there was *any* "good" in religion, he shot back, "Not very much, no. I don't. I mean, as long as there are people who think that this is the only way, you're going to have wars, and killing, and death." So religion can never be good, but rather "it's extremely dangerous," and it can never be fixed, because "of course you really can't fix an institution when it is religion. Because when you say religion, immediately you can get away with anything."

# **Elite**speak **alert!**

Religion Causes War: A favorite elite mantra, often espoused by comedian/writer/talk show host Bill Maher. The problem with the theory is that wars have many causes, most of which have nothing to do with religion. Bill's theory tells us nothing about World War I, World War II, Vietnam, Korea, the Peloponnesian War, or the Civil War. Another problem with the theory is that history's greatest mass murderers—Hitler, Stalin, Mao, and Pol Pot—were all militant atheists. ■

The elites' campaign to purge our culture of all religious images and references is often taken to such absurd lengths that it is difficult to believe. Take for example what happened in Madison, Wisconsin, after Mother Teresa was named to *Time* magazine's list of the 100 Most Important People of the Twentieth Century. This was reported by Bill Donohue of the Catholic League for Religious and Civil Rights. The Madison Metro System put a picture of Mother Teresa on its bus passes for a month in recognition of her inclusion on *Time*'s top-100 list. This obviously egregious violation of the rights of free people everywhere was protested by the "Freedom from Religion Foundation," which happens to be headquartered in Madison. The president of the organization stated that Mother Teresa's picture on the bus pass was "an insult to Madisonians who value women's rights, and the separation of church and state." Mother Teresa? Insulting? Ring the bell—I'm getting off the bus.

And now for something really stupid, consider the reaction of movie critics to the pseudoreligious aspects of the recent movie *Bruce Almighty*, in which Jim Carrey plays God. Again, as noted by Bill Donohue of the Catholic League, the critics did not appreciate the way religion made its way into this movie that is at least ostensibly about God. According to the AP, the tone of the movie went "from wacky to preachy." The *New York Times* did not care for the film's "preachy, goody-goody conclusion." The reviewer in the *St. Paul Pioneer Press* thought the movie was initially okay until the end when it got "all 'Patch Adams' on us, with an uplifting sermon on the importance of praying every day." Perhaps *Newsday* said it best: "Unfortunately, religious fervor moves in and sinks the last 20 minutes.... You don't have to be an atheist or an ACLU attorney to be creeped out by the movie's lip-service spirituality, which panders to the common denominator."

Most Christians will tell you that *Bruce Almighty* certainly does not represent a serious discussion of religion. And some Christians were even offended by what they viewed as a blasphemous attack on God in the film. But blasphemy has become piety in the distorted minds of the elites. And they do not react well to what they perceive—however wrongly—as piety. Message: Mention God in a movie and you lose. Elites are so sensitive to any positive mention of faith, in any context, no matter how frivolous, that their first reaction is to attack. Don't try to find any movie reviews that criticize a movie as insensitive to people of faith.

## ELITE SLANDER: CHRISTIANITY=BIGOTRY

The following is an extremely telling exchange between Sean Hannity of Fox's *Hannity & Colmes* and New York's liberal congressman Jerry Nadler, regarding the Catholic Church's admonition against homosexual acts.

**HANNITY:** Are they bigoted?

**NADLER:** I don't agree with their position.

**HANNITY:** Are they bigoted?

**NADLER:** I think that's a bigoted position.

So much for liberal "tolerance." Anyone who holds the Catholic faith and subscribes to its teachings on homosexuality takes a "bigoted position." All Catholics are bigots.

Recall the outcry against Pennsylvania senator Rick Santorum for his comment about the constitutionality of state laws against homosexual sodomy. Pending the Supreme Court's decision in *Lawrence* v. *Texas*, Santorum restated the reasoning of the governing Supreme Court precedent (which had upheld a similar statute), and said that he agreed with it. He added that he believes in the Catholic teaching of embracing the sinner but opposing the sin. For this the elites accused him of bigotry. He was viciously attacked and relentlessly ridiculed in the media. Some even called for him to step down from his leadership position in the Senate. And all this for simply publicly discussing his Catholic beliefs. Again, identify yourself as a Christian, and dare to speak about it, and the elite witch hunters will come for you. And they will do whatever it takes to silence you.

And the same treatment given to Santorum confronts that other religious public servant, George W. Bush, who the elites believe is, underneath the Ivy League pedigree, just another fundamentalist wackpot. "His use of explicitly Christian references is certainly problematic," says James Donahue, president and professor of ethics at the Graduate Theological Union in Berkeley, California. Donahue believes Bush's religious rhetoric is dangerous because "there is a presumption that God is on our side." Rather, "Good and evil cut a lot more subtly. I think the complexities are much more significant than the public rhetoric, specifically the Bush rhetoric, is portraying. It is insulting to thinking people that good and evil can be portrayed as so reductionist and so simplistic." Good and evil are for the simpleminded. "Thinking people," like the elites who run "Theological Unions" in Berkeley, have moved beyond such antiquated concepts. They've moved "beyond good and evil," and it's certainly not helpful for the leader of the free world to insist on employing this antiquated and simplistic view of the world. Question the subjectivist secular orthodoxy and be prepared for the consequences.

Bush's religious beliefs have been called "divisive," "simplistic," "a dangerous illusion," a danger to our liberties, and evidence that he "is claiming a divine mandate." Again, the president of the Freedom from Religion Foundation provides a winning quote, calling Bush "the most recklessly religious president we've seen." Protestant theologian Martin Marty is greatly concerned that "Bush's God talk will set the tinderbox that is the Muslim world on fire." Mr. Marty—remember, he's a "theologian" now—is appalled that Bush seeks to conform his actions with God's will: "The problem isn't with Bush's sincerity, but with his evident conviction that he is doing God's will." Again what the elite requires is that religion not affect what you do, or what you think, or what you say say publicly.

And when Bush's cabinet officials reference religion, they are attacked just as viciously. Take, for example, Secretary of Education Rod Paige, who had the temerity to suggest that Christian values are beneficial to schools. Imagine! Congressman Gary Ackerman quickly accused him of taking "the Taliban approach to education." So Christian values in schools are akin to terrorism—part of the Axis of Evil, I suppose. No surprise that Ackerman refused to support a nonbinding resolution declaring a day of prayer and fasting during Operation Iraqi Freedom. Pray for the safety of our troops? Sorry, it's offensive to elites.

In fact, if elites have their way, soon our soldiers won't even be allowed to pray for themselves. In a recent case against Virginia Military Institute (VMI), the traditional and long-standing prayer of the cadets before meals was challenged. Here again, a public expression of religion, no matter how nonsectarian, no matter how deeply rooted in tradition and history, must be attacked and eliminated. What about military chaplains? Are they unconstitutional? It may be that there are no atheists in foxholes, but if elites have their way, there may soon be no military chaplains or prayer in foxholes either.

## THE ELITE REJECTION OF OUR FOUNDING PRINCIPLES

This modern elite hostility to religion, and in particular to religious expression in public life, contradicts American history and tradition dating back to our founding. In our Declaration of Independence, our founders made clear that the rights they were declaring were God-given, and could not be legitimately taken away by kings or governments of any kind: "We hold these truths to be self-evident, that all men are created equal, and that *they are endowed by their Creator* with certain unalienable Rights, that among these are Life, Liberty and the pursuit of happiness."

These words, standing alone, repudiate the elite dogma. They establish that our founders believed: (1) in "self-evident" truths, truths that are objectively and universally true and can be known through reason; (2) that God exists; (3) that He is our Creator; (4) that our rights come from Him—that He created us with free will and liberty as an essential part of what it means to be human; (5) that these rights must be respected precisely because they are an inherent part of human dignity; (6) that our free will and liberty are constrained by God's law, which both individuals and governments are obliged to follow. (The founders described our God-given rights as "unalienable," meaning God has given them to us and they cannot be given away or traded by mere human choice. In other words, God's law and man's rights cannot be altered by subjective human will.) Lastly, the founders held that these beliefs were the central basis for our Declaration of Independence and the foundation of our new nation.

The "Representatives of the United States, in General Congress, Assembled," who signed the Declaration of Independence, not only cited as authoritative "the laws of nature and nature's God," but made a specific and direct appeal "to the Supreme Judge of the World for the rectitude of our intentions." They also made clear that they were establishing our independent nation "with a firm reliance on the protection of Divine Providence." Our founders did not rely on themselves alone. They did not adopt the elite self-image of total supremacy divorced from God's law. From the beginning, our independent America was founded on a belief in God, a recognition of our obligation to Him, and a reliance on His blessings.

Today—in the elite worldview—the Declaration of Independence would be an unconstitutional violation of "separation of church and state" and an offensive expression of religious belief by government officials. It directly contradicts all of the modern elite inventions: (1) that there is no God; (2) that in any event He is irrelevant; (3) that man is the supreme being; (4) that our choices are unconstrained by objective moral law and cannot be judged; (5) that our rights come from nowhere but the will of man; (6) that these rights come without obligations or responsibilities; (7) that we can "define" right and wrong subjectively, without acknowledging God's law, and it is logically impossible to do otherwise; (8) that belief in God is irrational, and dangerous to democracy, and has no place in our national life; and (9) that any mention of God in public life or as the basis for law or government action is irresponsible, illegitimate, and unconstitutional. These, of course, are all strange and false elite concoctions that were rejected by America's founders.

Far from seeing religious belief as a danger, the founders saw it as a precondition for a secure democracy. George Washington, in his Farewell Address, reminded his countrymen that "of all the dispositions and habits which lead to political prosperity, religion and morality are indispensable supports. In vain would that man claim the tribute of patriotism who should labor to subvert these great pillars of human happiness—these firmest props of the duties of man and citizens." Anyone listening at the ACLU?

Indeed, the American experiment in democracy presupposed a religious and moral citizenry. Washington was clear: "Reason and experience both forbid us to expect that national morality can prevail in exclusion of religious principle. It is substantially true that virtue and morality is a necessary spring of popular government." Cut to: Bill Maher, cringing. In fact, in 1789, Washington proclaimed a national day "of public thanksgiving and prayer, to be observed by acknowledging with grateful hearts the many and signal favors of Almighty God." In other words, God has richly blessed America and Americans should unite together annually, and in a public, official way, recognized by our government, to thank God for the many blessings He has bestowed on our great nation. Barry Lynn, call your office. What's next, a lawsuit by an elitist, antireligious interest group seeking an injunction to prevent our national observance of Thanksgiving Day?

As much as the antireligion elites would like to ignore our nation's history, they cannot. In his first inaugural address, Thomas Jefferson called upon "that infinite power which rules the destinies of the universe" for help and to "lead our councils to what is best." John Adams stated that our Constitution requires a "religious and moral" people and is wholly unsuited to the governance of any other. James Madison pronounced that "we have staked our future...upon the capacity of each of us to govern ourselves according to the Ten Commandments of God." Now our courts have ruled that the public display of the Ten Commandments on government property violates the very Constitution that Madison helped to author. Modern elites reject (and would be shocked by) Madison's belief that "before any man can be considered as a member of civil society, he must be considered as a subject of the Governor of the Universe."

Elites love to quote from Lincoln, but assiduously avoid his more "divisive" comments on his source of strength during the Civil War. Lincoln said it was his "constant anxiety and prayer that I and this nation should be on the Lord's side." Perhaps Lincoln should be posthumously declared unconstitutional and taken off the penny, along with the phrase "In God We Trust." Lincoln, like Washington, also established an official national day of prayer in Thanksgiving to God, issuing an order in 1863 to "set apart and observe the last Thursday of November next, as a day of Thanksgiving and praise to our beneficent father who dwelleth in the heavens." Thanksgiving Day has been observed since that time and was written into law by Congress in 1941. Again, a national official day of thanking God for his blessings and asking Him to continue to bless our nation is not the action of people who believe the elitist pap that religion has no place in our public life. The acceptance of the legitimacy—and critical importance—of religion in our public life has long been accepted in America, by leaders of all political stripes, until the modern elites began their campaign against religion.

Even elite icon Franklin D. Roosevelt took God's existence as a given and made reference to our national commitment to Him. In his 1942 State of the Union Address, for example, FDR spoke of Nazi Germany's godlessness compared with America's belief in God: "They know that victory for us means victory for religion. And they could not tolerate that. The world is too small to provide adequate 'living room' for both Hitler and God. In proof of that, the Nazis have now announced a plan for enforcing their new German, pagan religion throughout the world—the plan by which the Holy Bible and the Cross of Mercy would be displaced by *Mein Kampf* and the swastika and the naked sword." FDR knew—as did Hitler—that victory for America meant victory for religion, victory for the Holy Bible, victory for the "Cross of Mercy."

This view of America has now been utterly rejected by the elites. But more that that, they have embarked on a campaign to destroy that vision of America, indeed to make this vision of America illegal through their lawsuits, and to make this vision of America an object of embarrassment through their constant mocking attacks of religion in the media. To elites, a religious America is not the beacon for the world and the bulwark against tyranny and despotism but is itself the real danger, the real tyranny, the real despotism.

Listen instead to President John F. Kennedy, who affirmed in his inaugural address that "the rights of man come not from the state but from the hand of God." According to Robert F. Kennedy, in his

1966 speech in Cape Town, South Africa, "at the heart of . . . Western freedom and democracy is the belief that the individual man, *the child of God*, is the touchstone of value, and all societies, groups, the state, exist for his benefit" and "we must recognize the full human equality of all our people—before God, before the law, and in the councils of government." Again, we see the clear recognition by all these men that God exists, that religion and belief in God are part of the foundation of America, and that our rights, liberty, and equality are secured—and must be respected and protected—precisely because they are divinely ordained and established. They understood and accepted Jefferson's admonition concerning the protection of our precious freedom: "Can the liberties of a nation be thought to be secure when we have removed their only firm basis, a conviction in the minds of people that these liberties are the gift of God?"

This is something that elites reject without really thinking about the consequences. The protection of our God-given rights is not a matter of individual choice but is a requirement of justice and the natural law. But if elites reject all objective law and leave everything up to subjective individual choices free of all preexisting obligations, then where is the real support for our rights? If our liberties are supported only by current individual opinions and nothing more, then they are built on sand. None of our founders believed this dangerous idea. They believed that our rights were created by God, not invented by man. For if our rights are merely human inventions and human conventions, then they are passing. Different governments could choose without consequence to respect or deny these rights based on their own subjective beliefs. If there is no right and wrong that can be objectively known, that must be accepted as universal truth, then what makes freedom necessary? What makes liberty a requirement? What supports our rights throughout time, without regard to passing individual beliefs and temptations to tyranny?

If nothing objective supports our rights, then they are simply subjective beliefs imposed by human power. And if power is the only justification, then anything can be justified. You cannot logically distinguish between tyranny and liberty if power is the only basis for legitimacy. The bottom line

**Elite**speak **alert!**

When the elites talk about "separation of church and state" what they really mean is "extinction of church and adulation of state." ∎

is that when elites eliminate God in our national life, they eliminate the source of our rights and, at the same time, destroy their security. Elites remove the rock supporting our rights and instead seek to place the security of our liberty on the shifting sands of subjectivism. If no truth is possible, then "life, liberty and the pursuit of happiness" cannot be self-evident and true rights granted by the hand of God and demanding protection as a requirement of justice. This is the fundamental irrationality of the elite position.

If you have any doubt that this is the elite agenda, just consider the recent reaction to President Bush's clear statement—echoing our founders—in his 2003 State of the Union Address that "the liberty we prize is not America's gift to the world, but God's gift to humanity." This statement provoked an outcry among the elites, and the chief White House speechwriter was directly challenged by a reporter as to whether he understood why such a statement would be offensive. This reaction illustrates just how far elites have come in their extremist contention that belief in God has no place in our public life and our national discourse. The long-accepted truth that rights are God-given, a self-evident truth enshrined in our Declaration of Independence, may no longer be uttered by an American president because—according to the elites—such ideas are offensive to Americans. Our sacred truths have become "hate speech." Karen Yourish, writing in *Newsweek* about Bush's statement, warned that it "raised a red flag for supporters of separation of church and state." Beam me up.

## THE ELITE DISTORTION OF OUR CONSTITUTION

This elite conception of "separation of church and state" has become so distorted that it conflicts directly with and seeks to invalidate basic truths reflected in America's founding documents. Clearly, these radical ideas have no historical or logical basis. And you might be surprised to learn that they have no basis in our Constitution either. The words "separation of church and state" appear nowhere in the Constitution. The first amendment says that "Congress shall make no law respecting an establishment of religion, or prohibiting the free exercise thereof." So the Constitution prohibits our government from restricting the free exercise of religious faith, and from picking one specific religion and officially establishing that particular religion as the sole, state-sponsored religion of the American government. In other words, the government is required to be neutral *among* religions, in the sense that it cannot pick one and make it the official religion of the state. But it defies logic, history, and the Constitution to suggest that our founders required government to be neutral as between religion and irreligion. What elites now demand is that the government, in essence, establish the elite "faith" of secularism and atheism. They demand that the government at all levels acknowledge, de facto, that there is no God and prohibit all public expression of religious belief. Moreover, elites contend that such hostility to religion, such discrimination against people of faith, such violations of basic human rights are all mandated by the Constitution and its supposed requirement of "separation of church and state" that does not appear in the language of the document.

Ironically, the Constitutional protections that do exist regarding religion were intended to protect *religion* from encroachment by the state. In other words, our founders viewed government as a danger to religion and not vice versa. The notion of a "wall of separation between church and state" is traced back not to the Constitution but to a letter written by Thomas Jefferson. Pretty authoritative, huh? But again, Jefferson's concepts have now been grossly distorted to support elite arguments that religion represents a pressing and ongoing danger to the democratic state. For elites, God has become public enemy number one. But what elites depict as the central threat to our republic is, as understood by our founders, the only real guarantee of our national health and the true and sure support for a thriving democracy.

Unfortunately, the elites' distorted notion of this separation has become dogma. It is preached unceasingly in the media and universities, and enforced in our courts, our schools, and our communities to drive religion out of our national life. One of the most recent and radical court rulings illustrates this. The U.S. Court of Appeals for the Ninth Circuit essentially declared our Pledge of Allegiance unconstitutional, and prohibited its recitation by public school students, because it includes the words "one nation under God." The Pledge must be censored.

The natural progression of this elite position—it is difficult to call it reasoning—is the total secularization of America in the misappropriated name of the Constitution. Take it directly from Michael Newdow, the man behind the Pledge case, who published an article under the heading "The Freedom from Religion—Is Also Our Right." He stated, "I was looking at the money in my hands, and I noticed, as if for the first time, the words 'In God we trust' on every coin and every bill of every denomination. 'What's this?' I wondered. I don't trust in God. I'm an atheist." Profound. He goes on to argue that our money violates the Constitution. I guess our legal tender isn't legal anymore.

But this sort of absurdity is gaining ground. Consider the story of Zachary Hood, who was only six years old when he learned about religious tolerance—or the lack thereof—in the public schools. Zach's teacher asked each student to bring his favorite book to read aloud in class.[2] Zach chose to bring in the children's Bible that his mom read to him every night: *The Beginner's Bible: Timeless Children's Stories.* Poor Zach didn't know that the Bible would be considered contraband. Predictably, Zach was forbidden to read his book aloud "because it was religious." A sobbing Zach told his mother about his offense. When Zach's mother spoke to the teacher, principal, and other school officials, she was told that religious books were not allowed in public schools and she was ultimately informed that her family "was not public-school material." Zach's mother, Carol Hood, insisted, "I'm not trying to push religion into public school. I'm trying to push respect for religion into public school." Nevertheless, a federal district judge in New Jersey ruled that the teacher was within her right to forbid the Bible story. The Becket Fund for Religious Liberty took Zach's case and it was recently settled favorably. Also, President Bush's Department of Education recently issued guidelines aimed at protecting religious liberty and preventing discrimination in public schools. But these victories for common sense don't happen often enough.

Think about what happened to teacher's aide Brenda Nichol. She found herself in U.S. District Court recently watching lawyers measuring the cross she wears around her neck. Although the cross is only an inch wide and an inch and a half long, the elites attempted to get it declared illegal in her Pennsylvania classroom. Nichol was suspended from her job and told she would have to check her cross at the door if she ever wanted to return. Does this sound like America to you or like Soviet Russia? Thankfully, the federal district judge ruled in Nichol's favor.

A Wisconsin high school senior, Rachel Honer, also felt the jackboot of elitism recently. School officials rewrote the song she chose to sing at graduation to remove all references to God. Just another lesson in liberty brought to us by the wonderful people who run America's public schools. In this case, it's shut up and stop singing, at least when it comes to hymns. According to the Reverend Barry Lynn, "This is not some kind of illegal censorship."

No, Barry, I guess this is the "legal" kind of censorship you support. The kind elites engage in all the time. And by the way, what's with the "Reverend" anyway? Are you the high priest of the church of secularism?

And it only gets worse once you get to college—typically havens of antireligion elites. At Texas Tech University, for example, biology professor Michael L. Dini implemented a religious test for letters of recommendation to medical school. His philosophy: Those who believe God created the earth and mankind need not apply. In his specific warning to students, Professor Dini stated, "I will ask you: 'How do you think the human species originated?' If you cannot truthfully and forthrightly affirm a scientific answer to this question, then you should not seek my recommendation for admittance to further education in the biomedical sciences." You will bow before the god of evolution or you will be cast out into the outer darkness. If you believe in God, then you are unfit to study medicine. It's unclear what scientific method Professor Dini relies on to prove his thesis that God does not exist and had no role in creation. Dr. Dini told the *New York Times*: "I think science and religion address very different types of questions, and they shouldn't overlap." In other words, if you are irrational and reactionary enough to believe in God, you have no business studying science. So much for Gregor Mendel, Louis Pasteur, and other Christian biologists and scientists.

Examples like these abound, but the point is made. Elites have hijacked the Constitution and distorted it to support their campaign of discrimination against religion. These radical elite views have no basis in the Constitution and no basis in our history. Instead, they seek to transform a right to practice religion freely into a so-called right to be "free from religion." In their view, any discussion of religion is an establishment of religion, even when the expression is not by the government but by private citizens. Any exposure to religion at all, to religious expressions, to religious ideas, to religious texts is a violation of rights. Exposure to religion in the free marketplace of ideas, in the elite view, amounts to coercion, which equals establishment, which must be crushed. So they must shut down the marketplace of ideas—at least when it comes to religious expression—and ban religious belief from the public square. The free exercise of religion guaranteed by the First Amendment to the Constitution must give way to the elite vision of a Godless America.

## REMEMBERING WHO WE ARE

America is a country awash in religion. It was founded by men who believed in God and were committed to the protection of religious liberty. Religion was at the heart of America's greatest struggles against inequity. Leaders in the battles to overcome slavery, give women voting rights, and advance civil rights, were people of deep faith. The Rev. Martin Luther King Jr., was a preacher and the son of a preacher. His 1963 "I Have a Dream Speech" was rooted not in politics but in an unwavering belief that God expected us to treat each human being with equal dignity: "This will be the day when all of God's children will be able to sing with a new meaning, 'My country, 'tis of thee, sweet land of liberty...'" Also, he invoked God in what has become the most frequently quoted part of the speech—"Free at last! Free at last! Thank God Almighty we are free at last!"

Our most cherished national songs are infused with religion—from "America the Beautiful" to "God Bless America." My favorite is "The Battle Hymn of the Republic," written in 1862 by Julia Ward Howe, a leader of the antislavery and women's suffragist movements. Consider the Hymn's last verse:

> In the beauty of the lilies
> Christ was born across the sea,
> With a glory in His bosom
> That transfigures you and me;

*As He died to make men holy,*
*Let us die to make men free;*
*While God is marching on.*

Julia Ward Howe was a liberal in the true sense of the word. Like our founders, she understood that we owe our freedom to God, which meant that ending slavery would require God's grace and intervention. Today's so-called liberals claim people like Howe as their heroes, but that's just empty rhetoric. Howe inspired the nation by appealing to Americans' belief in our Creator. For Lincoln, it meant calling upon the "better angels of our nature." Today's liberals wince at this kind of "judgmental," "divisive" language tied to religious beliefs. If a nominee to the federal bench today were to write or speak words along the lines of Howe, senators like Chuck Schumer and Ted Kennedy would go ballistic, branding the nominee "out of the mainstream."

But Schumer and his cronies are the ones on the fringe. Following their frayed logic, most people of faith would be considered "too risky" for public service. The last thing today's liberal elites want is an explosion of morality in the United States. That would destroy the modern pillars of the left-wing agenda. The debate about abortion rights and homosexual marriage would take on an entirely new urgency. You don't have to be a Catholic to take heart in the words of Pope John Paul II: "If constitutional and statutory law are not held accountable to the objective moral law, the first casualties are justice and equality, for they becomes matters of personal opinion." Just days after September 11, almost every member of Congress gathered on the Capitol steps to show the world that they were united. Republicans and Democrats didn't stand side by side and sing "Imagine" or "This Land Is Your Land." They didn't recite Maya Angelou. They sang "God Bless America." It should not take a national disaster for us to remember where we came from and who we are: One Nation Under God.

# 6

# Flower Power, Take a Shower

▶ Antimilitary Elites

arly in 2003, I interviewed a twenty-something woman who identified herself as Maya Jones, a San Francisco–based activist for Not In Our Name (NION), the radical group that claimed to oppose "the war" but really opposes most of what America stands for.

The NIONistas' politics are best represented by its well-known full-page "Statement" in the *New York Times* of September 19, 2002, which paints the United States as the bad guy in virtually every paragraph. According to NION, the Bush administration is "unjust, immoral, and illegitimate." NION can't even express any pity for those murdered in the World Trade Center and Pentagon attacks without diminishing them. As the NION statement observes, "We too mourned the thousands of innocent dead and shook our heads at the terrible scenes of carnage—even as we recalled similar scenes in Baghdad, Panama City, and, a generation ago, Vietnam." You see, to the moral equivalency crowd at NION, there's no difference between September 11 and "Panama City." The statement, of course, also contains the usual gumbo of grievances about the Israelis and John Ashcroft bringing "down the pall of repression over society."

What's missing? Lots—if NION had any intention of making a serious case against the war on terror or the war in Iraq. For starters, the statement lacked any mention of Iraqi violations of UN resolutions, any mention of Iraqi torture and oppression, and, in fact, any mention of Saddam Hussein himself. Nor was there any mention of the danger posed to America by terrorists posing as legitimate immigrants, and of the necessity of America's being vigilant in defense of our borders and our security. That's because for NION, America itself is the problem, not America's enemies.

NION represents almost a perfect microcosm of the America Last attitude that drives so many people who claim to be "antiwar" but are really just anti-American. My conversation with Maya was truly illuminating, demonstrating the perversity, ignorance, and self-hatred that characterizes the anti-American left. I think I had more calls and e-mails about this than about any other subject I've ever covered on my show.

**LAURA:** Do you believe the Bush administration's actions, which ultimately toppled the Taliban in Afghan, is a war of repression?

**MAYA:** Yes, it is.

**LAURA:** So you think the people of Afghanistan would have been better off under the Taliban?

**MAYA:** I think the way the questions are posed are spun depending on who is posing them.

**LAURA:** [referring to a NION statement]: No, [your organization] called it a war of repression—

**MAYA:** [interrupts]: I'll answer the question but I'm not going to have a conversation where you cut me off every five seconds.

**LAURA:** We have a lot of time here, so I'll pose the question again. You said it was a war of repression and I'm asking, Is it repressive to release people from torture and bondage including women who couldn't leave their houses—

**MAYA:** To imply that the United States is releasing anyone from torture and bondage is ludicrous. They think that by leveling a

# **Peace**speak **alert!**

**Antiwar Activists:** Code words for an assortment of Stalinists, Communists, Maoists, Leninists, Marxists, and Socialists dedicated to subverting America.

**Human Shields:** When "shielding" Saddam's military installations, they were given free room and board by the same folks responsible for all those mass graves we have now uncovered. However, when they realized that the party was over, they bagged on Baghdad before the bombing began.

**200,000:** The number routinely given by "protest organizers" in the United States to reporters who inquire about the size of a particular demonstration. This number has been proven to bear no resemblance to reality.

**ANSWER:** Act Now to Stop War and End Racism, a.k.a Anti-American Marxist Front Group that Cozies Up to Dictators and Murderous Regimes (A.A.M.F.G.T.C.U.T.D.A.M.R.).

**Not In Our Name:** Another front group that opposes defending American interests and citizens from attacks by terrorists. Has not yet awakened to the fact that President Bush did not embark on war "in their name." NION can keep its name. Nobody else wants it. ∎

country by dropping thousands of bombs on a country that has already been under extreme repression and has been bombed in, you know, into a basic country of rubble. People there have been living in a war zone for the last twenty years and for the United States to go there and drop bombs on it yet again killing hundreds of people, actually thousands of people. As many people have died in Afghanistan as died in the World Trade Center. Is that releasing people from bondage?

**LAURA:** You don't think the people of Afghanistan are better off now than they were under the Taliban?

**MAYA:** No.

**LAURA:** What would *you* have done?

**MAYA:** You can ask me about what this government does to other countries and what we mean by "wars of repression." What other country has ever used nuclear weapons on another country?

**LAURA:** No, we're not going to play that game. You guys always go back to "using nuclear weapons." We're talking about the situation at hand, which is that America was attacked on September 11, and I want to know what Not In Our Name would propose we do about protecting Americans. What is your plan?

**MAYA:** Well, we believe that as people living in this country it is our responsibility to resist the injustices done by the government in our name. It is not going to make us any safer to go bombing Iraq, to go bombing Korea, to go bombing Colombia and Venezuela, and whoever else is on their list. You know what that says? It lets the rest of the world know that the United States is on a full rampage and has every intention of wrapping it up into a One World empire.

**LAURA:** Okay, but what is your plan? What will you do to keep *Americans* safe?

**MAYA:** We want to stop this country which is going to war with other countries.

**LAURA:** That's not a plan.

**MAYA:** What do you want me to say?

**LAURA:** You guys say what you *don't* like. You do have a right to say that the United States is repressive, that the United States is evil, that Bush is evil, but it would be helpful if you guys offered an alternative.

**MAYA:** We're not trying to come up with a plan. We're trying to stop a very ugly and serious juggernaut of war. We're trying to stop the attacks on Muslim and South Asian immigrants. We're trying to stop police-state restrictions—

**LAURA:** What about stopping attacks on *Americans*?

**Here's a sampling of the comments from my non-citizen-of-the-world listening audience. From William A.:**

"I am simply appalled by the views of your recent guest from 'Not in Our Brain.' Maya claims to not be an American, but rather is allied with the 'people of the world.' I presume the people of the world also include Muslim fanatics who stone women to death for being raped, throw hand grenades into Christian churches, or murder health workers in Yemen. She seems more allied with those who seek to kill all of us (including Maya) than with those who seek to protect us. What was so great about your interview is that these people are never challenged, and based on her last statement, she never would have come on the show had she known that you were not going to lob Katie Couric softballs at her."

**From Master Sergeant James S., USAF (Ret.):**

"We serve for three important reasons: Duty, Honor, Country!"

Unfortunately, those are three attributes completely absent from today's "antiwar" movement. ■

**MAYA:** We're trying to stop the government on its whirlwind rampage to take over the world.

**LAURA:** But Maya, filibustering about what is bad about the government is not proactive strategy for offering alternatives to make Americans safer.

**MAYA:** Is that what your problem is?

**LAURA:** Yeah, I'm concerned about Americans.

**MAYA:** Well, what's your solution?

**LAURA:** My solution is to do what we can, with our willing allies, to stop people from coming into our country and killing Americans. That's what I'm concerned about. I'm concerned about American people being murdered by terrorists.

**MAYA:** That's generally the tone of people like yourself who think only about Americans, but what we're saying is that there's millions of people around the world that live and breathe and eat and love in the same way we do—and we pledge common cause with the people of the world and not just look after our own backs as this government would have us do.

**LAURA:** Would the people of Poland or Hungary or Bulgaria have been better off if the United States didn't step in during World War II with the full force of the U.S. military to stop the progression of Nazism in Europe? What was the threat from Hitler?

**MAYA:** I have seven minutes left for you and I'm not going to get into what could have, what should have happened in World War II.

**LAURA:** But it goes directly to your point about our commander in chief—

**MAYA:** Okay, you want me to answer the question, I'll answer about whether the U.S. went into World War II as a humanitarian good deed—*Absolutely not*—

# **Peace**speak **alert!**

"**End the Occupation**": The new mantra of the Bring Back Saddam (a.k.a. "peace") movement." Thus demonstrating the utter depravity of the anti-American Left (we're "colonial aggressors," not liberators, you see).

"**Bring the Troops Home**": Their other tedious refrain is even worse. Here, the anti-American Left pretends that it actually cares about the lives of American soldiers.

"**Bush = Hitler**": Phrase commonly seen on placards waved at "peace marches."

"**Freedom for Iraq**": Phrase never seen on placards waved at "peace marches."

"**We were wrong**": Phrase never said by antiwar activists, despite the fact that their prognostications about the Iraq war were completely, miserably, and humiliatingly WRONG. ∎

[*Heated cross-talk*]

**LAURA:** Is there anything the U.S. has ever done helping other countries that has ever been good? I'm just curious.

**MAYA:** I can speak only for myself and not for NION.

**LAURA:** Should we have a military at all?

**MAYA:** The U.S. needs to have a military in order to protect its empire. Do I think that's correct? No.

**LAURA:** What empire are you talking about?

**MAYA:** The U.S. is the number-one world power. They have the most money, they have the highest economy—

**LAURA:** *They*? You're an American, right?

**MAYA:** I do not align myself with the United States government. I align myself with the people of the world.

**LAURA:** The people of the world? I thought you just said the U.S. wants to create a One World superpower order.

**MAYA:** The U.S. wants to dominate the whole world. Not in an equal way so that everybody has safety and health and the ability to live and prosper. They want to be the number-one dog on the block. A gangster mentality is what it is.

**LAURA:** What was the Soviet Union? What was Nazism? What was Fascism? All three of which, with our military and our desire for freedom and to protect the U.S., we defeated?

**MAYA:** Well, you tell me who lives free in this country? I don't know how often you sit down and talk to a young black man, and I'm sorry, he does not live free.

**LAURA:** You tell that to the Marines I saw at Camp Pendleton not so long ago. They lived pretty free to me. And they're very excited about serving their country and protecting liberty and being a proud member of the U.S. military. Are you saying they're all brainwashed and stupid?

**MAYA:** Yes. They only have two options, you can go to jail or you can go into the military. There's no funding for schools and no funding for higher education. This government sets it up very specifically so that targeted communities have to go into the military. I have many friends who joined the military because that was their option. They wanted to get out—

**LAURA:** Maya, I gotta tell you, we're going to get flooded with calls from people in the military who listen to this program. They are going to be insulted by this. They support defending freedom and liberty—

**MAYA:** I'm going to have to go—

**LAURA:** Appreciate it.

**MAYA:** You guys should let people know when you get them on your show that you're in opposition to what they're saying so that they can come more prepared.

**LAURA:** Perhaps you should just do some research, which is what you don't do on your historical—

[*Click*].

Now Maya Jones is just one representative of one "peace organization," but her answers are fairly typical of what passes for intelligent conversation in the coffeehouses of Berkeley, Hollywood, and other liberal hangouts. But for the rest of us, they smacked of a smug elitism disguised as empathic global populism. Scratch the surface of the bumper sticker slogans—"America the empire builder," etc.—and you won't find rational arguments. No, what you'll get is peacenik belligerence and accusations of intolerance.

## AN ARMY OF NONE

Because they hate America—we'll be getting to that in a minute—antiwar elites are naturally convinced that those serving in the military are "stupid" or "baby-killers." After all, in their world, America is not something to be protected, it's something that other people need to be protected *from*. To people like Maya, no decent person could ever volunteer to defend such an evil, racist, sexist empire. Thus, anyone in the military must either have no other options or must truly be evil himself. When they look at our mil-

# **Peace**speak **alert!**

**Fox News:** Right-wing wackos. Liars, liars, liars. How dare they call "antiwar activists" leftists! How dare they claim that the groups have Marxist ties! Oh, wait, that's true.

**Talk Radio:** Repeat above.

**BBC, ABC, The Nation, etc.:** Former propaganda outlets for Iraqi Ministry of Information. Now working for North Korean and Cuban Intelligence. ■

itary, they don't see brave and honorable Americans. They just see wave after wave of Darth Vader's storm troopers.

Because they don't really think America is worth protecting, they don't really see any need for an efficient military. In their world, the only good use for the military is the same use they find for so many other U.S. institutions: to advance the revolution. And so back in the 1990s, Bill Clinton—perhaps our most unsoldierly president—decided to treat the armed services as his personal social engineering experiment.

This was a dear cause for liberal elites, most of whom thought that the military had held out for far too long. After all, in almost every other sphere of public life, the elites were succeeding in transforming society to reflect their own image. They had kicked God out of the public schools. They had turned our universities into hotbeds of political correctness. They had corralled the media to promote their agenda. Even Big Business had bought into many of their ideas—if only to protect itself from the inevitable lawsuits. But after gender integration at our military academies, the military refused to budge. Liberal elites were furious that any institution in America still refused to implement "gender equality" and "diversity training" and "sensitivity programs." When military spokesmen argued that allowing women in front-line combat roles or submarines would lower standards and reduce unit cohesion, they were sloughed off by the elites as being out of touch and "unprogressive."

And so Clinton overruled the military experts, and tried to turn our armed forces into yet another playground for elite tinkering. The elites didn't care whether afterward the military would be capable of defending the lives of Americans and protecting the United States from attack. They shortsightedly believed any such attack to be utterly impossible. Besides, they felt that somehow there was something "wrong" about military culture and the warrior ethos, and they wanted to change the armed services to make them "look like America." Well, *their* vision of America anyway.

But the United States military has a culture of its own. And that culture rests on the deeply felt belief that evil is real, that it is present in the world, and that it threatens the very existence of this country. As a result, everything the military stands for is in direct opposition to elitist me-myself-and-I liberalism. Fortunately, there is no constitutional right to serve in the military, which allows it to pick and choose the few good men (and women) it needs. If the Joint Chiefs feel that admitted homosexuals would detract from their unit's ability to fight, then they should bar them from service.

While the U.S. military is—properly—subject to civilian control, we civilians should be very careful about imposing our values on the military. Military life is, of necessity, completely different from civilian life. To put it bluntly, the military exists to kill people—and to sacrifice the lives of its own members—in order to protect the rest of us. In no avenue of civilian life, even in risky fields like police work or the fire department, are men *expected* to fight to the death in foreign countries and undergo the trauma of war. It was simply cruel and absurd for the Clinton administration to implement politically correct policies intended to "correct" military culture, thereby increasing the already high risk to the lives of American soldiers, sailors, airmen, and marines by reducing unit morale and cohesion and preventing them from operating at peak effectiveness. It is simply not fair to endanger our servicemen so that the elites at home can feel good about themselves.

There is nothing inherently political about the culture of the American military. The U.S. military—in fact, any military—must have order, discipline, and authority to survive. Liberal elites apparently cannot understand that liberal society needs to be defended by sometimes *illiberal* means. The military is no more racist or homophobic than the rest of America. If anything, the military from top to bottom is a hell of a lot more "diverse" than, say, the rich, virtually whites-only boards of People for the American Way or New York's Metropolitan Museum of Art. Blacks, Hispanics, Asians, whites, rich, poor, Southern, Northern, Midwestern—they all serve with equal distinction in the U.S. military.

# **Peace**speak **alert!**

**George W. Bush:** Warmonger, dope, dupe. The most evil man in history. In the pocket of Big Oil.

**Saddam Hussein:** Yeah, he might be a bad dude, but we all have our faults! Plus, he was only protecting his country from the American imperialist onslaught.

**Sean Penn:** Famous international statesman. His previous marriage to Madonna gives an indication of the level of intelligence he brings to the debate.

**Janeane Garofalo:** Acclaimed geopolitical expert and Middle East analyst. Some people believe she should stick to comedy. Others think that her foray into foreign policy is the best stand-up she's ever done.

**Ramsey Clark:** Head of the International Action Center, former U.S. Attorney General. Never met a blood-soaked dictator he didn't like. But only if they're anti-American, of course. ■

Too many of our elites fail to see that every aspect of military life, even something like parade ground drill, serves a legitimate purpose and isn't meant to turn men into brainwashed automatons. Drill, for instance, trains individuals to see themselves as part of a group, whether platoon, company, or division. It teaches them to put the unit before the self, which is crucial in battle to keep discipline and reduce casualties. Elites may not understand why men and women volunteer by the thousands for arduous, muddy training in camps instead of going to spin class at the tony gym down the street, but let us all be thankful that they do.

Of course, soldiers make these sacrifices because they take their oaths of loyalty to country and God seriously. Unfortunately, many of our elites laugh at displays of patriotism and faith. If you're an elitist who's spent his entire career working for the Ford Foundation, the *New York Times*, or a Hollywood studio, concepts like valor, bravery, and sacrifice are probably alien to you. You don't take them seriously, you don't know anyone who does, and you naturally think that anyone who does profess to live by them must be mentally defective, even evil.

It would be nice to think that our elites could at least practice the virtue of "tolerance" that they are so often proclaiming to the rest of us, and could respect the military's unique culture. But, alas, such is rarely the case. Consider Saint Xavier University Professor Peter Kirstein (a "teacher" of American history, God help us), who wins the award for penning the most military-hating screed in recent history. One day late in 2002, Kirstein received a polite e-mail from Robert Kurpiel, a young cadet at the Air Force Academy, asking whether Kirstein could help advertise an upcoming academic conference on international relations. No big deal. This is what Kirstein wrote in reply. (By the way, I've kept all the bad grammar, spelling errors, factual inaccuracies, illogical assertions, etc.)

*You are a disgrace to this country and I am furious you would even think I would support you and your aggressive baby killing tactics of*

*collateral damage. Help you recruit. Who, top guns to reign [sic] death
and destruction upon nonwhite peoples throughout the world? Are you
serious sir? Resign your commission and serve your country with hon-
our. No war, no air force cowards who bomb countries without AAA,
without possibility of retaliation. You are worse than the snipers. You
are imperialists who are turning the whole damn world against us.
September 11 can be blamed in part for what you and your cohorts
have done to Palestinians, the VC, the Serbs, a retreating army at
Basra. You are unworthy of my support.*

> *Peter N. Kirstein
> Professor of History
> Saint Xavier University*

Now, after a firestorm of epic proportions and thousands of
angry calls engulfed Saint Xavier University, Kirstein was forced to
apologize for his crude and tasteless e-mail, and was suspended
for—get this, folks—an entire semester. But the whole affair just
goes to show how ingrained antimilitary sentiment is within the
elite classes.

Elite suspicion and loathing for the military were not invented
yesterday. The great poet and author (of *The Jungle Book*, among
others) Rudyard Kipling skewered the army-hating liberals of his
day who liked "makin' mock o' uniforms that guard you while you
sleep." And George Orwell wrote in his novel *Coming Up for Air*
about a young man who volunteered ("listed") for the army to the
horror of his well-bred neighbors. "'Just think of it! A fine young
fellow like that!' It just shocked them. Listing for a soldier, in their
eyes, was the exact equivalent of a girl's going on the streets."

Nothing's changed. The elites still think volunteering for the
military is for losers. Try laying that line on young Joe Robert, a
PFC in the Marine Corps—now training as a recon specialist—
whose father, Joe Robert, is one of the wealthiest men in northern
Virginia. His boot camp class at Camp Pendleton "looked like

America," he told me, "with young men of all colors, from all backgrounds."

The elites antimilitary condescension was brilliantly skewered in a November 2002, op-ed in the *Washington Post* written by Frank Schaeffer, a novelist who lives on Boston's upmarket, Volvo-loving North Shore. He described what happened when his son John enlisted with the Marine Corps.

Frank recalled that "John's enlisting was...deeply unsettling. I did not relish the prospect of answering the question 'So where is John going to college?' from the parents who were itching to tell me all about how their son or daughter was going to Harvard. At the private high school John attended, no other students were going into the military." Then there was the mother who asked, "But aren't the Marines terribly Southern?" (What is it with the elites and the South?), and another parent (echoing Orwell), who commented, "What a waste. He was such a good student."

These people assumed that the military was a dead-end career suitable only for redneck sociopaths. How can they be expected to support our troops when they think the Marines are "terribly Southern," and think "Southern" is the equivalent of evil? Trying to get them to appreciate the patriotism, pride, and drive of those who volunteer to serve their country is like asking a tone-deaf person to perform at the Met. There's a gulf between military culture and elite culture, and it's getting wider by the minute. One is proud to be American, the other isn't.

## WHEN BEING "ANTIWAR" IS THE NEW BLACK

"Have we gone to war yet? We f—ing deserve to get bombed. Bring it on," shouted Chrissie Hynde of The Pretenders at a March concert in San Francisco. "Let's get rid of all the economic sh— this country represents! Bring it on! I hope the Muslims win!"

The aging rocker Hynde, inevitably described as a "veteran peace activist" by the media, was *cheering* for the deaths of American soldiers at the hand of an enemy. She was encouraging Saddam to kill and mutilate them. She thought we "deserved" to lose. She wanted Saddam to defeat America, to stay in power so that he could continue tormenting his own people. She was supporting a tyrannical, murderous regime at the expense of an open democracy.

Shocking as it seems to us, Hynde's vile comment is nothing out of the ordinary if you're a member of the "antiwar" left. It's regarded as perfectly acceptable to spew venom at America while standing up for our enemies. "The United States government poses as the great defender of human rights, but... there is no greater violator of human rights in the world than Washington," declared Richard Becker, the International Action Center's Western Region Coordinator, at a Palestinian rally in 2000. When America faced off against Iraq, the antiwar movement portrayed Saddam Hussein as the victim.

# **Peace**speak **alert!**

**America:** A country that had become so arrogant, so drunk on its superpower status, that it was begging to be attacked by terrorists. (sorry, "freedom fighters.")

**Morality:** Ick.

**Patriotism:** Ditto.

**September 11, Destruction of World Trade Center, attack on Pentagon, loss of thousands of lives:** That is soooo 2001!

**American troops:** Ignorant servants of the devil himself, George W. Bush. Mostly poor hicks or minorities with no other options. Soldiers of Global Capitalism. Instruments of mindless killing.

**Israel:** A tiny country intent on taking over the entire Middle East and enslaving the Arabs. Blamed by the elites for everything that goes wrong anywhere. ∎

Put simply, the so-called antiwar movement isn't really antiwar. The very same people often support, for instance, the Palestinians' "war of liberation." Many of them are Cold War relics who supported the Soviet invasion of Afghanistan. Their objections have nothing to do with peace. These so-called "peace activists" would be saying, "See, we told you so!" if we were struck again by terrorists. *Violence* is excused—after all, we're the bullies!

Do you think I exaggerate? Consider the case of Lynne Stewart, a manically leftist lawyer who defends terrorists in the courts. In 2002, John Ashcroft indicted her for allegedly helping her jailed client Sheikh Omar Abdul Rahman to communicate with his terrorist cronies in Egypt. In 1995, she told the *New York Times*, "I don't believe in anarchistic violence, but in directed violence. That would be violence directed at the institutions which perpetuate capitalism, racism, and sexism, and at the people who are the appointed guardians of those institutions, and accompanied by popular support." Basically, she means attacking America is A-okay because Americans apparently run the "institutions which perpetuate capitalism, racism, and sexism."

Creatures like Stewart have many friends abroad who wish to harm Americans. At a "peace" demonstration in Italy in November 2002, for instance, *every* random terrorist group was welcome. Yasser Arafat's puppet, Mustafa Barghouti, pledged to a sympathetic crowd that "we as Palestinians will never, ever stop our struggle. Nothing will break our will." The audience, recognizing these phrases as code for "we will continue suicide bombings against Israel," went nuts. Also present was the Basque terrorist front (the ETA) and friends of the drug-running, Marxist Revolutionary Armed Forces of Colombia. There were doctored posters of Osama bin Laden in the famous Che Guevara pose, and pictures of the Kurdish terrorist and Stalinist psychopath Abdullah Ocalan (whose terrorist group PKK was responsible for murdering several thousand Turks *and* Kurds in the name of "freedom"). And then there were the inevitable fans of Venezuela's dictator Hugo Chavez and Sub-Comandante Marcos, the creepy head of Mexico's Zapatista National Liberation Army.

For the type of people in this crowd, the confrontation with Iraq was only a convenient excuse to organize protests attacking America. Once the war was over, the "No Blood for Oil" zealots just moved on to something else. In this case, they instantly switched slogans to "End the Occupation" (referring to American soldiers in Iraq) and "Bring the Troops Home," as if they gave a damn about the troops' lives. (This touching sentiment was also belied by the San Francisco protestors who held aloft a sign reading, "We support our troops when they shoot their officers.") Instantly, America was depicted as an all-conquering, bloodthirsty colonialist occupying power of Iraq, rather than as a liberator. Without missing a beat, the group ANSWER, or Act Now to Stop War and End Racism—the extreme leftist umbrella group that organizes most of the protests—advertised a "Conference Against War, Colonial Occupation and Imperialism" just after the war ended. According to its literature, "The invasion and occupation of Iraq has created a U.S. military dictatorship in a country that possesses ten percent of the world's oil supply. This occupation is meeting widespread resistance throughout Iraq." (By the way, note the implied approval of "resisters" sniping and killing American soldiers.) For July 4, 2003, a protest was organized in Philadelphia featuring the usual mishmash of complaints, like:

- "*No* to U.S. wars at home and abroad"
- "*No* to colonialism and Empire"
- "*No* to the Occupation of Iraq"
- "*No* to racism, attacks on civil rights and immigrants"

But lest you think they say no to everything, they're in favor of "funding for social programs—not the Pentagon's war machine."

As usual, we're the Bad Guys.

There's nothing new about the ability of the "antiwar" types to turn on a dime as circumstances dictate. Only a couple of years ago, even before September 11, these same "antiwar" agitators were running riot in Seattle and Washington. Back then they had disguised themselves as opponents of the "American-backed" IMF and American-style "global capitalism." But we haven't heard too much about the WTO lately, have we? And what happened to all those evil (American) corporations allegedly exploiting "sweat-shop labor" in Asia and sucking Africa dry?

Before they lost interest in human rights, the radicals were all over animal rights and went around claiming McDonald's was exploiting the world's bovine population. And whatever happened to all those anti-AIDS red ribbons the fashionistas used to wear? All that boring stuff's been forgotten in the rush to condemn President Bush as the "new Hitler" and volunteering to do Saddam's bidding by acting as human shields. It's as if they have Issue Deficit Disorder—every year or two, they lose interest and move on to something Newer! Trendier! More tear-inducing!

Even with the antiwar material, we've been here before. Some of us are old enough to remember 1983, when there were huge "peace marches" here and in Europe demonstrating against Ronald Reagan's installation of defensive missiles in NATO countries to counterbalance the Soviet Union's SS-20s, which were poised to strike the capital cities of Western Europe. The millions of peace marchers—the cultural ancestors of today's peace idiots—claimed America was the aggressor and that the Kremlin was just "misunderstood." In the end, NATO refused to budge and the USSR collapsed. Just think, if we had listened to the pacifists, the good old USSR might still be going strong.

Then as now, the antiwar brigade hated democracy and loved dictatorships. Name me a single "pacifist" or "unilateral disarmer" from the 1980s who lifted a finger to help political dissidents in the Soviet Union. How many of today's "antiwar" activists spare a thought for those Iraqis executed and tortured for daring to question Saddam's authority? How many of them care about the dissidents rounded up and jailed in Castro's Cuba? Well, the

International Action Center (IAC) *was* outraged—but not about the thuggery rife in Castro's funhouse. No, they raised howls of protest (and I am not making this up) about President Bush's 2002 call for "free and fair elections" in Cuba. "George Bush and the U.S. government have no right to lecture any other country on the issue of democracy," exclaimed Castro apologist Gloria La Riva of the IAC. The IAC does not mention the long list of democracy activists, independent journalists, and other dissidents from Castro's Communist tyranny, who have been rounded up, "tried," and found guilty of "treason" and sentenced to long prison terms. At least we know where the antiwar movement's priorities lie (and the UN's, which reelected Cuba to the human rights commission at the same time).

And look at the names of the Democrats who backed Teddy Kennedy's peacenik-inspired "nuclear freeze" scheme of the 1980s. Teddy's idea was that both the United States and the Soviet Union would agree to "freeze" any further production of nuclear weapons—thus guaranteeing Soviet nuclear superiority and relieving the Soviet Union of an arms race it couldn't afford. Gosh, I wonder why President Reagan didn't sign on to that scheme? But lots of Democrats did, including Dick Gephardt, Tom Daschle, Harry Reid, Barbara Boxer, Chuck Schumer, Barbara Mikulski, Carl Levin, Patrick Leahy, Robert Byrd, and many, many more. Do these names sound familiar? They should—they're the same ones who accused another Republican president of "playing with fire," "rushing to war," and "threatening stability."

Without even admitting that they'd been completely and embarrassingly wrong about their friends in Moscow, the antiwarriors moved on attacking America in the run-up to the first Gulf War in 1990–91. Once again, we saw peace marchers around the world ranting that America's aggression against poor little Iraq would lead to "tens of thousands" of body bags coming home. Ted Kennedy was there, of course, giving us the benefit of his sophisticated military analysis:

"When the bullets start flying, 90 percent of the casualties will be American," he informed the Senate on January 10, 1991. "It'll be brutal and costly. It'll take weeks, even months, and quickly turn from an air war into a ground war, with thousands, perhaps even tens of thousands of American casualties. The administration refuses to release casualty estimates, but the 45,000 body bags the Pentagon has sent to the region are all the evidence we need of the high price in lives and blood that we will have to spare... We're talking about the likelihood of at least 3,000 American casualties a week, with 700 dead for as long as the war goes on."

Good call, Teddy. There was even a man called Gerhard Schroeder in Germany who took the lead in denouncing us in front of various demonstrations. According to his predictions, America would be forced to use its nuclear weapons on Iraq, "with terrible consequences." There would be hundreds of thousands, even millions, of casualties, and turmoil throughout the Middle East. His advice? Do nothing and negotiate with Saddam; under no circumstances must America wage war on Iraq. Today, he's chancellor of Germany. And what was his advice this time? Let the inspections continue (i.e., do nothing) and negotiate with Saddam; under no circumstances must America wage war on Iraq.

As for Kennedy, he's still banging the same tired old drum. On January 21, 2003, he warned that "an assault against Iraq will not advance the defeat of al Qaeda, but undermine it. It will antagonize critical allies and crack the global coalition that came together after September 11. It will feed a rising tide of anti-Americanism overseas, and swell the ranks of al Qaeda recruits and sympathizers. It will strain our diplomatic, military, and intelligence resources and reduce our ability to root out terrorists.... It could quickly spin out of control." Wrong, wrong, wrong.

If we'd listened to the peace idiots after September 11, there would have been no war in Afghanistan, home of the Islamofascist Taliban. They'd like to forget about it now, but I remember that MIT professor Noam Chomsky (lauded by the liberals' house paper, the *New York Times,* as "arguably the most important intellectual alive") warned that if America attacked the Taliban, it would lead to "genocide." Of course, that would be America's fault. Even the *New York Times* ran opinion columns purporting to be "news analyses" that claimed America would drown in the "Vietnam-like quagmire" of Afghanistan. Remember all those articles about how the Russians and the British had never been able to conquer Afghanistan? All these pundits wanted us to sit still and do nothing. They didn't care that America had just been attacked and that a gang of fanatics had slaughtered thousands of civilians in cold blood. To them, America was wrong to "seek revenge." And what happened? Bush ignored the America-bashers and blew the Taliban out of the water in what, three weeks? The "unbeatable" Taliban were history. They didn't even know what hit them. When they sat cowering in their caves the last thing that went through the terrorists' heads was not a vision of the seventy-two black-eyed virgins they'd be meeting in Allah's paradise, but a high-velocity round fired by a member of the U.S. Special Forces.

I think George Bush—actually, the Iraqi people as well and all those slandered and abused by the "peace at any price" crowd—are owed a lot of apologies from all those antiwar activists who got it so spectacularly wrong. That would be the polite, honorable thing to do. But it's never going to happen. It's a little like those Hollywood buffoons who invariably claim they're going to leave the country if the Republicans win the election—but never do (much to our dismay). Janeane Garofalo, for instance, promised that she would apologize to Bush in person if she was wrong about how disastrous the war was going to be, only to refuse to do so after a particularly nondisastrous war. And where are the cringing apologies from the likes of Eric Alterman of *The Nation*, who wrote sarcastically, "Is Wolfowitz really so ignorant of history as to believe the Iraqis would welcome us as 'their hoped-for liberators'?" No, Eric, the Iraqis loved being brutalized.

Or how about Columbia University's Edward Said, Palestinian

activist and the darling of the anti-American left? He lashed out at other Middle Eastern writers (such as Lebanese academic Fouad Ajami, the Iraqi exile Kanan Makiya, and the exiled Iraqi leader Ahmed Chalabi) for their "rubbish" because they dared to say that the war would be a quick one. As Eddie pointed out, "The idea that Iraq's population would have welcomed American forces entering the country after a terrifying aerial bombardment was always utterly implausible." Hmmm. The only utterly implausible aspect of this whole affair is that fools like Alterman are still employed.

No number of mass graves uncovered by our troops will convince antiwar pols like Howard Dean that the war in Iraq was necessary. Dean, former Vermont governor and Democrat presidential candidate for the disenfranchised left, is banking his presidential run on the WMD issue—positively gleeful at the prospect that weapons might have been destroyed or hidden, never to be found. When CNN's Wolf Blitzer asked him whether the Iraqi people were "better off" without Saddam, Dean replied, "We don't know that yet." To his credit, Blitzer kept his composure, and followed up: "You think it's possible . . . that whatever emerges in Iraq could be worse than what they had for decades under Saddam Hussein?" According to Dean, "I do, I do."

## ELITE HYPOCRISY: GOOD WARS VS. BAD WARS

The "antiwar" crowd has never been right about anything, ever. (They weren't even right about Vietnam. That poor country is still suffering from the economic misery imposed upon it by Communism.) But to them, that doesn't matter. It's not important whether they're right or wrong. The point is to make America look bad by using scare tactics and issuing pro-enemy propaganda. If it's not Iraq, it'll just be something else.

If they care about peace so much, why were the elites so quiet, and even supportive, about our military intervention in Bosnia or

Kosovo—or even when we last dealt with Iraq back in 1996 and 1998? There are two reasons.

First, their compatriot Bill was our commander in chief. That makes all the difference. Many of the attacks on "the war" are actually disguised assaults on the Bushies—the Rumsfelds, Cheneys, Wolfowitzes, etc. The elites lost to Reagan and they lost Florida in 2000, so now it's payback time, and if that means opposing war at the risk of jeopardizing national security, then that's just "politics."

Consider the shifting words of Tom Daschle. This is Daschle back in 1996, after Saddam had attacked the Kurds in northern Iraq: "Saddam Hussein's actions will not be tolerated. . . . We intend to make that point clear with the use of force." Then in February 1998, Daschle went positively Patton about hitting the Iraqi dictator where it hurt. "Look, we have exhausted virtually, our [sic] diplomatic effort to get the Iraqis to comply with their own agreements and with international law. Given that, what other option is there but to force them to do so? . . . The answer is, we don't have another option. We have got to force them to comply, and we are doing so militarily." You go, Tom!

But with Bush in the White House, Daschle suddenly went touchy-feely. Before Operation Iraqi Freedom, Daschle felt that America was "rushing to war without adequate concern for the ramifications of doing so unilaterally or with a very small coalition of nations." (Actually, America didn't do anything of the sort, unless you think the support of more than thirty countries is a "very small coalition." It's also larger than the one that backed Clinton in 1998.)

And Daschle isn't the only flip-flopper. John Kerry, a strong contender for 2004's Democratic presidential nomination, talked tough in 1996. "If the history of the last six years [since the Gulf War] has taught us anything, it is that Saddam Hussein does not understand diplomacy, he only understands power, and when he brandishes power in a manner that threatens our interests or violates internationally accepted standards of behavior, we must be prepared to respond—and with force if necessary." Down, boy! But before this war, he was distinctly ambivalent about it; during it he declared he wanted to have "regime change" in Washington; and after it, he accused the Bush administration of "laying out enormous plans" in Iraq and said that "it is time for us to demand that they lay out a plan for us here in America." In other words, let's ignore the whole Iraq thing and talk about raising taxes.

And finally, let's not forget the Master of Foreign Policy himself. It's unbelievable that during the 1996 presidential debates, Bill Clinton said this: "Sometimes the United States has to act alone, or at least has to act first. Sometimes we cannot let other countries have a veto on our foreign policy." Or this: "We have learned that if you give [Saddam Hussein] an inch, he'll take a mile. We had to do something. And even though not all of our allies supported it at first, I think most of them now believe that what we did was the appropriate thing to do." Or how about Clinton in 1998: "The hard fact is that so long as Saddam remains in power, he threatens the well-being of his people, the peace of his region, the security of the world." Clinton added, "The credible threat to use force, and when necessary the actual use of force, is the surest way to contain Saddam's weapons of mass destruction program [and] curtail his aggression."

How can anyone reconcile those words with what Clinton said in the lead-up to war? "The real thing we have to worry about is whether we have enough support in the world so that it's obvious that we were implementing the UN will and not doing a preemptive attack," opined Clinton. In any case, it's North Korea, not Iraq, that poses the "biggest short-term threat" to global security and America. In other words, Clinton suddenly wanted to do nothing about Iraq. The Democrats' hypocrisy on this issue was beyond shameful.

The elites also found it easier to support military action in Kosovo and Bosnia because those conflicts weren't primarily about protecting American security. (The same analysis applies today to

Liberia.) They were more akin to "humanitarian" efforts. The elites had no problem with our military building roads or repairing bridges in Haiti. They had no problem with soldiers putting their lives at risk to protect the Bosnian Moslems. They just don't like military endeavors that are designed to benefit *America*. If Somalia had been on the verge of becoming a nuclear power, and was pleading its case to the UN bureaucracy that America was only trying to grab its "strategic" sheep herds, we would have seen celebrities and leftists falling over themselves to volunteer as human shields for General Mohammed Aideed. No War for Wool!

## THE SADDAMITES

We faced exactly this scenario in the lead-up to war in Iraq. The "antiwar" elites backed a dictator over our president. They trusted Kofi Annan over George W. Bush. They said their concern was for the lives of innocents, "the children," etc., but they were willing to prolong the war, which kept Saddam's torture regime in power longer, devastating the very population the peace pushers say they care so much about. To them, the Iraqi people were only pawns in their quest to subvert America. They weren't antiwar protestors—they were protesters *against* freeing Iraqis from their bondage.

That's why you never saw placards saying "Freedom for Iraq" at their protests but thousands about chanting "Fight the Power," "No Imperialist War against Iraq," and "No Blood for Oil." Liberation wasn't on the anti-American agenda. They didn't give a damn about what happened to the oppressed Iraqis. For the sake of attacking America, the Saddamites aligned themselves with one of the most violent regimes on earth. The moment that made most Americans the happiest—the sight of Iraqis celebrating Saddam's fall—was humiliating and embarrassing to them.

But the Saddamites deserved to be humiliated. They talk about human rights while they're busy defending dictators whose hands drip with the blood of murdered thousands. They scream about "rights" but they have no sense of right. They pander to the most disgusting forms of barbarism seen since World War II. These are people who think Yasser Arafat is a terrific guy, even though he's responsible for the murder of American citizens. (In the Palestinian Authority, by the way, one way of executing gays is to stand them up in neck-deep pools of fetid water with sacks of feces on their heads before throwing them into dungeons infested with insects. Next time there's an "antiwar" riot, look closely at the placards being waved and count how many feature pro-Palestinian slogans. The same people waving those slogans go back to their college campuses *the next day* and complain that "right-wingers" are oppressing homosexuals. Once again, we see that the only *consistency* among the "antiwar" crowd is that they are consistently anti-American.)

The International Action Center, the biggest of the hardcore leftist, anti-American, "antiwar" groups, recently issued a dispatch from North Korea that reads: "The army-first policy has guaranteed a strong, healthy, well-disciplined fighting force despite several years of arduous conditions for the people of socialist North Korea. It represents a sacrifice the people are proud of, and their respect for those in uniform is unmistakable, as is the élan of the fighting forces.... The land, factories, homes, hotels, parks, schools, hospitals, offices, museums, buses, subways—everything in [North Korea] belongs to the people as a whole." Tom Scahill wrote a piece lauding "the accomplishments made by North Korea despite generations of colonial occupation, war and threats of outside intervention." What we in capitalist, imperialist, genocidal America forget is that "goods and services in North Korea, like health care, education and housing, are virtually free." Well, yes, that is true, but then again, the health care, education, and housing in America are infinitely superior to anything you can find in North Korea. Don't believe me? Try getting a CAT scan there. Try finding an apartment that's not dingy, tiny, cold, and situated in some hideously ugly 1960s Stalinist building. Try buying a book not approved by the authorities. Try finding a copy of the U.S. Constitution. North Korea is so far behind its southern neighbor in terms of freedom, wealth, and quality of life that it is hard to imagine that they share the same peninsula. Yet, the IAC is an outfit that thinks Pyongyang is a paradise. These are the same people organizing "peace marches" in big cities, people who claim to "speak for Americans."

Well, let's just look at some other facts about North Korea. Between 1995 and 2000, according to a human rights report issued by the State Department in February 2001, "approximately a million" North Koreans died because of famine. The only reason that figure isn't hovering around the eight-million mark (or nearly one-third of the population) is that other countries (including this one) have sent North Korea masses of food. Moreover, the North Korean health "system" (run by the state, of course) has flatlined, with even basic health care hard to come by. Clean water is a rarity, electricity is available for just a couple of hours a day, and *63 percent* of children are stunted because of chronic undernourishment. But hey, the IAC and its "antiwar" partners can't get enough of Kim Jong Il and his Fightin' Forces—the very same ones who are poised to attack American troops based in South Korea and who are currently threatening the world with nuclear weapons. That's giving peace a chance.

Antiwar rallies are really hate rallies. Hate-America rallies, that is. If you actually attend one of these rallies, you'll notice that the speakers (and their unshaven and unwashed listeners) assume that America is the "Fourth Reich," that all the world's problems can be traced to George W. Bush, that America's goal is to dominate, not liberate. I wish I were exaggerating, but it's impossible to do so with this crowd. At a San Francisco rally before the war, there were signs depicting Bush administration officials as Nazis in SS uniforms. Underneath the various photos were such tag lines as:

- "The Fuhrer, Already in his Bunker" (Dick Cheney)
- "House Negro" (Powell)
- "Will Kill Africans for Oil" (Condi Rice)
- "Faith-Based Fascist, Sexless Sadist" (John Ashcroft)
- "Jew for Genocide" (Paul Wolfowitz)

Those signs give you a sense of what passes for humor and cleverness among the "antiwar" crowd.

As for the president, he's regularly depicted as a blood-crazed, money-obsessed sadist intent on murdering millions of innocents with his genocidal policies. (Speaking of genocide, wasn't it Saddam who oversaw the murder of 100,000 Kurds, and inflicted police roundups, mass executions, and anonymous burials on his own people? Weird how the "antiwar" movement never mentions that.) Other times, Bush is portrayed as a moron wearing a cowboy hat and six-shooters and chug-a-lugging glasses of oil. He's a member of the "Axis of Evil," the other members being Tony Blair and Ariel Sharon (of course—gotta have a Jew in there). Protesters turn up wearing Bush masks and waving baby dolls splattered with red paint. They carry signs reading "Soldiers Are Terrorists" and "America Is HeartleSS, RuthleSS" with the two last letters of each word copied from the Nazis' lightning-bolt "SS" runes. (More examples of "antiwar" humor.) On the *Tonight Show*, Dennis Miller offered the perfect response to the peaceniks' love of Nazi imagery: "If you're in a peace march and the guy next to you has a sign that says 'Bush is Hitler,' forget the peace thing for a second and beat his ass."

But in the twisted world of the Hate America crowd, George W. Bush is the modern Hitler and creeps like Saddam are Genuine Lovers of Peace. (Now that Saddam's out, Kim Jong Il and that hardy perennial Fidel Castro are back.) The hate-America crowd suppressed the mountains of evidence about the cruelties of Saddam's regime. (And let's not forget good old CNN, which admitted it glossed stories in return for access to Iraq.) Here was a dictator who targeted Iraqi minorities, like the Kurds, for destruction, and who massacred the Marsh Arabs of southeastern Iraq so that during his reign their numbers fell from 250,000 people to 40,000. Tortures, bombardments of villages, "disappearances," arbitrary arrests, and summary executions went on every day while Saddam was in power. They would still be going on if the "antiwar" crowd had its way. But instead of complaining about this brutality, the antiwarriors worked themselves into a frenzy over the fear that somehow, some way, some American would get access to cheaper oil as part of Saddam's fall.

Not wanting to have their message interfered with by the facts, the "antiwar" crowd often banned Iraqi exiles from speaking at "peace marches" ostensibly devoted to "helping the Iraqi people." For example, Amir Taheri, one such exile, attended a protest in London. He and his fellow exiles wanted to use placards with "Freedom for Iraq" on them, but the organizers were only allowing what he called "official" placards reading "Bush and Blair: Baby-Killers," "Not In My Name," and "Freedom for Palestine." "Not one placard demanded that Saddam should disarm to avoid war," recalled Taheri. "The goons also confiscated photographs showing the tragedy of Halabja, the Kurdish town where Saddam's forces gassed 5,000 people to death in 1988." When Salima Kazim, an Iraqi grandmother whose three sons had been murdered by Saddam for being "dissidents," asked Jesse Jackson if she could borrow his microphone to tell the protestors about Iraqi abuses, the good reverend angrily snapped, "Today is not about Saddam Hussein. Today is about Bush and Blair and the massacre they plan in Iraq." At least we know whose side he's on now.

Of course the antiwar/anti-America gang never stops to think about what would happen if they tried the same "demonstration against authoritarian rule" in any of their beloved dictatorships (Cuba, North Korea, Libya, the Palestinian Authority, Communist China, the old Soviet Union, Khmer Rouge Cambodia, etc., etc.). Faster than they could say "Not In Our Name," they would be dragged off by the secret police and tortured for fun. The lucky ones would die quickly.

I wish these "peace activists" would remember that the next time they whine about how "oppressive" America is. They've forgotten that the only reason they're allowed to go out and protest in the first place is because of the sacrifices Americans have made over more than two centuries—and are still making today—to protect our hard-won freedoms. We're the freest country in the history of the world and these idiots think they're living in Nazi Germany. Maybe they can go live in "free" Cuba or Iraq and we can have jailed Cuban and Iraqi political dissidents (otherwise known as democrats) come over here. At least *they* see America as a beacon of freedom and tolerance—and what's more, they've actually suffered, *really* suffered, for their beliefs, unlike the marching college kids who equate "suffering" with Daddy not paying off their credit cards on time. Even Norman Mailer, the novelist who's an old "antiwar" leftie, snorted in derision at the new breed of protestor during a speech in Los Angeles. "Look at all those protesters, those young professionals pushed into the side streets by the police in the New York march," he hooted in Los Angeles "They all got bored and took out their cell phones. Probably on the phone with their brokers! No war for oil! Ha!"

But these are the type of protesters you get when your guiding principle is to Blame America First. If something's wrong in the world, then obviously it must be our fault. Sorry, *your* fault. The elites, remember, are above all criticism. So their White House Clinton-Gore Dream Team can't be blamed for not taking custody of bin Laden when they had the chance to in 1996. (Imagine if Clinton pursued bin Laden with the same tenacity that he pursued other—ahem—interests.) His Secretary of State Madeleine Albright can't be blamed for seeing North Korea through rose-colored glasses when she celebrated the Agreed Framework prohibiting nuclear production, which Pyongyang never had any intention to abide by. She could also not be blamed for clapping while sitting

# The**Rogues**Gallery

The so-called elites come in all shapes, sizes, colors, and party affiliations. Although they don't all share the same views, they do all wield disproportionate influence in American society. So what does this mean for the rest of us?

## ▶ THE ENTERTAINMENT ELITES

*Associated Press/Nick Ut*

▲ "I'm not the president but I play one on TV!" In a duct tape moment, **Martin Sheen** never sounded better (at an antiwar rally in Los Angeles, March 26, 2003).

*AFP/Corbis/John Mabanglo*

*Associated Press/Michael Green*

▲ **Natalie Maines:** The lead Dixie Chick is proud to be loud, but not that President Bush is from Texas. She wept in a post-incident interview with Diane Sawyer. We weep when she talks politics.

◀ "Life partners" **Susan Sarandon** and **Tim Robbins**. True love, true peaceniks, truly tedious.

# ▶ THE ENTERTAINMENT ELITES

Zuma Press/Beth Schneider

▲ Stupid White Man: Elite fave **Michael Moore** has made millions playing the "regular guy," while portraying "regular Americans" as moronic and unsophisticated. Nice work if you can get it.

Reuters

▲ And you thought **Sean Penn**'s talents were limited to acting, punching photographers, and losing handguns? On CNN's *Larry King Weekend*, Penn said that as a celebrity he had a "heightened responsibility" to travel to Iraq on a December 2002 "fact-finding" mission.

# ▶ THE ENTERTAINMENT ELITES

▶ **Barbra Streisand:** A very funny girl when she talks politics, foreign policy, military affairs, or when she tries to spell. Streisand is desperately concerned about the "trickle down immorality" of the Bush era! (This from a woman who is close pals with the guy who was impeached, played doctor with a White House intern, and bombed an aspirin factory.) If you're feeling down, her "truth alerts" on barbrastreisand.com are a scream.

▲ Bush-bashing actress **Janeane Garofalo** smelled a blacklist when her recent sitcom pilot *Slice o' Life* was axed by ABC. Maybe it wasn't as funny as her political analysis.

▶ "Banana Boat" crooner **Harry Belafonte** likened Colin Powell and Condoleezza Rice to "house slaves" for working in the Bush administration and supporting the war in Iraq. In a later "clarification" he said he meant that Powell is a "tragic failure."

▶ Buddha made him do it! **Richard Gere** was booed at the post–September 11 "Concert for New York City" when he called for "peace and tolerance."

# ▶ THE ANTIRELIGION ELITES

Getty/Frazer Harrison

▲ Playboy mansion devotee **Bill Maher** says he believes in "a god" but has contempt for "organized religion." With that sort of original and bold thinking you might get your own HBO show, too!

EFE Photos/Dan Smith

Getty/Justin Sullivan

▲ California Dreaming: **Michael Newdow** claims his daughter's First Amendment rights were violated by the words "under God" in the Pledge of Allegiance. The wacky left Ninth Circuit Court of Appeals agreed. God help us.

◀ Papa Don't Preach: **Madonna** says "Catholicism is a very masochistic religion . . . there are some very beautiful rituals in Catholicism, but there is a certain darkness within it. It's not a very loving religion. It's not very flexible. It doesn't make room for human error." (Don't worry, Madonna, you're forgiven for *Swept Away*.)

# ▶ THE UNIVERSITY ELITES

Zuma Press/Cristiano Laruffa/La Presse

▲ Writer for the elites **Susan Sontag** outdid herself when not long after September 11, she wrote that the attacks came "as a consequence of specific American alliances and actions." Translation: We asked for it.

Reuters News Media Inc./Corbis

Corbis/Christopher Felver

▲ Prof. **Noam Chomsky** is an anti-American hack wildly popular among Euro- and academic elites. The MIT linguistics professor blasts the U.S. as a "leading terrorist state." He's still defending Nicaragua's Sandinistas.

▲ **Cornel West** is an amiable fellow but unintelligible as a scholar and writer. After many years on the Harvard faculty, he bolted to Princeton after he felt unfairly pressured to do some real academic work.

# ▶ THE ANTIWAR ELITES

Reuters News Media Inc./Corbis

▲ Traitor Watch: No, it's not the Iraqi Information Minister, it's former attorney general (what was LBJ thinking?) **Ramsey Clark** at a Baghdad press conference (Sept. 2002), calling for the impeachment of President Bush. Note the portrait of one of his closest Iraqi supporters, the late Qusay Hussein.

▲ Rocker **Sheryl Crow** accessorizes with antiwar slogans before the war in Iraq. So why did she hang with Hillary in Bosnia after our military efforts there? And where was the T-shirt during the war in Kosovo?

▲ Hub of the antiwar wheel: **Brian Becker** is everywhere at once, as head of international ANSWER and an activist with the Marxist Workers World Party. He's a self-described radical socialist. Agreed.

# ▶ THE INTERNATIONAL/EURO-ELITES

Reuters Photo Archive/Andy Clark

▲ With friends like these . . . French foreign minister **Dominique de Villepin** claims to "love Americans and America," but he stabbed America in the back when he reneged on his pledge to Colin Powell to support a UN resolution authorizing military force against Iraq.

▶ **Fidel Castro:** The dictator the entertainment elites just can't resist. He's not perfect, but he loves American culture! He appreciates good music! He even looks good in a pair of Oakleys!

AFP/Corbis/Christophe Simon

▶ Legal elite Supreme Court Justice **Stephen Breyer** thinks our Constitution will need to evolve to "fit" with the documents of foreign nations. I guess Jefferson and Hamilton forgot to include the "judiciary shall consult France" provision in Article III.

Reuters Photo Archive/Evan Richman

AFP/Corbis/Gerard Cerles

▲ **Kofi Annan:** The UN secretary-general who hails from Ghana loves the Manhattan social circuit, but not America's "unilateralism." He'd rather be secretary-general of the world.

# ▶ THE IMMIGRATION ELITES

AFP/Corbis/Tim Sloan

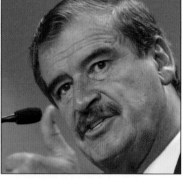

Reuters Photo Archive/Monika Fleuckiger

▲ Mexican president **Vicente Fox** wants to keep the flow of illegals into the U.S. moving. It's much easier than fixing the Mexican economy.

◀ **Ted Kennedy** and **George W. Bush** have one thing in common—they favor amnesty programs for illegals. It's the open-border elites versus the people.

# ▶ ELITE INSPIRATION

Getty/Quique Kierszenbaum

Condé Nast Archive/Corbis

▲ **Jane Fonda** chilled out with the enemy during the Vietnam War, setting a standard that even few of today's Hollywood elites can live up to.

▲ Reporter and columnist **H. L. Mencken** started from the premise that Americans were stupid. He once called democracy "the worship of jackals by jack asses" and coined the famous phrase, "No one ever went broke underestimating the intelligence of the American people." He's foremost among the twentieth-century elites.

alongside Kim Jong Il at a stadium rally during her visit to Pyongyang in October 2000 as 100,000 performers did routines lauding such themes as "If the Party Decides, So We Do" and "We Will Support Our Powerful Nation with Rifles." There was even a video image of a long-range ballistic missile taking off projected onto a giant screen. When she stood up to leave, the audience of 50,000 (and the 100,000 drafted performers) leapt to their feet to cheer wildly. Half-bright said North Korea was preparing to open itself to the world. But she can't be blamed for that. *Au contraire*, the North Korea nuclear blackmail game is George Bush's fault because he "offended" the Dear Leader by including his country as part of the Axis of Evil.

## IT'S ABOUT SECURITY, STUPID

Most of all, the views of the "antiwar" movement are insane. They're impossible to take seriously. Literally, they make no sense. Their "assertions" are absurd and their "arguments" childish. If Operation Iraqi Freedom was all about oil, for instance, then instead of going to all the trouble of attacking Iraq, why didn't Bush call up Saddam and tell him that he would lift sanctions without disarmament? Once the sanctions were lifted, and Saddam was allowed to open the spigots, we would have had all the Iraqi oil we could wish for at knockdown prices. How long do you think it would have taken for Saddam to agree and ensure he stayed in power? Ten seconds? Half a minute, maybe? In any case, the Middle East is shrinking as a supply of our oil, and we've gotten along just fine for the last decade, and . . . oh, never mind, the "antiwar" brigades wouldn't listen anyway.

Or what about Yvette Clarke, a Democrat on New York's City Council who backed an "antiwar" resolution in a city that witnessed 3,000 dead and suffered untold billions in damages on September 11? What's her justification for stabbing America in the back? "If we're going to be looking for a fight, let's fight poverty, let's fight firehouse closures, let's fight racism and sexism," she says. But how are we going to "fight poverty" when we're paying enormous sums to nuclear blackmailers? How are we going to fight "racism and sexism" in cities that have been reduced to rubble by nuclear terrorists, or cities that have been abandoned from fear of chemical weapons? Until we've secured our own safety, we can't possibly solve any other problem.

Clarke is backed up by people like Olga Vivas, the "Action Vice President" (as opposed to all her fellow vice presidents for "inaction," presumably) of the National Organization for Women. She said at an October meeting of the Prominent Citizens Oppose War with Iraq (among whom were advertised the usual humdrum leftists like Barbara Ehrenreich, author of *Nickel and Dimed*; Bob Edgar, general secretary of the National Council of Churches; Ben Cohen, the ice cream guy and founder of something called Business Leaders for Sensible Priorities; Jonathan Dean of the Union of Concerned Scientists; Linda Fuller, Habitat for Humanity International; and Richard Falk, Princeton University) at the National Press Club that radical Islamism isn't the cause of the Middle East's repressive policies toward women, but rather "U.S. foreign policy" is. It gets even more oppressive at home, evidently. "Isn't there terror being inflicted on the women and children of the United States?" by Bush's domestic policy, she asked.

Uh, no. You see, "terror" is when bad men come to your house and kill you for your beliefs. "Terror" is when you can't say what you think for fear of being shot. "Terror" is when you huddle in your basement night after night, wondering which of your neighbors is a spy. Ask the folks who lived in Saddam's prisons if they think American women and children are living under terrorism. Or don't, if you're worried about being laughed out of the room. Clarke and Vivas, and those like them, are not just idiots, they are moral morons.

Now, I know that not everyone who attends an "antiwar" protest is stupid, or even an elitist. There were sensible arguments against a war in Iraq, just as there were many sensible arguments in favor. The problem is that the "movement" has been hijacked by hard-line fanatics posing as caring, sharing, "antiwar" believers.

If you ever think about going to one of these "antiwar" protests, just think about the crowd you'll be hanging with. These are people who constantly compare George Bush to Adolf Hitler. These are people who censored and suppressed facts and criticisms that got in the way of their fairy tale of Iraqi innocence and American wickedness. Such people have no interest in the truth. They are only interested in getting America. And people like that have no compunction—absolutely none at all—about exploiting Hollywood's legions of useful idiots and manipulating well-meaning church groups and youth organizations—and even you—into parroting their anti-American line. Yes, people who fall in with this crowd are exercising their legitimate right to dissent—a right protected by the strength of the U.S. military—but they are also unwittingly acting as puppets and mouthpieces of the anti-American crowd.

And when you look under the rocks where these anti-American groups live, you see some really scary and dangerous characters. Take the organization Not In Our Name (NION), represented by my radio guest Maya. It's split in half. The first "public" half is called the "Not In Our Name Statement," which is the ostensibly "acceptable" face of the "antiwar" movement. The Statement recruits celebrities and assorted dumbbells to sign petitions that are published in major newspapers. But behind the statement lurks the "Not In Our Name Project." That part organizes the protests and is controlled by such members of the Revolutionary Communist Party (RCP) as Mary Lou Greenberg. Now, Greenberg is *also* a founder of Refuse & Resist!, another front for the RCP. So when low-wattage celebrities like Martin Luther King III or Casey Kasem sign the NION petition, they're indirectly doing the RCP's dirty work. The beauty of the scam is that King and Kasem (and Susan Sarandon and Danny Glover and Jane Fonda, etc.) don't even know they're being used for more nefarious purposes than just "dissent." The elites are being sucker-punched into espousing an even more virulent form of anti-Americanism than the garbage they usually come out with. What they don't realize is that the hard-core anti-American left has no principled opposition to war; all it cares about is making tactical attacks on America, and any cause—Iraq included—will do.

## KNOW THY ENEMIES—AT HOME

While liberal elites still harp about the "vast right-wing conspiracy" that is allegedly controlled by the NRA, the Federalist Society, Operation Rescue, the Christian Coalition, and [fill in the blank with the conservative group of your choice], the really insidious collaboration is happening among the antiwar left.

Liberal are quick to dismiss any mention of the background, history or membership of these groups as red-baiting. Fox News Channel's Alan Colmes blasted such a comment by author David Horowitz: "You go on to talk about how this was done under the auspices of the Communist Workers World Party, meaning the march in Washington last Saturday, which to me is red-baiting." Hint to Alan Colmes: it's not red-baiting if they really are reds. Other "mainstream sources"—like Reuters, the *Washington Post*, and CNN—treat these outfits as if they're legitimate pressure groups instead of Marxoid manipulators.

It's no surprise that these news organizations have fallen for the trick. The leftists have been perfecting these kinds of tactics since the 1930s, when they worked to persuade Americans that Stalin was just a cuddly guy with a mustache and that all those stories about man-made famines and mass deportations to the Gulag were "American propaganda." Walter Duranty, the *New York Times* man in Moscow in the 1930s, won a Pulitzer for reporting that everything was just great in Stalin's Russia when he knew perfectly well it wasn't. The Pulitzer Committee is finally considering revoking his prize. I'm sure he'll be crushed. Replace "Stalin" with "Saddam" and you'll see that nothing has changed in the intervening decades. The elites closed their eyes to the Soviet Union's evils, just as they wanted to keep giving Saddam another chance.

The "antiwar" faction is still Stalinist. It tolerates terror, and uses deception for power.

Let's take a look at the real "antiwar" movement. The first thing you need to know is that absolutely everybody is connected. Senior members of one particular group habitually turn up on others' boards; much of the time, even the group itself is a front for a still more shadowy group lurking in the background. For instance, Brian Becker is a spokesman for ANSWER, a Marxist front for "antiwar" groups that the *Washington Post* blithely calls an "activist coalition." And what activists they are. Becker sits on ANSWER's steering committee, but he also happens to be the National Co-Director of the International Action Center (IAC) and an executive of the World Workers Party (WWP). He's also, by the way, chairman of the U.S. Troops Out of Korea Committee. Kim Jong Il just loves him. But Brian doesn't love America. He thought that the war against the Taliban was "one of the great crimes and acts of terrorism in our era."

The real nerve center of the "antiwar" movement is the WWP. It is considered by experts to be a hair's-breadth away from being classified as a terrorist group. Which experts? Let's hear from former FBI Director Louis Freeh: "Anarchists and extremist socialist groups—many of which, such as the Workers World Party—have an international presence and, at times, also represent a potential threat in the United States."

The Stalinist WWP was founded in the wake of the Soviet invasion of Hungary in 1956—as a *pro*-Soviet outfit celebrating the crushing of freedom. In the same spirit of repression, the WWP cheered on the Chinese government when it drove its tanks through Tiananmen Square. So, basically, it rants against imaginary American "imperialism" while lauding real, live Communist imperialism. It hails Fidel Castro and Kim Jong Il as great leaders, claimed before the fall of Saddam that "Iraq has done absolutely nothing wrong," and protests the war-crimes trial of Slobodan Milosevic ("Milosevic has earned the respect of working-class activists worldwide," says the WWP newspaper *Workers World*). Many articles from *Workers World* are reproduced on the IAC website.

Now, why would that be? Because the IAC is an offshoot of the WWP founded by Ramsey Clark, who was once—hard to believe—Lyndon Johnson's attorney-general. Clark skidded off the mental rails about thirty years ago and has never quite got back on track. Clark acted as counsel for Pastor Elizaphan Ntakirutimana, indicted for his role in the Rwandan genocide; and defended Radovan Karadzic, a wanted Serbian war criminal, in a civil suit filed against him in New York brought by Bosnian rape victims. During the Kosovo war, Clark flew to Belgrade and told his audience, "It will be a great struggle, but a glorious victory. You can be victorious." By shooting down American pilots, presumably. These days, Clark is cochairman of the International Committee to Defend Slobodan Milosevic. Shaking hands with bloodstained dictators and psychopaths is nothing new to Ramsey, so it's not too surprising he was in the forefront of the campaign to get Saddam off the hook.

The most important aspect of the IAC's activities is ANSWER, which is basically a project that it secretly runs with the WWP. ANSWER sponsors and organizes marches, and serves as a "convergence point" for the various anti-American groups like the Free Palestine Alliance and the Mexico Solidarity Network, as well as assorted kooks (such as Leslie Feinberg, who describes herself as a "lesbian-gay-bi-transgender movement activist") associated with the WWP. And so on and on it goes: front after front after front dedicated to destroying America.

## METASTASIZING ANTI-AMERICANISM

There's one major distinction between the WWP-IAC-ANSWER crowd and their colleagues in the Not In Our Name (NION) movement. While they're both fanatically anti-American organizations, the NION people don't worship at the feet of Kim Jong Il, though they do blame America for North Korea's troubles. Because they've got more Hollywood celebs on their roster, NION needs to be a little bit more respectable in public than the WWP, which wouldn't mind liquidating whole swaths of NION signatories as "class enemies" when the revolution happens. That's not to say that NION is not controlled by some very shady figures, chief of which is C. Clark Kissinger (no relation to Henry Kissinger).

Kissinger is a longtime Maoist and member of the Revolutionary Communist Party (RCP). The RCP backed the Khmer Rouge's mass murders in Cambodia ("a legitimate revolutionary action") and cheered Mao's insanely murderous "Cultural Revolution." Its mission, from what I can gather, is to foment revolution in the United States. The RCP's new Marxist-Leninist-Maoist Programme is "a battle plan for destroying the old and creating the new. . . . As Mao said: 'Who are our enemies? Who are our friends? This is a question of the first importance for the revolution.'"

First on the list of "enemies" are Americans. Which explains why the RCP and its dupes in the NION have jumped onto the "antiwar" bandwagon. It's the height of irony that an outfit that applauds violent revolutionary upheaval in the name of Mao is suddenly a great believer in pacifism. Actually, it may be a toss-up for that distinction. It's also pretty ironic that all those well-meaning Hollywood liberals signing up for NION have no idea that for years gays were banned from the RCP. The Party's "chairman," a bearded wonder named Bob Avakian who lives in exile in (where else?) France, called homosexuality "a degenerate disease from rotting capitalism."

As for Kissinger, in 1987 he helped "initiate" Refuse & Resist!, another front for the RCP. These days, R&R! helps out at the peace rallies by undermining America in other ways. John Ashcroft is their favorite whipping boy, and R&R! agitates to highlight his "concentration camps" and subvert our anti-Muslim "wartime police state." It comes out in force to protest *any* measures aimed at keeping terrorists from entering America or detecting them once they're here. R&R! claims that "with an unjust, immoral and illegitimate war planned on a major Arab country, what the government has set out to do is terrorize a source of potential opposition." Illegal Muslim immigrants, terrorists, al Qaeda money launderers . . . that kind of thing.

The insidiousness of these groups is disturbing. These revolutionary "vanguards" are also in the recruiting business—and that means your sons and daughters. Take the otherwise silly Books Not Bombs campaign, when school and college kids took a stand "for peace" by not attending classes on March 5. Now, that's what I call sacrifice: skipping off school on a spring day to hang out with your friends "for peace." It certainly helped that dozens of "anti-war" college profs and teachers said they wouldn't punish marchers for playing truant.

Most of these "rallies" consisted of a couple of hundred kids standing around with handmade banners reading "Bush Is Dumb and So Is War" and "War Is Terror" as they listened to amplified hip-hop. (I strolled around one such gathering at Stanford in spring 2003.) Other times, the earnest book lovers went on miniature rampages, got drunk, or robbed convenience stores.

What happened at these baby-rallies was less interesting than who was running the show—namely, something called the National Youth and Student Peace Coalition (NYSPC). The *Washington Post* described it as including "15 student groups that joined forces after the Sept. 11, 2001, attacks." Sometimes I wonder whether reporters lack any sense of skepticism—or do they just type whatever's handed to them in the press release? The NYSPC is not some after-school get-together club. These are just some of the "student groups" involved in the NYSPC: the Black Radical Congress, the

Young Communist League, Students Transforming and Resisting Corporations, the Young Democratic Socialists, the Young People's Socialists League, and the Student Peace Action Network.

They may sound like a bunch of marginalized kooks, but groups like the IAC, ANSWER, the WWP, the NYSPC, and so forth gain immense power by controlling, organizing, and manipulating the "antiwar movement." By treating them as normal, respectable special interest groups, the elite media foolishly do propagandistic work for them. As a report on MSNBC noted of one protest, "a growing number of people are speaking out against a war with Iraq—students, grandparents, businessmen, politicians, teachers, actors, and activists, standing shoulder to shoulder in protest." Just normal, everyday folks, right? If you think so, go check out one of these protests for yourself. Read the "literature," the placards, listen to the speaker. (Torture, I realize.) There are very few "mainstream Americans" present.

Worse, even when the radical politics of the anti-American left are exposed, the elites refuse to purge them from their ranks by asserting that "they want the same thing." According to Stephen Zunes, an associate professor at the University of San Francisco and experienced "antiwar movement" watcher, the WWP's hijacking of the movement "causes division among the non-authoritarian left groups. They say, 'Do we march at a rally organized by a group like this? I don't feel comfortable with this, but it's the only game in town.'" Well, they shouldn't. Then there's Scott Lynch of Peace Action, who says, "Good for them for having the wherewithal to call the demonstrations. . . . This is ANSWER's dance, and they get to call the tune." But the only reason it's "ANSWER's dance" is because more moderate groups keep making excuses for ANSWER's bad behavior.

Imagine what would happen if it was reported that a mainstream Republican gathering was quietly orchestrated by the Ku Klux Klan and the American Nazi Party? There would be an uproar. Yet, when we have proof that the left-wing equivalents of the KKK and the Nazis are running the "antiwar movement," the media and the elites say nothing. As always, the elites give themselves a pass.

## WINNING THE BATTLE

The most important thing to remember about the "peace protestors" is that while they're vocal and powerful, there are many more of us than of them. (Their organizers always vastly exaggerate their strength. In San Francisco, aerial photos of one protest proved that rather than the 200,000 protesters the antiwarriors had claimed, the real number that showed up was 65,000.) Casting ballots in democratic elections is morally purer than attending a march choreographed by anti-American zealots. We support America; *they* do not.

We need to ask, Do they have no shame—not even an inkling that they're doing the devil's work? Is there no dictator's hand they won't shake? Why, if they value freedom, do they attack the American Republic, the staunchest defender of liberty that has ever existed? (Or maybe that answers the question: they don't value freedom—except maybe their own freedom to oppress others.) Tens of thousands of American soldiers in the last 230 years have put their lives on the line and died to protect our values and our lives. Our blood has been spilt and our treasure has been spent fighting for this Republic.

The elites don't respect that, because when it comes to America, they just don't get it. They don't understand that America is different, that we are *the* exceptional nation, the world's last best hope. We are not greedy, and we are not imperialist, and we are not evil. We are not infallible, but we mean well and do well. We are a lion, slow to anger but ferocious when attacked. We are the Good Guys.

We are not France. We are not China. This is not North Korea. We are a free people. We are a fiercely independent country. We will do whatever it takes to defend America and its citizens wherever they are in the world, and we will not take orders from anyone. We do not need France's "permission" to protect the lives of Americans.

American soldiers did not die because they were selfish but because they were selfless. They sacrificed their lives not to gain territory for an imperialistic country, but to protect the freedom of Americans and to bring freedom to millions of others around the world.

# 7

# Bordering on Insanity

▶ Open-Border Elites

America's immigrant work ethic is something I learned about at a very young age. My mother loved to regale my brothers and me with stories about her Polish immigrant parents' long hours in the thread mills of Willimantic, Connecticut, during the Depression. They were among America's working poor, but happy to be here, to have work that put food on the table. Their English wasn't perfect but they insisted their children's would be, so they could have a better life. My grandparents were proud of their Polish heritage, and my mother and her brother and sister carried on the Polish traditions—the cooking, the music, the holiday gatherings.

My mother was a waitress for almost thirty years and so worked with many recent immigrants. Like her, they were waitresses; others were dishwashers, busboys, and maids. One of the maids, a Polish woman I knew only as Mary, cleaned floors during the day, and was a seamstress at night. My mother befriended her, and occasionally gave her work. Mary would send any extra money she made to her daughter in Poland. I don't ever remember Mary in a bad mood. That was my early impression of America's immigrants—they were

**181**

law-abiding, hard-working, respectful people grateful for the opportunities America afforded them. Life was tough, no doubt about that, but not as tough as in the Old Country.

Indeed, almost all Americans celebrate this country's immigrant heritage, and remain remarkably willing to extend a welcoming hand to those immigrants who obey our country's laws. Unfortunately, the United States is currently being hit with a flood of illegal aliens. And on the issue of how to deal with illegal aliens, the gap between most Americans and our elites could hardly be greater.

Each year the Chicago Council of Foreign Relations conducts a wide-ranging and respected survey of what the "public" and "opinion leaders" think about a host of different issues. "Opinion leaders" are defined as including CEOs of the Fortune 1000 corporations; presidents of the largest labor unions; TV and radio news directors, network newscasters, newspaper editors and columnists; leaders of all religious faiths; presidents of large special interest groups and think tanks with an emphasis on foreign policy matters; university presidents and faculties; members of the U.S. House and Senate; and assistant secretaries and other senior staff in the Administration.

On the issue of immigration, the results proved what the rest of us had already suspected. The elites live in a completely different world than you and I.

The late 2002 poll found that 60 percent of the public believes that the current level of immigration is a "critical threat to the vital interests of the United States." Not a *serious* threat, or a *possible* threat—a *critical threat*. And what did our elites think? Only 14 percent of them felt it was critical. That's a 46 point gap. This gap was enormous even before September 11. In 1998, for example, the figures were respectively 55 percent and 18 percent. After September 11, even *fewer* of the elites saw immigration as a critical threat.

Regarding legal immigration, 55 percent of the public wants it to be reduced, and 27 percent said it should stay the same. For the elites, only 18 percent of them said immigration should be reduced, and 60 percent wanted no cuts. Even more bizarrely, while 70 percent of the public wants *illegal* immigration reduced, only 22 percent of elites agree. In other words, they don't care whether our immigration laws are enforced or not.

Given the attitudes of the elites—and the disproportionate influence they have in American life—it is hardly surprising that we constantly hear calls from politicians for blanket amnesty of "undocumented workers." The phrase "undocumented workers" was created by the immigration lobby to supplant the more accurate term—"illegal aliens." Clever, but despite what Bill Maher thinks, America is not that stupid. The media are willing partners of the pro-illegal alien lobby, when they showcase tearjerker stories about illegals who cross the border. They do it so they can send money home to their poverty-stricken native village and support their sick grandparents. Take this example from Kelly McEvers reporting for NPR from Jakarta: "Timbull Adrian Sahad left his cruise ship after ten months, and then worked in factories and restaurants in Philadelphia. Earlier this year, Sahad heard about the new program that required him to register with the INS. He immediately caught a plane back to Jakarta for fear of being jailed or deported. He reunited with his wife, who works in an Indonesian factory for about an eighth of what he made in the U.S. Sahad himself is having trouble finding work." Mr. Sahad: "We are not terrorists. We love to stay in the United States for work, for the money. American people don't like the job like in—you know, one hour, six dollar or seven dollars. Only us, illegal people, you know?"

If only the "mainstream media" spent as much time alerting the public to the other side of the issue—including the recent lawsuit filed by Mexico in a Texas court against citizen groups in the United States that took steps to protect their private land from trespassing by Mexican illegals. Imagine that, our citizens actually defending their property against intrusion and trashing! Our good friend Mexico strikes again.

Nobody doubts that the vast majority of illegals are hard-working and enterprising. But there are also hardworking and enterprising thieves among them (20 percent of all federal prisoners are illegal aliens). There are also people violating the securities laws so they can support their families. The law is the law, and these people are here *illegally*. They've jumped the line and pushed past other hardworking and enterprising people who are actually trying to respect our laws. And our elites want to reward these lawbreakers at the expense of honest immigrants—not to mention honest Americans.

## THE TERROR CONNECTION

Illegal aliens take advantage of the decency of Americans, gambling that we won't have the heart to deport them. But this decency makes it easy for would-be terrorists to take advantage of us. The Center for Immigration Studies in Washington, D.C., conducted a survey of the forty-eight foreign-born, radical Muslim terrorists who have been charged, convicted, or admitted involvement in terrorism between 1993 and 2001. The report makes frightening reading. It's astounding how easy it is to manipulate the U.S. immigration system.

Of the forty-eight, sixteen were on temporary visas (primarily tourists) at the time they committed their crimes, seventeen were Lawful Permanent Residents or naturalized U.S. citizens, twelve were illegal aliens, and three had pending applications for asylum. Most of the terrorists had broken immigration laws, either because they held jobs illegally, sneaked across the border, overstayed their visas, arrived as stowaways, used false passports, provided "inaccurate" information for their green cards, or contracted fraudulent marriages. Others had even been granted amnesty or were applying for "asylum."

Those who don't care about illegal immigration say that we shouldn't allow our concerns to be driven by the fact that a very small percentage of illegal aliens intend to hurt this country. But we learned on September 11 just how much damage a few illegal aliens can do. The record is clear that energetic enforcement of existing laws would have stopped the September 11 hijackers before they even got here. United States law plainly states that individuals who are young, unmarried, unemployed, or lack strong attachment to a residence overseas are to be denied temporary visas. Under this provision, Mohammad Atta and his accomplices should have been kept out of this country. But thanks to the type of lax enforcement of our immigration laws that results from elite indifference, they got their visas and the rest is history.

Here's another example of how stopping illegals at the border should be our number one priority. By official tally, 355,000 people issued *final deportation orders* over the years seem to have absconded. After September 11, the government decided to find at least some of them. Of those 2,256, an anemic 696 have been actually deported. That is ABSURD! Are we supposed to feel reassured, because, as Barry Newman reported in the *Wall Street Journal*, "the [government] is concentrating on younger men with criminal records from countries that breed terrorists....It may no longer be safe to tear up deportation orders as if they were parking tickets." Whew! I feel so much better.

One man, a thirty-six-year-old from Sudan, who had two drug offenses to his credit, said that when he was picked up for possession of marijuana a second time, he was subject to deportation, but "I ignored the order....I came to New York City [for his deportation hearing]. I didn't give them any address."

For some stupid bureaucratic reason it has been the practice for the government to release nearly half of all deportable aliens after their hearings. The reason? There was no room to house these people—only 20,000 beds are available throughout the U.S. for this purpose. These beds are filled with foreigners who have the right to an appeal to yet another bureaucratic trap, the Board of Immigration Appeals. Even then, 87 percent of those who've been ordered deported flee. Among aliens from terror-friendly countries, that figure is a staggering 84 percent. Under the new "get tough" approach, it will take until 2006 to enter the 355,000 names into the crime computer at the FBI.

Once illegals make their way into the U.S. it's extremely difficult, time-consuming, and expensive to send them home. That's why an aggressive border enforcement policy is so desperately needed.

There are encouraging signs that the administration is getting tough. For instance, 82,000 foreign Muslims came forward earlier this year to register with immigration authorities as required by Congress post–September 11. Of those 82,000, about 13,000 now face deportation because they were here illegally. Foes of tough border and immigration enforcement wail that only eleven of the foreigners had links to terrorism so why are we "punishing" and "stigmatizing"all the rest? First, it took fewer than two dozen men with terrorist ties to kill thousands of Americans and take down three of our nations prized buildings. Second, let's not forget that the 13,000 were here illegally.

"There has been a major shift in our priorities," Jim Chaparro, acting director for interior enforcement at the Homeland Security

# The Big Lie

Speaking in support of the 1965 Immigration Reform Act, a younger, trimmer Senator Ted Kennedy of Massachusetts confidently predicted, "our cities will not be flooded with a million immigrants annually." That wasn't the only thing he was hopelessly wrong on. Kennedy also assured Americans that "no immigrant visa will be issued to a person who is likely to become a public charge," and that mass immigration "will not cause American workers to lose their jobs." You're batting 0 for 3, Teddy. ∎

Department, told the *Chicago Sun-Times*. "If a loophole can be exploited by an immigrant, it can also be exploited by a terrorist." That makes perfect sense. But of course the usual suspects have waded in to complain about institutional racism in targeting Arab and Muslim illegals. "The identical violation committed by, say, a Mexican immigrant is not enforced in the same way," said Lucas Guttentag, director of the immigrants' rights project at the ACLU. Yes, that also is true. But the solution is not, as the ACLU implies, to *relax* enforcement for Muslims and Mexicans, but to treat Mexican illegals in exactly the same manner. If a Mexican is here illegally, he should be deported—just like a Muslim, a European, a Canadian, a Vietnamese, an Australian, or a Martian. It's good that the new government policy will mean an improvement, but given how lax things had become, that's not saying much.

## OPENING BORDERS, SHUTTING DOWN DEBATE

One other problem resulting from elite indifference to illegal immigration is that most Americans have no clue how serious a problem it is. It is not too much to say that media elites are effectively engaged in a cover-up to prevent the widespread anger that would undoubtedly result if the facts were widely known. In a country of roughly 280 million people, there are *10 million* illegal aliens registered by official data-keepers (and probably several million more). The U.S. Census Bureau estimates that each year there is a net increase in illegal immigrants of 500,000—enough to make a fair-sized city. At current rates of immigration, America's population will explode from today's 280 million to 450 million in fifty years time.

The influx is going to have a major impact on the rest of us. Someone has to pay for the impact of illegal immigration on American life. And I know who's going to be expected to shell out and shut up—us. Unremitting illegal immigration automatically means higher taxes, with higher spending on education, social services and health care, higher crime rates and urban crowding, a lowering of wages for American workers, increased unemployment among American workers, and a greater risk to national security. But just you try and explain these plain facts without being heckled by the media elite and its accomplices for being an intolerant, racist immigrant-basher. They'll even try to silence you.

Back in October 2000, ProjectUSA, a group that wants to restrict immigration to manageable levels, put up a billboard at the foot of New York's Brooklyn Bridge. It read: "Immigration is doubling U.S. population in our lifetimes." The U.S. Census Bureau was cited as the source. Not a big deal, right? It's a straight, unadorned *fact*. Can't complain about that, right?

Well, evidently you can. The New York and New Jersey Port Authority ordered the billboard removed—after exactly thirteen days of uproar by Manhattan's Great and Good. Apparently, the New York elites thought it counted as race-baiting and equated it to "Nazism." (Come on, guys, you need a new shtick!) But for once, there's a happy (ish) ending to the saga. In July 2001, ProjectUSA sued the Port Authority successfully on First Amendment grounds and received an out-of-court settlement. Strangely, those tireless defenders of free speech, the ACLU, were nowhere to be seen. Maybe all its legal eagles were too tied up vacationing in the Hamptons. In fact, ProjectUSA asked the ACLU for support three times but the group declined, saying there was "no case." But ProjectUSA reports that an ACLU staff attorney let slip the real reason, saying off the record that "a large and growing immigrants' rights faction within the organization" made it impossible to help.

## THE VAST LEFT-WING CONSPIRACY

Our nation's media elites, of course, agree wholeheartedly with the agenda of pro–illegal immigration groups, so they gladly swallow their lies whole and regurgitate them unquestioningly. What you don't know about these advocacy groups—and what their partners in the media won't tell you—will shock you.

The pro-immigrant lobby, not those Americans who want our laws and borders enforced, is the extremist bunch. The hidden connections that exist among pro–illegal immigrant groups are undeniable. Remember, what all these lobbying organizations have in common is their support of law-breaking. Remember, they are working toward a "borderless world." These elites claim they want to "strengthen" America by opening the floodgates. In truth, they want to weaken it by using the flood to sweep away border controls.

All this takes quite a lot of organization and the commingling of efforts. The same activists keep popping up in different "immigrant rights" groups. The Washington, D.C. executive director of the American Immigration Lawyers Association (AILA), a vocal group of over 8,000 attorneys and law professors, is Jeanne Butterfield. She was once the director of the Palestine Solidarity Committee, a Marxist group connected to the terrorist Popular Front for the Liberation of Palestine. She was also previously involved in the "Nov. 29 Coalition," a radical umbrella organization for eighty rabidly anti-Israeli groups.

Is it not illogical to believe that, given Butterfield's connections, the AILA might have a private agenda when it comes to immigration? Is it really a humanitarian organization dedicated to bettering America and looking out for our interests? Can we trust its opinions when it comes to the touchy subject of Muslim immigration? Do we really want more of Jeanne's radical Palestinian friends coming here?

And then there's the National Immigration Forum, which "advocates and builds public support for public policies that welcome immigrants and refugees and that are fair and supportive to newcomers in our country." Butterfield is on the board of directors. Lucas Guttentag is closely associated with the National Immigration Forum, as was Stephen Moore of the libertarian open-borders think-tank, the Cato Institute. The National Council of La Raza—

the histrionic Hispanic rights advocacy group—and the National Lawyers Guild are hooked up to the Forum as well.

The National Lawyers Guild (NLG)—a Communist front-group formed in 1936—is especially interesting. Back in the happy days of the Cold War, when we knew who the bad guys were, the NLG was working alongside those very same bad guys. Even today, the NLG sneakily declares that it is an "association dedicated to the need for basic change in the structure of our political and economic system." It should just come out and say it: We Want to Overthrow the United States of America.

In the 1980s, the NLG's "National Immigration Project" began examining "immigration issues." More recently, its website says, "Guild members were playing an active role in encouraging cross-border labor organizing and in exposing the abuses in the *maquiladoras* on the U.S.-Mexico Border." One of the Project's former members, Amy Novick, is now working as the American Immigration Lawyers Association deputy director in the Washington office under. . .Jeanne Butterfield![1]

- The incestuous relationships between pro–mass immigration elite groups are astounding. The most elitist of elite enterprises, the Ford Foundation, funds a huge number of them. Of course, some of them have other "legitimate" aims, but these only serve to obscure their pro–mass immigration bias. Robert Locke, an associate editor of *FrontPageMagazine.com* provided a partial list of some of the beneficiaries of Ford Foundation largesse in a 2002 article entitled "The Open-Borders Conspiracy." There are nearly sixty—repeat, sixty—of them.

## THE BORDER CULPRITS

You should be aware of the groups that work night and day to loosen our border controls and facilitate the lives of those who violate our immigration laws. Here is a partial list:

- The National Council of La Raza
- American Immigration Lawyers Association
- National Immigration Forum
- National Lawyers Guild
- National Coalition for Dignity and Amnesty for Undocumented Immigrants
- The Ford Foundation
- ACLU's Immigrants Rights Project

Put together, these groups and dozens of others like them are working to undermine America's resolve when it comes to illegal immigration. But illegal immigration is only one part of this crowd's larger agenda. Buried underneath all the emotional rhetoric is a core of dedicated anti-American propagandists. For instance, there's a pro–illegal immigration outfit calling itself the "National Coalition for Dignity and Amnesty for Undocumented Immigrants." It is comprised of no fewer than 300—repeat, 300—organizations based in twenty-five states all quietly working toward the same aim of legalizing illegal aliens and eroding border controls. Its members attend anti-capitalist and "antiwar" riots where they agitate for an unconditional amnesty for all 10 million or so "undocumented immigrants," giving work permits to anyone who wants to come here, plus an end to INS raids, border patrols and deportations. They have two broad aims:

- Blame America for all the world's problems. They scream that the reason why immigrants flock here in the first place is because Americans exploit and despoil their home countries. As always, we're the bad guys.
- Force America to lose its distinctiveness. These guys hate America so much they want to annihilate our cultures and traditions by making us take tens of millions of "refugees" from around the world against our will.

Take a look at the list of Ford Foundation recipients and remember what the pro–illegal immigration campaign is *really* about the next time you hear some bitter old Clintonista complaining about the "vast right-wing conspiracy." The right-wing conspiracy is nothing compared to the Elite Anti-Democratic Left-Wing Conspiracy. The elites always stick together to stick it to you.

## MUGGING AMERICA

The actual costs of illegal immigration and high legal immigration are staggering, maybe as high as $22 billion a year—or even higher. Nevertheless, the elites will tell you with a straight face that illegal aliens actually *save* us money because they pay taxes but don't take welfare. This is deliberately misleading. Yes, illegals have their wages garnished (if they're "on the books," unlikely as that is), but the amount is tiny. Unskilled illegal aliens aren't even in the minimum tax bracket. And yes, they don't claim much welfare, but this is because they're generally barred from doing so. In any case, every American worker who loses his job because of illegals undercutting his hourly wages *can* collect welfare. So, somewhere along the line, taxpayers pick up the tab.

But where the costs really stack up is that illegals rely heavily on government social services for education, criminal justice, and emergency medical care. On top of that, Americans have to pay for all the border chaos illegal immigration creates. These costs are substantial. Each year, California alone blows $3 *billion* taxpayer dollars subsidizing its immigrant habit.

But that's not all. If the elites have their way, these costs will be going up. Consider the following examples of elite efforts to circumvent our immigration laws by making life easier for illegals once they're here:

**CONSULAR IDENTIFICATION CARDS.** Through its U.S. consulate offices, Mexico has handed out hundreds of thousands of "consular ID cards" to illegals living in the U.S. to help them blend into society, and many of the elites in the U.S. are delighted. These cards have been accepted nationwide by hundreds of municipal governments as identification for obtaining government services, by many police departments when detaining someone, and by banks and other businesses in order to lure immigrant customers. Our very own Treasury Department proposed regulations allowing these cards to be used at federally guaranteed banking institutions! (The Homeland Security Department, thankfully, disagreed.) The U.S. House of Representatives voted to enact more stringent standards for these cards—including that the Mexican government must verify that the recipients are *legal* U.S. citizens. But that begs the question: why would legal U.S. citizens or Green Card holders need these cards? (They can get a driver's license and/or use their Green Card as legal identification.) The cards should be prohibited altogether—they pose a security risk and have one purpose and one purpose only—to make it easier for immigration lawbreakers to live here.

**THE "DREAM ACT."** This monstrosity should actually be called Orrin Hatch's Nightmare Act. The usually conservative Republican senator from Utah proposed that illegal aliens should be allowed to pay subsidized in-state fees for higher education at state universities. Say what? In California, the state—i.e., California's long-suffering, taxpaying legal residents—would be required to shell out $11,000 a year for every illegal under twenty-one who wants to go to college to major in Gender Politics and Binge Drinking.

But only an idiot, or an elitist, could not see that the Dream Act will break an already tottering system. For every illegal who gets into these highly competitive state universities, there's a *legal* teenager playing by the rules who gets rejected. There are only a finite number of places. Why can't illegal aliens who want a college education take courses in their native countries? More to the point, why is Hatch rewarding lawbreakers at the expense of law-abiding Americans and legal immigrants?

Proponents of the schemes claim that by acquiring a college education, illegals will be able to break out of their low-paying jobs and start paying taxes as higher earning professionals so that they'll eventually repay the costs of their tuition. It's a brilliant idea, flawed only in one important respect: Current labor laws prohibit hiring illegal residents, so a college education will bring no tangible benefits to once low-skilled illegals. The elites' reaction is to push for "reform" of current labor laws to allow companies to hire illegal residents. And so the elites continue making a mockery of our immigration laws for their own benefit.

Thankfully, there are some legislators who retain a sense of reality. In Virginia, they strongly considered making illegals pay out-of-state charges, even if they live there. Lawmakers in both chambers overwhelmingly approved the measure. "Particularly in this time of budgetary uncertainty, it is unwise to provide taxpayer subsidies of an average of over $6,000 per year per student to those who have not followed our laws," said Republican state attorney general Jerry Kilgore.

Then again, even in Virginia, there's always some mush-headed elite making excuses for those who break the law. "If you require these kids to pay out-of-state tuition, even though they live here, they will not go," said Democrat state senator Leslie Byrne. But Leslie, that's the whole point. They're not *supposed* to be living here in the first place. That didn't stop Democrat governor Mark Warner from vetoing the legislation requiring illegals to pay out-of-state tuition. Nevertheless, Kilgore struck back, pointing out that Warner's veto was irrelevant because state and federal law prohibits illegal aliens establishing legal residency or the intent to create a permanent domicile. That automatically makes them ineligible for in-state tuition. As Gina Munoz, a nineteen-year-old attending California State University, Sacramento, says, "I don't think they should be able to [qualify for financial aid].... They're not legal citizens. Though they work hard and get good grades, they're still not here legally." Nicely put, Gina.

**DRIVE-TIME.** Now in Democrat-heavy Maryland it's a different story. Both chambers of the state legislature have already approved in-state tuition for illegals at public universities. So now they're moving on to providing driver's licenses for immigrants without proof of residency or a Social Security number. Worse still, driver's licenses are often accepted as identification for everything from boarding a plane to opening a bank account to "getting past security." Keep in mind that all this is happening *after* September 11. Before that date, seven of the nineteen hijackers exploited lax state regulations to obtain Virginia driver's licenses and official documents fraudulently. Virginians have closed the loopholes (a coalition of twenty-nine immigrants' rights groups warned that the move could lead to "human and civil rights violations against ethnic minorities"—always with the hyperbole!) but Maryland apparently intends to ensure that illegals can always obtain whatever document they need. It's simply another example of the elites putting anyone but Americans first.

**HOSPITALS IN NEED OF CARE.** The Federal Emergency Medical Treatment and Active Labor Act directs that hospitals with emergency-room facilities must treat anyone who turns up, but does not state who is liable for the cost of treatment. As a result, rural hospitals in Texas, Arizona, New Mexico, and California are being crippled by huge demand for their services by illegals. There are even reports that Mexican ambulance companies are sneaking across the border with uninsured patients and dumping them at American emergency rooms. "Hospitals in Mexico are pointing the ambulances north when they discover a patient can't pay for services and has no insurance. They know they can get treatment in this country," said one federal law enforcement official.

No fewer than seventy-seven hospitals in the Southwest have been designated as facing "a medical emergency" because their budgets can't cover the uncompensated expenses. The Southeast Arizona Medical Center in Douglas is heading toward bankruptcy, while the Copper Queen Hospital in Bisbee, Arizona, has a net operating income of just $300,000 but has been whacked with $200,000 in costs due to illegal alien patients. In San Diego, Scripps Memorial Hospital shut its doors after losing $5 million a year giving unreimbursed medical care to illegals. American hospitals cover *$1.45 billion* in costs each year treating people who have injured themselves (heatstroke, broken ankles, and dehydration) illegally crossing the border. You and I pay the bill with higher costs for hospital care. Nobody wants to see another human being with a near-fatal injury heartlessly turned away at a hospital. But once again, pro-immigration fanatics are taking advantage of our charity. In Washington State, "depression" and "high blood pressure" have been classified as medical emergencies. Guess who antes up the cash for any illegal feeling a little blue or stressed out? In Ohio, they've even introduced bilingual cards informing their holders that free healthcare is available at their nearest hospital. The cards helpfully add that hospitals are prohibited from asking about the bearer's immigration status.

Every single dollar of that money comes out of American taxpayers' pockets at a time when our own health costs are rising. And why are they rising? According to Steven Camarota of the Center for Immigration Studies, "immigrants and their children account for nearly two-thirds of the increase in the population lacking health insurance over the last decade. By dramatically increasing the uninsured population, immigration creates significant costs for taxpayers, and it drives up costs for insured Americans as providers pass along the costs of treating the uninsured to paying customers." So now you know.

**GET INTO JAIL FREE.** While most illegals may exist honestly and work hard when here, there is a significant number of foreign criminals who take advantage of the 1,940-mile border to smuggle drugs. Simply stated, open borders are an open invitation to criminals. About 80 percent of the cocaine and half the heroin consumed in the United States is hauled across the Mexican border. Moreover, American law enforcement agencies have to spend money on processing and prosecuting illegals who commit crimes while living here. In the twenty-four border counties alone, this sum has been estimated at $125 million a year. That's a lot of money, but not as much as the $500 million it costs us to *keep* these thugs in jail. In California, one in seven inmates is an illegal alien. Nationwide, one in five federal prisoners is an illegal alien. Think about that for a second. One. In. Five. It's costing us a lot of money to keep them inside.

**EDUCASHUN.** Federal law prohibits denying any child free public education. Yes, even if they are here illegally in the first place. As always, we pay through the nose so President Vicente Fox of Mexico can keep his education budget under control. Right now, 15 percent of all K-12 children in California are illegal aliens, costing Granola State taxpayers a cool $1.6 billion a year to build additional schools and hire extra teachers. About the same percentage of schoolchildren in New Mexico, Arizona, and Texas are illegal aliens.

## I'VE GOT A COUNTRY I'D LIKE TO SELL YOU

The political elites know perfectly well that our immigration laws are not being enforced, and that we can expect millions of additional illegal aliens over the next few years. But they're not going to do much about it. They have too much invested in turning a blind eye to the problems caused by unrestricted immigration. Besides, no politician wants to be tarnished with the accusation of racism or "xenophobia." It's always easier to go with the flow.

The leaderships of both parties are equally at fault. Democratic and Republican elites are obsessed by what they think is a massive pool of Latino votes just waiting to be grabbed. They believe that whichever party succeeds in becoming the favored party of immigrants will win every election for the foreseeable future. Imagine, ten million fresh votes ready for the picking—with more coming all the time. Furthermore, the vast majority of these votes live in key battleground states like California, New Jersey, Texas, Florida, New Mexico, Pennsylvania, and New York.

You can see why the politicians are drooling to pick them up. Pollsters predict that a few million Hispanic votes could change the national political landscape. If the Hispanic vote tilted to the GOP, California could come home for the Republicans and places like Berkeley would be left high-and-dry as isolated elite strongholds in a sea of conservatism. On the other hand, the Democrats could use this vote to make whole areas of the country off-limits for Republicans, boxing them into the South and a shrinking part of the West for a political eternity.

There's just one small problem with this dream. Those millions and millions of votes don't exist. They belong to people who aren't eligible to vote.

Political elites are terrified of offending the Hispanic vote so they have refused to disavow amnesty programs for illegal aliens (at least publicly). Even after September 11, they're calling for *more* immigration, not less. They're cutting deals to ensure the law doesn't get enforced. They're playing the usual legislative tricks to score points with ethnic activists. Teddy Kennedy, for example, cunningly managed to insert a provision into the Senate's appropriations bill that would have shut down funding for the National Security Entry-Exit Registration System. (NSEERS has caught some 350 known foreign criminals and terrorists from entering the country.) Kennedy's provision was excised only at the last minute.

They're doing all this in the face of massive public opposition.

Before September 11, President Bush was so eager to appease Mexico's President Vicente Fox and Hispanic voters in the U.S. that he proposed granting amnesty to about 3 million illegals meeting certain minimum requirements. He even planned to ask Congress to get rid of the laws banning employers from hiring illegal aliens. "The truth of the matter is that if somebody is willing to do jobs others in America aren't willing to do, we ought to welcome that person to the country, and we ought to make that a legal part of our economy," Bush said at a ceremony honoring his Mexican counterpart. "We ought not to penalize an employer who is trying to get a job done, who hires somebody who is willing to do that kind of work."

After September 11, the Bush administration put amnesty on the back burner. Plus, there was the little matter of the polls—that showed Americans were solidly against amnesty of any kind. One poll showed that 56 percent of Americans thought the 3 Million Man policy was a "bad or very bad idea." Most of us understood that there are millions of people from around the world who fill in all the forms and wait for years in their home countries for the INS to process them—all in order to immigrate here *legally*. Handing out amnesties to border-jumpers undercuts their efforts and punishes them for being honest, patient, and law-abiding.

But it didn't take long for President Bush and his politically savvy strategist Karl Rove to swing back toward the elites on this issue of illegal immigration. They are positively giddy at the prospect of all those potential new votes, as evidenced by Rove's description of their "Hispanic outreach strategy." "[The President's popularity is] the result of careful work through a lacework of communications strategies, policy initiatives, high-level appointments and foreign visits." Let's translate all those catchphrases into one word: AMNESTY. What the White House is doing to shore up immigrant votes is a kind of Sneak Amnesty. Okay, so aiming for 3 million in one shot was a little ambitious. Instead, smaller, quieter efforts are being undertaken to weaken immigration and border controls. In fiscal 2001 alone, *215,000* illegal aliens were granted legal status and another 970,000 cases were pending. We're being hoodwinked, folks.

The new U.S. Ambassador to Mexico, Tony Garza, gave the game away when he told Mexico's *Reforma* and *El Universal* newspapers that Bush wanted to legalize up to *15 percent* of all aliens who have been here longer than a decade. That would amount to hundreds of thousands of border-jumpers rewarded for rigging the system. "What I would like to see is us have a debate to establish some criteria to legalize these people who have been part of our community," Mr. Garza told *Reforma*. "I believe we should recognize them, giving them some sort of status."

In 2002, the Bush administratoin tried slipping what amounted to an amnesty clause into the Enhanced Border Security and Visa Entry Reform Act (which authorized tracking immigrants suspected to be terrorists). That provision—colorlessly known as "245(i)" of the immigration code—allowed legal and illegal aliens who have employer or family sponsors in this country to remain here while they applied for residency. Previously, such applicants had to do so in their home countries. On the face of it, 245(i) didn't look like a big deal. After all, only about 200,000 people were covered by it. But its effects would have been far-reaching. Every person who has obtained residency status or citizenship can import his entire extended family. The Bush administration tried to wrap 245(i) into a "family values" gift box, but that didn't fly.

None other than West Virginia Senator Robert Byrd put a hold on reinstating 245(i) (once in a blue moon, the old fellow actually does the right thing), noting that many of the illegals receiving amnesty would not have undergone background or security checks. Message to elites: the people don't want partial, full, mini-, or semi-amnesty. They certainly don't want our immigration laws to be relaxed without a debate.

The Democrats are all over immigration. They won't hear a word said against it. The Democrat leadership seems to have decided that illegal immigrants are the only way they're going to be winning elections anytime soon. Not a single Democrat presidential candidate or congressional leader wants to enforce the law. If anything, they *celebrate* the act of illegality. Democrat Congressman Barney Frank of Massachusetts, for instance, moved a bill through the House Judiciary Committee to make it easier for immigrants convicted of felonies to remain here.

Dick Gephardt told a meeting of the National Council of La Raza that he supported a bill to allow illegal aliens who have evaded capture by authorities for five years to qualify for permanent residency status. He claimed that "our proposal will bring undocumented immigrants out of the shadows and into the light of accountability and greater cooperation in our fight against terrorism." He never explained why granting residency to illegal agricultural workers from El Salvador would bring "greater cooperation" in the fight against Islamist terrorism. But Hispanic activists love what they hear from Gephardt. He "is putting down a marker that we are getting back to the legalization debate in a serious way," said Cecilia Munoz, a vice president of La Raza.

Gephardt was not about to be outdone by the former Senate Majority Leader Tom Daschle, who also wanted to extend an amnesty and actually make *more* illegal aliens eligible for residency. (At one point, the Democrats even proposed that any immigrant who had worked here for ninety days in a year-and-a-half time period could get his amnesty stamped, no questions asked.) Daschle claims that most of those who would benefit already have children born here. "In my view, it ensures we send as clear a message as possible: Democrats support family reunification," he said. It's good that Tom Daschle has suddenly discovered how important it is that families stay "united." He's a regular Dan Quayle when it comes to the families of illegals.

And where would we be without Nancy Pelosi? In 1990, she voted against an amendment that would have kept caps on most categories of immigration. Since then, the number of immigrants has skyrocketed. She also voted to extend an amnesty to certain illegal aliens from El Salvador, Guatemala, Honduras, and Haiti. It gets worse—she then voted against allowing members of the armed forces from helping the border control in their duties. More recently, she even voted in favor of preventing local and state police from enforcing certain immigration laws. Thanks a bunch, Nancy. Nice to see you sticking up for Americans. Or maybe that should be, "sticking it to."

If Dem-elites had their way, amnesty would be like abortion—legal and easy to obtain.

## "ILLEGAL IMMIGRATION IS AN ECONOMIC PLUS"

This is where businesses start whining, "But we can't find Americans to do the manual labor and service jobs that are available!" "What about the free market!" Nice try, but "market forces" are why Americans avoid certain low-paying jobs in what is still a high-tax environment. But what caused wages to fall and taxes to rise in the first place? That's right, a flood of unskilled illegal aliens undercutting wage-levels and making huge demands on hospitals,

**Dave C. of Utah wrote me:**

*"My wife and I, from Canada, are in the final stages of processing our permanent residency applications. Ever since arriving in the States six years ago we have followed U.S. immigration laws to the 'T' and spent thousands of dollars on having green card applications processed. It is disconcerting to see politicians giving big breaks to people who emigrate here illegally. These 'breaks' send the wrong message to people who want to come to America—it reinforces illegal immigration. Hey, maybe I should have jumped off a boat near the Florida coast and applied for graduate school in Texas instead of following immigration laws."* ■

schools, and other expensive social services. As one of my listeners pointed out, "in the hospitality industry...employers brazenly hire illegals at substandard wages, telling us to accept similar pay or not work at all. They and others then hide their shameful practices behind the insulting cliché, 'Immigrants take jobs that no one else wants.' We in fact want such jobs, but we need to earn enough to feed our families. Worse, illegal aliens compete for what little affordable housing there is."

Because the majority of illegal aliens crossing the border are single males, many of whom share living expenses with other illegal aliens, their costs of living are tiny compared to what an American worker needs to earn to take care of his family. They don't need to put away money in a Roth IRA or save up for a down payment or sock away cash for the children's' college fund. Just about everything they make is sent back home to their village, where even a day's wage goes a very long way. So they can afford to work for much lower wages than their legal counterparts. These painful facts of life are obvious to any regular American, but somehow the elites can't see the big picture.

Instead, they rely on the cliché that illegal aliens contribute more to the economy than they suck out of it; so, all in all, we're better off with a large (the larger the better) population of illegals. In fact, that's not true at all. Even the liberal *Los Angeles Times*—the paper of record in a town that runs on illegal labor—was forced to confess this fact, all the while trying desperately to explain it away in typical elite style. In 1997 the National Research Council was asked by Congress to investigate the question of how much illegal aliens cost (or benefited) the economy. According to the *Los Angeles Times*: "*the council found that overall, legal and illegal immigrants indeed receive more in publicly funded services than they pay in taxes* (italics added)." Here comes the "but" (remember the elite agenda): "But that's no more true for immigrants than for low-paid Americans; low wages are expensive to society as a whole. And a straight services-for-taxes calculation doesn't tell the entire story. Whole industries—such as hospitality, textiles and agriculture—'would not exist on the same scale without immigrant workers,' the academy found. Immigrants add as much as $10 billion to the U.S. economy, the study found, mostly due to their willingness to do the kind of hard, dirty, dangerous, and low-paid work Americans don't want."

Let's bear two points in mind here. First, let us remember what liberals always forget: we are talking about immigration that is *illegal*. Drug dealers, prostitutes, and loan sharks all contribute a lot to the U.S. economy, but we still prosecute them because we don't want their money. Or is money more important than the rule of law? If people want to openly advocate changing the laws to have open borders so that we can all have freshly pressed hotel sheets, fine. Let them try—although no one thinks they would succeed. But don't simply break the law and then try to defend lawbreaking on economic grounds.

Second, we can't know what would happen to the hospitality, textile, and other industries if our laws were enforced. One thing we do know is that the people working in those industries would be paid a higher wage and would have more legal protections. It is absurd to say that Americans won't do jobs that are "hard, dirty, and dangerous." Aren't there American coal miners, and American factory workers, and American cowboys, and American firemen? Aren't all these jobs hard, dirty, and dangerous? Don't we have millions of Americans who have no job at all? Don't we have millions of Americans trying to survive on less than $20,000 a year? Don't you think some of these people might be willing to take these jobs—especially if they paid a living wage? I don't know how many Americans want these jobs, but I do know that a lot of these employers don't want to hire Americans. They want people they can exploit. That's why illegal immigration is illegal. And that's why these laws should be enforced.

This is pretty obvious. But maybe the elites simply don't want to see the obvious. It's not in their interest. After all, you're not going to see too many illegal aliens practicing law (thanks to the bar exam) or medicine (thanks to licensing boards) or owning large businesses (thanks to the maze of regulations surrounding business ownership). In other words, the elites are protected from competition with illegal immigrants. *Their* wages won't be going down. *Their* jobs won't be at risk. So it's not surprising that they don't get too choked up about this issue.

## DON'T CRY FOR ME, AMERICA

Whereas previous generations of immigrants—illegal or not—were encouraged to adapt to American life and to accept our traditions and values, modern elites are teaching exactly the opposite lesson to our current crop of immigrants.

Instead, it is clear that American society is expected to adapt itself to the immigrants. Has anyone noticed that ATMs have started asking whether we want to "proceed" in English or Spanish? Or that specialty ethnic media no longer broadcast and print in English? Or that police departments, hospitals, courts, schools, and government agencies now prefer hiring multilingual employees owing to the number of illegal and non-English speaking immigrants in the community?

Now by this point, I can hear the immigrant special-interest groups moaning and whining. What about the Statue of Liberty? What about being a "nation of immigrants?" But the issue isn't immigration; the issue is whether our laws are going to be enforced. After all, every country is a nation of immigrants if you think about it. Even if America has been more welcoming than most, we must always maintain a careful balance between welcoming new immigrants and protecting the interests of Americans who are already here. That balance is found in the laws that Congress has passed and the president has signed. These laws should be enforced, not undermined by a tiny minority that doesn't like them. And as for Lady Liberty, she celebrates just that—Liberty. *Not* Open Borders.

But even those immigrants who are here legally are not being encouraged to devote themselves fully to this country. For most of American history, immigrants were expected to hunker down and blend in as part of a larger American family. They were taught to revere the Founding Fathers and to celebrate Thanksgiving. But today's elites have no intention of providing such teaching. Thanks to "multiculturalism" propaganda, immigrants don't even learn the basics of American history. (No, the little quiz given to those seeking citizenship doesn't count.) Turn-of-the-century immigrants were taught in English and steeped in shared American traditions by public schools. Any learning about native culture and language was done at home.

Because we were such a disparate—and to this day, thankfully, a multiracial—nation, English helped bind us together. According to Marian Smith, historian for the Immigration and Naturalization Service, in the 1920s "there were lots of English courses...adult 'Americanization programs' offering English and citizenship instruction. Churches, local schools and communities pushed English instruction. Companies like Ford Motor Company provided English classes. It was considered good business, and all this was very popular. Congress later expanded the effort by creating what was called the National Citizenship Education Program."

Today, "Americanization programs" and English-language requirements are regarded as "white cultural oppression" by our multicultural elites. In turn, the radicals who run groups claiming to represent immigrants play up "ethnic separatism" as a virtue. Learning English would accelerate immigrants' assimilation into American society, and that's the last thing they want. It's gotten to the point where even official naturalization procedures are being conducted bilingually. At Arizona District Judge Alfredo Marquez's direction, seventy-five Mexican immigrants were recently sworn in as citizens in a ceremony held largely in Spanish. And of course there's more. A growing number of counties and districts are being forced to introduce bilingual ballots for voters. In the 2002 election, the federal government ordered 300 municipalities to offer a foreign-language option.

For example, Berks County in Pennsylvania recently fell afoul of the Unrestricted Immigration brigade when officials didn't hire Spanish-speaking poll workers or print ballots in Spanish. In court, the county claimed that bilingualism would harm efforts to assimilate the large number of Hispanics who have come to the area, but the Bush Justice Department cracked the whip, completely disregarding the concerns of local officials.

**Elite**speak **alert!**

The elites trot out a myriad of lame justifications for pushing for more open borders, among them: "We need to raise the quotas on legal immigration." ∎

Not surprisingly, the Department of Justice found a compliant judge. Federal District Judge Michael Baylson, who ruled against Berks County, wrote: "Even if the voter, illiterate in English, may be able to distinguish one candidate's last name from another, the voter illiterate in English may not understand the office for which the various candidates are running, and surely cannot understand the various propositions, ranging from bond authorizations to constitutional amendments."

But this reasoning ignores the most critical point of all: these naturalized citizens who "have been unable to exercise their right to vote," are apparently unable to read a simple ballot form in English. In the words of the judge, they are actually "illiterate in English." What we need to ask is, first, how did they get naturalized? And secondly, why have they not learned the most basic English? If someone emigrates to America, is sincerely devoted to his adopted country, and wants to participate in the most sacred right of being an American, the least he could do is be able to "distinguish one candidate's last name from another." What happened in Berks County—and what is happening throughout this country—is that instead of putting the onus of citizenship on immigrants, the elites are heaving the burden of adaptation onto *our* shoulders. Americans are supposed to adapt to the language and culture of immigrants, immigrants don't have to adapt to the language and culture of America. Why? Some elites (on the left) don't much like America so why force new immigrants to learn our traditions? And other elites (amnesty-loving Republicans) don't want to push too hard for fear of offending a potential Hispanic voting bloc.

The great Theodore Roosevelt addressed the issue of "Americanization" in the first years of the twentieth century. It was a time when the debate was raging over the "melting pot" and what it meant to be an American. "There is no room in this country for hyphenated Americanism," he boomed in a 1915 speech. "The only absolute way of bringing this nation to ruin, of preventing all possibility of its continuing to be a nation at all, would be to permit it to become a tangle of squabbling nationalities."

Try voicing the same concerns as T. R. did all those years ago today, and the elites are likely to brand you a bigot. Since the 1960s, when the immigration laws were relaxed, the elites have focused on downplaying the *citizenship* aspect of immigration. Elites on the far left don't like the idea of a united and patriotic America—after all, it might do things like overthrow Saddam Hussein or stand up for itself at the United Nations. So they prefer to balkanize it into a "tangle of squabbling nationalities." Just as T. R. predicted. To the elites, pledging allegiance to America is obsolete. They want to destroy borders between countries to create a globalized world in which "transnational citizens" drift back and forth whenever they feel like it. They *do* want it to cut both ways.

The best way of achieving this objective is to loosen our domestic controls on the numbers of immigrants, legal and illegal, coming to and living in America.

- "Undocumented workers shouldn't be prosecuted or deported."

- "Mexico is our friend. We don't need to patrol the border so heavily."
- "The undocumented workers already here should have an amnesty."
- "All workers, even so-called 'illegal' ones, have a right to medical care, education, and other social services at taxpayer expense."
- "Bilingual education helps the children of immigrants come to terms with life in this country."
- "Since they work here and live here, immigrant workers should have the right to vote."
- "And don't forget, of course, the canard that anyone who's 'anti-immigrant' is a 'racist.'"

We must resist the elites every step of the way—and refuse to be intimidated by their name-calling. We're not racist, and we're not "anti-immigrant." We *are* in favor of regulating illegal immigration, enforcing the laws of this country, and protecting the rights of those who are here legally. There is nothing "racist" about that. We cannot fall prey to the twisted blandishments promoted by elitist anti-American organizations.

## RISKY BUSINESS

If there's one lobby that is even more craven and cynical than the political elites when it comes to immigration, it's got to be Corporate America. Something called the "Essential Worker Immigration Coalition," which describes itself as a "broad-based coalition of national businesses and trade associations from across the industry spectrum," lobbies the parties to redress the "shortage of both semi-skilled and unskilled ('essential worker') labor." In other words, let 'em all in. The only "essential" thing about EWIC is that it thinks it's essential to price Americans out of jobs through amnesty and guest worker programs.

Long gone are those days when Chambers of Commerce hammered home to their members the patriotic need to Americanize their employees. Believe it or not, there was even a time when Henry Ford set up a school for immigrants that taught them on the first day how to say in English, "I am a good American." Nowadays, for that kind of "racism" he'd be hauled in front of a court by some lawyer in hock to the immigration lobby.

The elites tell all sorts of lies to explain why immigrants are not being turned into Americans. One of these lies is that "imposing" American values and culture on immigrants "oppresses" them. According to this view, the children of immigrants suffer from "self-esteem problems" and become "stressed" when they are not taught in their native languages. So, of course, they need bilingual education in schools.

But there's no evidence that this is true. Every kid gets stressed and worries about what other people think of him. Why should immigrant children be any different? If anything, keeping them linguistically quarantined from the rest of the school stresses them out more than normal. Teaching in Spanish (or any other foreign language) doesn't even help the kids' grades. "The accumulated research of the past thirty years reveals almost no justification for teaching children in their native languages to help them learn either English or other subjects," concluded linguistic expert Rosalie Pedalino Porter.

The only "justification" for bilingual education is that the elites want to keep immigrants firmly in their place. Being locked into a foreign language by "caring" teachers' unions is like being locked in prison. Without knowing English, immigrants and their families don't have a hope of completing school, let alone college, or improving their standard of living. The facts prove that our current policies with respect to the "education" of immigrants simply aren't working. Adult Mexican aliens are *seven times* more likely to be high school dropouts than are native-born Americans. They're permanently mired in poverty and semi-literacy. The only jobs awaiting them out of school are unskilled ones paying the lowest of low wages—and/or welfare. Even after living here for more than two decades, half of Mexican immigrant families live at or near the poverty line. A third are uninsured. And they are twice as likely to rely on welfare than are American-born citizens.

That's the bad news. The good news is that you always have someone cheap and handy around to look after the kids, clean the pool, and mow the lawn. At last, the elites can re-create what they've seen on PBS's *Masterpiece Theater*! The gilded world of nineteenth-century Europe, where the rich could lord it over dozens of maids, butlers, and footmen. The only difference between then and now is that the servants were better paid than the coolies exploited nowadays by the elites.

Which means that if you're part of the business elite, you've got a huge labor force that will work for peanuts and never complain. The editorial board of the *Wall Street Journal* just can't get enough of that cheap labor, which is why it supported a constitutional amendment requiring open borders. The *Journal's* pals at the Cato Institute, and the Club for Growth, a free-market lobbying group, think the same, and supported the idea with adulatory "reports" proving that America's economic health depended on mass immigration. September 11 temporarily silenced these corporate cheerleaders. Stephen Moore, a senior fellow at Cato and president of the Club for Growth, recommended that they "lay low and don't talk about it a lot."[2] Nevertheless, the Immigrant Hustle continues. Only recently, executives at Tyson Foods—the country's largest meat processor— were indicted for allegedly arranging with a "smuggler" (actually an undercover border patrol agent) to import illegals with falsified documents to work on their poultry production lines. "I'm going to need to replace 300 or 400 people—maybe 500. I'm going to need a lot," said one of the co-conspirators on the phone to the agent. According to prosecutors, at one point there were more illegal workers at Tyson plants in Shelbyville, Tennessee, and Wilkesboro, North Carolina, than legitimate ones.

The business elites have a vested interest in promoting amnesty and other scams designed to cover up how illegal immigration benefits them. Even if they were given proper visas or naturalized, low-skill laborers from Mexico and South America would still drag down the wages of the most vulnerable American workers, including American blacks. I am reminded of the words of Frederick Douglass, who in the mid-nineteenth century, commented that "every hour sees the black man elbowed out of employment by some newly arrived emigrant, whose hunger and whose color are thought to give him a better title to the place."

In every way, illegal or unrestricted mass immigration hurts Americans, erodes American values and benefits the elites.

But some regular Americans aren't taking it anymore. One group that calls itself the American Border Patrol is planning its own "shock and awe" public awareness campaign that includes getting a live video stream on the Internet of immigrants crossing illegally into the U.S. Another small assembly of landowners have signed up to patrol the border on their own, as part of the "Citizens Border Patrol Militia." Arizona native Chris Simcox, who started the group, was all over cable television, proclaiming that he wants to "embarrass the government into doing its job" at the border.

These efforts have, predictably, triggered a backlash among immigrant "rights" groups such as the Tucson-based Border Alliance Network that gathered nearly 2,000 signatures petitioning for a state investigation of citizen border patrols in southern Arizona. And Southern cowboys taking the law into their own hands are easy targets for the media elite. The April 1, 2003, issue of *The Progressive* stereotypically described citizen patrols as "gun toting cadres" who are comfortable with "racist rhetoric." Xenophobes in Stetsons! And let's not forget our pal to the south, Mexico's President Vicente Fox, who's always willing to help us keep the border secure. In May, his government filed a lawsuit in federal district court in Texas against two citizen patrol groups—Ranch

Rescue and Border Rescue—for their treatment of Mexicans cross-ing the border illegally.

But one doesn't have to endorse all aspects of these homegrown illegal immigration efforts to understand the enormous task before us. The new Homeland Security Department now oversees all bor-der enforcement, but there is little reason to think that the current, hodgepodge approach will be improved. David Stoddard, a twenty-seven year veteran of the U.S. Border Patrol, believes the only way to really stop the illegal tide is with the military's help. He envi-sions a scenario with 100 helicopters outfitted with infrared scopes, and a large number of surveillance stations across the bor-der from Texas to California.

There are some major problems with this idea. The Posse Comitatus Act, as well as Naval regulations, prohibit using the mil-itary to "execute the laws" unless authorized by Congress or the Constitution itself.[3] Things have gotten so out of control with the influx of illegals, some are calling it an "invasion" that only the military is equipped to thwart. Hard to see that this would fly in Congress, unless, heaven forbid, we were to suffer a terrorist attack from someone who crossed either our northern or southern bor-ders illegally.

So, what can we do? First, we need energetic enforcement of existing immigration laws. That means prosecuting businesses that employ illegals and deporting as many illegals as necessary to deter other would-be lawbreakers. No more accepting as legal identifica-tion "consular identification" cards handed out to any illegal off the street at Mexican consulates nationwide. Additionally, we need to clarify all our immigration law. Currently the courts favor illegals' "rights" to education and medical attention while government authorities simultaneously warn illegals they're subject to deporta-tion. Which is it? The feds need to decide whether America is still going to be a soft touch or if we're going to get tough on illegal immigration.

# 8

# Busting the Greed Creed

o you remember *Wall Street*, the Oliver Stone movie that attacked the excesses of 1980s-style capitalism? There is a great scene in which Michael Douglas (playing the slimy über-capitalist Gordon Gekko) is defending his plan to take over an old-fashioned corporation against charges that he is only pursuing his own selfish interests at the expense of the company as a whole. Explaining his vision to the shareholders, Gekko argues that he is not ashamed of his motives because, as he explains, "Greed, for lack of a better word, is good. Greed is right. Greed works. Greed clarifies, cuts through and captures the essence of the evolutionary spirit."

Now, there can be little doubt that Hollywood leftie Oliver Stone intended Gekko to be the villain of his piece, but like so many of Hollywood's ideas, it didn't exactly work out that way. In Gekko—and particularly that speech about greed—Stone had perfectly captured the changing attitudes of a country that was turning businessmen into stars. As the boom of the 1980s morphed into the go-go years of the 1990s, more and more Americans came to agree with Gekko that greed, in fact, was good. And because of

**215**

this belief the business elites have become immensely powerful in American life.

But wait a minute, I hear my conservative friends saying. Businessmen can't really be compared with the mostly liberal elites we've been discussing throughout this book. They've worked hard to build their businesses. They employ their fellow Americans. They've helped to make this the richest country in the world. Who are you Laura, to attack businessmen, some type of crazy Naderite? What would you do, have us squash the free market?

For all of you are having these thoughts, take a deep breath, and remember the thesis of this book. America is supposed to a country with government of the people, by the people, and for the people. But that will not happen if we allow an elite few to dictate to the rest of us. We don't need to worry about those who make their way on merit and who are respectful of the traditions and beliefs that have made this country great. But the trouble with the elites is that they ignore or repudiate their obligations to our country, its traditions, its independence, and its history. Too many businessmen need to be reminded that the dollar is not the symbol of America. The flag—representing our one nation under God—is.

And let's not forget, as we saw during the Clinton years, greedy businessmen and corporations love a corrupt president like Bill Clinton, who was only too eager to waive all sorts of rules— including the lifting of restrictions on selling sensitive military technology to Communist China—for Corporate Friends of Bill. Corporate America is not a straight Republican ticket. Many of Clinton's generation went from college and grad school draft deferments to work in the same corporations that they had vilified at teach-ins and protests just a few years earlier. For these Dem-elites, self-interest always trumps principle. The elites sing in one key—"Me, Me, Me." God and country they can do without. "Me" they can't.

Hillary "Cattle Futures Queen" Clinton, who laid down the new line in White House etiquette—"If it's not nailed to the floor, it's mine"—should be example enough to remind us that greed and liberalism go together like oppression and Communism. But by the same token, conservatives need to remember that lust is not the only deadly sin; tradition tells us that there are six others, including avarice and gluttony. After all, Jesus Himself taught, "it is easier for a camel to go through the eye of a needle, than for a rich man to enter into the kingdom of God" (Matthew 19:24). And Paul warned Timothy that "the love of money is the root of all evil" (1 Timothy 6:10). Certainly liberals have utterly failed to draw reasonable distinctions between a free market and greed. They prefer to regulate things in favor of their friends. Conservatives prefer economic freedom, while always recognizing the moral obligations that all of us owe to one another, and to our country. When we violate those obligations in the pursuit of money, we have crossed the line into greed. And as the events of the last few years have taught us, greed is not good. In fact, it is usually very, very bad.

## THE WRECKAGE OF WALL STREET

In the 1980s, there were corrupt traders, bond salesmen, and corporate raiders. But today figures like Ivan Boesky and Michael Milken seem like small potatoes compared to today's corporate crooks. The great bull market turned out to be full-of-bull market when we felt the full brunt of the deception and fraud perpetrated by the business elites of the tech-bubble era.

The crooks of the 1990s were con men and snake-oil merchants who left behind nothing but economic chaos and bankrupted investors. Don't be fooled by the kinder gentler environmentalism and wishy-washy politics espoused by many of these well-heeled cheats—these guys out-Rockefellered Rockefeller when it came to scalping and predatory behavior. In hindsight, the stock market bubble they helped to create—with the help of some clever accounting devices—was perhaps the largest scam in the history of American business.

The Business Elite—from the ponytailed liberals to the check-your-morality-and-patriotism-at-the-door-libertarians—betrayed our fiduciary trust. And the problems of the late 1990s can't just be attributed to a few bad apples like WorldCom, Enron, and Global Crossing. Many established and respectable companies also admitted cooking the books. In 1995, for example, only fifty companies had to "restate their financials" (meaning that the original figures were seriously incorrect). In 2001, this figure jumped to 270, then leapt again to 330 in 2002. That's an orchard of bad apples.

## WHEN BAD PEOPLE DO BAD THINGS

Unfortunately, too many people in Washington don't want to acknowledge the seriousness of the problem. In February 2002, former Bush Treasury Secretary Paul O'Neill said that "while we may need to do some repair work, I don't believe that our system is broken. We have the lowest capital costs of any place in the world because we've demonstrated that investors' money is safer here." He's right, of course, but only up to a very important point. America is the best place to invest—largely because of a culture that rewards success and punishes failure—but his tone-deaf acclamation of low—sorry, *lowest*—capital costs at a time of widespread disillusionment and outrage sent exactly the wrong message at a time when many investors were feeling duped by the wiseguys on Wall Street.

The scandals of the late 1990s are a perfect example of why greed is bad, why it doesn't "clarify," as Gordon Gekko claimed, but instead clouds the judgment. In every one of the major corporate scandals that have been uncovered, corporate insiders put their own selfish interest ahead of that of the clients and shareholders they were supposed to be concerned for. On November 8, 2001—the very day that Enron acknowledged it had overstated profits by nearly $600 million over the preceding five years—ten out of fifteen analysts were rating the stock a "buy" or in some cases, a "strong buy." The deception perpetrated by the Enron insiders in this case was complete and thorough enough to avoid detection from even industry research specialists for years. In turn, it was these specialists in whom the general public then placed their trust. The words of Saul Cohen (of New York law firm Proskauer Rose) ring true: "There has never been anything at the level of these scandals and it is symptomatic of cultural issues. The people who were managers in the 1950s, '60s, and '70s came out of the era of depression. They weren't selfless, but they weren't greedy either."

It's true that there is a sucker born every minute, and certainly many regular investors themselves deserve some blame. Too many of us were greedy for instant profits and didn't bother to do basic background research before buying into dot-coms launched by twenty-two-year-old whiz kids promising to revolutionize the way we bought shoelaces online. But, there are also countless examples of Wall Street analysts who touted companies to the public with "strong buy" recommendations—all the while being fully cognizant that these stocks were worthless or at best wildly speculative. And we believed them. Suckers.

Between 1995 and March 2002, Morgan Stanley used four ratings to evaluate stocks: "strong buy," "outperform," "neutral," and "underperform." As a Securities and Exchange Commission investigation revealed, however, four senior analysts maintained an "outperform" rating on at least thirteen stocks even as they precipitously declined during 2000 and 2001. For example:

- Morgan Stanley kept its "outperform" rating on drugstore.com for thirty months while the price fell by 95.4 percent.
- Priceline.com fell by 92 percent during the thirty months it was rated "outperform."
- Akamai plunged by 82.8 percent as an "outperform" stock in *ten* months.

The question here should be, What did Morgan Stanley—or for that matter, other guilty firms like Goldman Sachs, Salomon Smith Barney, Credit Suisse First Boston, and Merrill Lynch—think these companies would be "outperforming"? The Iraqi air force? The box office of Madonna's *Swept Away*? Al Sharpton's poll numbers? Put it this way: if you had stapled a newspaper listing of New York Stock Exchange companies to a wall, used a monkey to throw thirteen darts at it, and bought whichever companies the darts randomly hit, you would probably have done better than if you had listened to the overpaid clowns at Morgan Stanley.

How about this example from disgraced Tyco CEO and corporate looter Dennis Kozlowski? In a 1999 *BusinessWeek* interview, Kozlowski claimed, "I own more stock today that I've ever owned. Ninety percent of my assets are in Tyco, and I've been adding to my position." But as the Manhattan DA recently discovered, Kozlowski was secretly selling stock worth $280 million. He wasn't the only one. Kenneth Lay at Enron got rid of $100 million worth of Enron shares over three years while insisting in public that he wasn't. Gary Winnick, chairman of bankrupt telco Global Crossing, miraculously managed to sell $735 million in company stock when the market was at its height. No doubt it was all a coincidence that the chairman succeeded in timing his exit so adeptly.

Unfortunately, poor recommendations were just the tip of the iceberg. The SEC, market regulators, and state prosecutors exposed many more tricks of the trade, so to speak, used by the country's largest investment companies. The Street was rife with corruption, insider dealing, and conflicts of interest, as thousands of pages of internal e-mails used as evidence amply demonstrated. Companies hoping to get their stock listed as a "buy" would secretly pay off analysts for positive "research." Brokerage analysts lied to investors about a company's prospects so the investment banking side of their bank could profit when they took these investors on as corporate clients. And once they were clients, investment houses gave the companies' senior executives special early-bird access to IPOs that the public was encouraged to buy! buy! buy! even as the executives locked in huge profits by dumping the stock. They even had a name for the latter practice—"spinning."

Nice. Everyone was a winner—except you and me.

In fact, the interests of you and me meant nothing to many people on Wall Street. Investigators found that an analyst at Lehman Brothers told a large institutional investor that while "ratings and price targets are fairly meaningless" and the " 'little guy' who isn't smart about the nuances may get misled, such is the nature of my business." A Bear Stearns analyst bragged that he had attended a conference by SonicWALL (ever heard of it?), whose stock Bear Stearns had sold to investors. During the conference, he asked complimentary questions to fool people into believing that SonicWALL was a *really great* company with a *terrific future*. Said he, "we got paid for this...and I am going to Cancun tomorrow because of them." Even as Bear Stearns maintained its "buy" rating, SonicWALL stock collapsed from $66 to $3.75 between 1999 and April 2002.

Over at Salomon Smith Barney, the star telecom analyst Jack Grubman gave himself a "C" in stock picking for a disastrous 2001. ("C" is the lowest grade that the company allowed in self-evaluations.) "We missed some opportunities to downgrade certain of our stocks during the year," he wrote. He's referring, undoubtedly, to the companies that went bankrupt that he had been hyping all along. As far back as 2000, however, Jack's colleagues had their misgivings about his abilities. It was well known within Salomon circles that Grubman—who was paid $14.2 million that year in salary and bonus—was a terrible stock picker; it was an open secret that he pumped companies whose stock prices kept plummeting. In e-mails between themselves quoted in the *New York Times,* Salomon brokers sniggered about Grubman's woeful performance. One said that Jack "should be publicly flogged," adding that "under the category, Bonus for Creating Tax Loss Carry Forwards for Retail Clients, Grubman should be recognized accordingly as our best analyst." Ha, ha, ha. Unfortunately, the joke was on the investors. Grubman kept his job until August 2001 and no one seems to have spared a thought for the poor saps who kept sinking money into his picks.

## ELITES COVERING FOR ELITES

What was the result of the SEC's investigation into these problems? A $1.4 billion settlement with ten firms and two analysts (including Grubman) in which the accused neither admitted nor denied the allegations. But is Wall Street getting the message and changing its ways? No. At a Manhattan financial conference on April 29, 2003, Morgan Stanley CEO Philip Purcell was asked about the $1.4 billion settlement and crowed, "I don't see anything in the settlement that will concern the retail investor about Morgan Stanley. Not one thing." The bravado got worse: "So far, so good this year. We have maintained our standards in market share as well as our reputation, in my view." Hear that, small guys? Nothing here to concern you.

Pressed to comment on Purcell's comments by reporters, SEC chairman William Donaldson huffed that they showed a "troubling lack of contrition." Yet Purcell's reaction in a way seems perfectly calibrated. No one went to jail. Yeah, so some embarrassing e-mails surfaced. Yeah, so Morgan had to pay $125 million. Big whoop. For Purcell and other top dogs, it's all just a rounding figure, a cost of doing business. They'll make it back when the dust settles. At the end of the day, though it sounds like a big sum to you and me, $1.4 billion amounts to just 7 *percent* of Wall Street's 2002 profits, which was its worst year since 1995. It later emerged that four out of the ten firms were planning to file insurance claims for a portion of the fine owing. So in other words, the bad guys are getting someone else (as usual) to foot part of the bill. Even Jack Grubman only had to shell out $15 million for his sins. Of course he was also banned from the profession, but don't worry about him—he still has about $15 million left to scrape by on.

In comparison to this wrist slapping, the general public lost $8.6 trillion dollars in market capitalization of the DotCom Index and $5.25 trillion in the NDX between March 2000 and September 2002. Combined, these losses equal $13.85 trillion, which is 130 percent of the GDP that the entire country produced in all of 2002. The fine levied was less than one-hundredth of one percent of this number.

Even many pro-business congressmen and senators don't believe enough has been done. "I am not convinced that the global settlement has done enough to change attitudes at the top of these banks," remarked Senate Banking Committee chairman Richard Shelby, a Republican from Alabama, during a hearing on the global settlement. "Without holding executives and CEOs personally accountable for the wrongdoing that occurred under their watch, I do not believe that Wall Street will change its ways or that investor confidence will be restored."

In Senate testimony, the SEC chairman insisted that nothing in the settlement precluded future criminal charges, and that wronged shareholders still have recourse in the courts. Yes, the ten that were targeted will be defending against class-action lawsuits from individual investors for years to come. The $387.5 million in restitution to shareholders (part of the global settlement) is pocket change to investors whose life savings tanked. Let's face it, if any of the top executives at the ten banks had gone to jail, the investors' suits would have been guaranteed to pay out huge windfalls. Instead of admissions of culpability, lawyers for investors are relying on damning e-mails and other documents produced in discovery and as part of the settlement.

Sadly, we have grown accustomed to corporate defendants buying their way out of admitting any wrongdoing, which is what happened here. Several of the top executives issued nonadmission admissions once the settlement was announced. Elite tycoon Sanford I. Weill, chairman of Citigroup, casually stated that "certain of our activities did not reflect the way we believe business should be done." You don't say, Sandy.

Like most conservatives, I think the impulse to regulate must be kept in check. All manner of havoc is created when the regulators run wild with ill-considered legislation. You can't legislate honest behavior. But in this case Wall Street just doesn't seem capable of getting it unless there are real laws with real penalties in place. Though they don't carry guns, white-collar criminals are *criminals who financially mug people*—and they should be treated as such by not being allowed to buy themselves out of trouble. New York State attorney general Eliot Spitzer—*Time*'s "Crusader of the Year" and the subject of an adoring *60 Minutes* profile in May 2003—had a golden opportunity to really teach Wall Street a lesson during his investigation of its crooked practices. But he botched it. No one admitted wrongdoing, let along went to jail. Spitzer did say that from now on "they are being watched" (oooh, scary) and high-mindedly intoned that "rules are meaningless unless there is dedication to complying with them." Now, I'm a conservative, and I don't think I'm naïve, certainly not naïve enough to believe that introducing a raft of new regulations into a corrupt culture will miraculously turn Wall Street crooks into saints. The ever-present danger with the regulatory option is that someone inherently antibusiness such as Ralph Nader, will be in charge and use his powers to prevent the Street from carrying out its legitimate, wealth-creating business for years to come. The key is to steer a course between heavy-handedness and do-nothingism. Clearly, Spitzer's shadow campaign for governor and fear of alienating too many of the business elites unfortunately guided him decisively toward doing nothing.

In other words, we first need to try to persuade Wall Street *to police itself* and punish the thieves in its midst—the threat being that if it does not, then we (or maybe Ralph Nader) will be forced to do the policing for it and then things will start getting really tough. As for the government, for the moment, the most valuable thing it can do is strictly enforce *existing* laws, not pile on new laws that won't be enforced.

The business elites have already made a mockery of the American traditions of hard work, thrift, and honesty. They cheated to get what they wanted and took advantage of people's good natures and lack of detailed financial knowledge. They acted like typical elites in looking out for themselves and screwing the rest of us. And in the end, they were just given a light slap on the wrist as punishment. Naughty boys! The public trust was looted and all they had to do was pull out their fat wallets, slide some cash across the counter, and be done with it. And they're still getting paid the big bucks. In April, shareholders of the Goldman Sachs Group approved a plan to allow twenty-nine executives to pick up annual bonuses of up to 1 percent of operating income. Doesn't sound like a lot until you take into account that the shareholders capped these bonuses at a mere $35 million annually. The bank stated that it wanted "to perpetuate the sense of partnership and teamwork that exists among our senior professionals." Hmmm, nice work—if you can get it.

But while they're blowing their millions on the French Riviera, corporate bigwigs might want to keep in mind the early results of a poll commissioned by *Investor's Business Daily* in May. It shows that public trust in business has collapsed. Of 715 respondents, just 8 percent said they had "high" or "very high" confidence in the honesty and integrity of these CEOs and CFOs. Just 11 percent said the same of brokerage firms. And 12 percent for Wall Street analysts. Half of all respondents said they had "low" confidence in CEOs and CFOs.

Spitzer and Co. can talk as much as they like about "watching" Wall Street while handing out the financial equivalent of parking tickets, and liberals can agitate for wide-ranging legislation to regulate ethics, but the base problem is that the business elites have betrayed Americans. "Corporate leaders are going to have to convince that they really are operating their organizations with integrity," said Michael Hoffman, director of Bentley College's Center for Business Ethics (and no, that shouldn't be an oxymoron). "Those organizations that can develop an ethical advantage are going to have a competitive advantage, particularly in this environment where there is such a crisis of confidence and trust."

The business elites should be put on notice, or they'll be going to jail and not collecting $200 million. One place where we can start is pushing business schools, the places where budding members of the Business Elite start their careers, to take teaching business ethics more seriously. According to a January 2003 article in *BusinessWeek*, Wharton alone expels about five MBA candidates each year for such tactics as cheating in exams and lying on application forms. Young Leaders of Tomorrow, no doubt. At the moment, ethics is treated as a marginal subject in courses, but it should be up there with marketing, finance, and strategy at the top of the curriculum. Employers should be encouraged to place as much value on a student's scores for ethics as they do on his abilities. True, these policies won't solve the problem root-and-branch, but they can at least weed out a few "ethically challenged" future scions of the business elites.

## IT IS OUR BUSINESS

As for the rest of us, even as these guys were raking in hundreds of millions of dollars, we were being asked to work longer hours at a time when our job security was eroding fast and our salaries were nowhere near keeping pace with executive "compensation." Since 1970, the average annual salary has risen from $32,522 to $35,864 (in 1999, expressed in constant 1998 dollars)—an increase of only 10 percent. At the same time, corporations have become less averse to laying off larger numbers of employees, who do not receive anything like the prizes handed out to unsuccessful or sacked senior executives.

When it comes to working long hours, Americans are the world leaders. In the 1990s, we added nearly a full week (or 36 hours) to our work year, which now lasts on average 49.5 weeks. We now work even harder than the famously workaholic Japanese by 137 extra hours per year.

This is not entirely bad news. One reason we work so hard is our hard work ethic, and it doesn't hurt either that we're highly productive. Long hours can be a signal of economic success and higher income, not necessarily that we're wage slaves being worked to death.

But while I understand the importance of hard work and long hours to the American economy, I'm worried about the noneconomic effects on our families. Mothers with young children are returning to work far more quickly (and working longer hours) than they did even a decade ago in order to make up for lost income. Families where the mother and father both work are more prone to divorce than ones where mom takes care of the kids and the house while dad brings home the paycheck. And if both parents are out at work, what do their children do? They are underexposed to their parents but overexposed to the reams of pornography and violence churned out by media companies looking to make a quick buck.

Just as CEOs have an obligation to their shareholders not to pick their pockets, companies have a responsibility not always to put their profits before doing the right thing. That is not to say that corporations should act as do-gooding charities or be subjected to ill-conceived legislation to "make" them do good. The corporation's primary goal must be to maximize its earnings in a free, open and competitive market. Without profits, obviously, there would be no employees or products and services for consumers. But still, there are times when the acquisitive instinct needs to be tamed. This is for two basic reasons.

First, the business community would be shooting itself in the foot if it continued to propagate a heartless, cynical image—even if it translates into higher profits in the short term. Just as the robber baron tactics of the late nineteenth century eventually provoked a public backlash, our modern scandals could lead to a similar result. Even Republicans, traditionally more favorable to business, realize that they cannot defend corporations engaged in corrupt dealings. If we have too many Enrons, business will find itself strangled by reactionary regulation and corporate taxes to "promote a more just economy" (i.e., higher taxes, more regulation). This time around, how can we be sure it would be temporary?

A July 2002 *Washington Post*–ABC News poll found that 42 percent of 1,024 respondents said they trusted Democrats to make "sure that large business corporations properly account for their financial situation," while only 36 percent said they trusted Bush. About 37 percent thought the Dems could make corporations more "honest" with the public compared with 34 percent for the Republicans. This poll was taken at the height of the Enron debacle, so the figures may be skewed slightly. But still, if you're a CEO, it should make pretty frightening reading.

Secondly, American corporations—even if they span the world with networks of subsidiaries and factories—owe their first loyalty to America. Corporations, like individuals, are citizens. They have rights, but they also have duties. One of the duties, for corporations, is paying taxes in the United States and not setting up your headquarters offshore to avoid your rightful financial obligations. Enron, for example, set up 700 "partnerships" based in the Cayman Islands for the purposes of tax "avoidance." And Stanley Works moved headquarters to Bermuda for similar reasons. According to some estimates, some $800 billion originating from America is stashed away among the 400 banks and 47,000 registered or licensed partnerships in the Cayman Islands alone.

While such moves may seem clever in the short run, they will cripple American support for business over time. Essentially, if a company doesn't have any loyalty to the country, why should we have any loyalty to it?

## BUSINESS AND OUR ENEMIES

Another corporate duty is not putting profits before national security and not dealing with enemies of the United States. The dubious satellite technology sales to China by Loral during the Clinton years is a case in point, as is the suspiciously high number of American companies pressuring Congress to liberalize trade with Cuba and end the embargo. In 2001, for example, American firms shipped $2.3 million in goods to the island nation, but between January and September 2002, that figure rocketed to $109.4 million. Trading with the enemy is good for profits, I guess. "Once you give companies a taste, they're going to want more," said John Kavulich, president of the U.S.-Cuba Trade and Economic Council, Inc. You bet they are.

The usual excuse trotted out is that ending the embargo would force Castro to open up his closed society. Well, maybe. Proponents of the Internet a couple of years ago said the same thing about bringing the Web to Cuba: once Cubans discovered the outside world they would agitate for internal change. It didn't happen. What did happen is that in 2002, Castro banned the sale of computers and computer accessories to the public. A Cuban who wishes to get online these days must spend a week's wages buying a state-determined e-mail address and then join a government-supervised computer club (obviously run by the secret police). Unfortunately, in order to ensure that no one can surf the Net and learn the truth about Castro's government, the Cuban network of computers is "unplugged" from the Web so the censors can read your e-mail and control which sites you visit.

Given Castro's behavior—and what we have seen from his years of dealing with Canadian and European businesses—it is absurd to believe that trading with Cuba would open that country's political process. What would happen is that some corporations would make a killing by shipping goods to Castro's cronies, but few Cubans would reap the benefits. America's free market depends on our free political system to nurture and protect it: corporations, no matter how tempting the potential profits, should not do business with a government that denies free elections.

Companies do not exist in a vacuum. Like responsible, civic-minded individuals, they have a duty, if not a legal obligation, not to promote society-harming ideas like teen sex, illegal crossing of borders, and violence. They should have, to put it briefly, an attitude of noblesse oblige to their home communities.

Businessmen and women who put their entrepreneurial talents to work, spend long hours building a company from scratch, and get rich are the epitome of the American dream. Likewise, individuals who join an established company, work their way to the top, and get paid a lot of money should be praised, not condemned. Wall Street brokers and analysts who honestly evaluate companies' prospects and direct their clients to buy or sell stock are doing admirable work. They may get it wrong, and their clients may lose money, but that is the nature of the market. Sometimes it goes up and sometimes it goes down. Experienced investors calculate the risks and act accordingly on the principle that greater risk entails greater reward. When it works properly, capitalism spins wealth out of benign self-interest.

But sometimes capitalism itself needs to be restrained. The members of the business elite believe the free market is where American life begins and ends. Conservatives champion the free market champions and usually we are right to do so. But not when what is called the "free market" results in a market force so overwhelming that meaningful competition is thwarted. As the ever-incisive William Safire recently noted, "The concentration of power—political, corporate, media, cultural—should be anathema to conservatives."

## THE MEDIA CONSOLIDATION SCAM

And to that end, not all regulation is bad. There is nothing "unconservative" about believing the government has a responsibility to protect the public interest. Would we really want to live in a country where the federal government did not write regulations covering the dumping of toxic materials into our rivers and streams? Or where the FDA merely allowed any drugmaker's product onto the market regardless of its efficacy? There are some libertarians and business elites who would say yes—let the market decide! But the fact is we need some government regulation for the public good: for safety, for honesty, and even to enforce truly free competition.

One area where the public can be served much better is in the media. You know, the *public* airwaves, which are supposed to be administered "in the *public* interest." Fact: The elites who run media corporations are *always* going to push the envelope when there is money to be made. Although the bottom-line approach is often good for the shareholders and for the wallets of top corporate executives, it is not always in the "public's interest."

In June, the Federal Communications Commission (FCC) approved a proposal to allow wider cross-ownership of newspapers and television stations. In other words, the nation's biggest media corporations got a big wet sloppy kiss courtesy of the commission and the broadcast lobby. This means media ownership is now poised to become increasingly concentrated in fewer hands. The *New York Times*, an immensely wealthy outlet, can buy up television stations and use them to broadcast the *Times* perspective on the news, showcase its reporters (the ones who don't fabricate stories), and highlight its left-leaning editorial slant. Smart fellows like Rupert Murdoch and Viacom's Mel Karmazin are set to assume an even more prominent role in deciding what we see, read, and hear, and when we see, read, or hear it.

Once again the American public has been done a great disservice in the name of the free market. It is no surprise that the Republicans on the FCC (led by Michael Powell, Colin's son), whose instinct is to deregulate first, ask questions later, were responsible. Powell is a perfectly nice fellow with a public interest blind spot. The commission's Democrats, listening to us rather than the National Association of Broadcasters, voted against ending the ban in most cities on cross-ownership of newspapers and television stations. "Ninety-nine percent of the individual comments coming in here from concerned citizens have said, 'Please don't relax the rules further,'" Michael Copps, an anticonsolidation commissioner, told the *Washington Post*.

Unfortunately, the situation looks very similar to what happened when the FCC relaxed its rules on radio station ownership. Remember when you could travel from city to city and you could find a great radio station that would actually play the seven-minute version of "Stairway to Heaven"? Now, with rare exceptions, it doesn't matter where you are in the United States, all the choices are the same—one station is Top 40, one is country, one is oldies, one hip hop. How did this happen? Again, the FCC's impulse to deregulate smothered its common sense—and once again the "public interest" was given short shrift. So today just three companies own half of the stations nationwide. Radio giant Clear Channel owns 1,200 stations! The main point: There is nothing "conservative" about this type of market concentration. As conservatives, we should support the greatest number of individual, localized media owners as reasonably possible. Opening the market to more voices makes it that much harder for elites to control the airwaves.

The elites' counter-argument is invariably that no regulation of consolidation of ownership is necessary, because the market has provided new, exciting media alternatives—cable television, the Internet, even satellite radio. But that argument only works if the audience consists entirely of literate, sophisticated people. The truth is, we all know that most Americans are not up all night scouring the London-based *Daily Telegraph's* website for a more balanced approach to foreign affairs. Most still get their news from major newspapers, television, and traditional radio. And we need more choice and competition in these markets, not less.

## THE BUSINESS BOTTOM LINE

America was built on capitalistic risk-taking. Nearly 10 percent of all Americans have started their own business at some time. That's an amazing number and a testament to the best that is American. In recent decades, the influence of business over our lives and careers has grown. Fewer people nowadays work for the government, which is all to the good, and at some point in our lives, nearly everyone works for a company, large or small. The corporation is here to stay, though it has changed its spots over time. Previously, people often stayed with their employer until retirement, whereas today employees change jobs with dizzying frequency. Corporations these days evolve far more rapidly than they used to as they merge, split, spin off, sell, acquire or shut down units of the whole. We are living in an age where loyalty to the firm is in fast decline (and the same goes for the loyalty of the firm to us). But at the same time, there are infinitely more opportunities open to us. In America, we are free to move from one region to another in search of greater opportunity for ourselves and our families. There is nothing new about this. Americans have always been a people on the move. When Americans found the East Coast too claustrophobic, they hitched their wagons and sought to improve their lives in the West.

Americans work to support their families, and we can afford all those vans, DVD systems, gas grills, and enormous houses because we work hard. What happened in the 1990s is that a small clique of business elites turned moneymaking into an obscene obsession. When the tech boom imploded, the markets fell, and unemployment rose, we were the ones left holding the bag by these greedy, selfish elites.

We need to recreate an ethos of public trust in business. This requires that the business elites must be subjected to the same rigorous enforcement of the laws as the rest of us. And ideally, business will understand that it needs to reform itself to better reflect America's—and its own—traditional values.

# 9

# The Ivory Tower Goes Red

▶ The Education Elites

Call me controversial, but there's nothing wrong with liberals teaching our kids. Liberals can make great educators—as long as they keep their politics out of the classrooms and lecture halls. The problem is, they don't. Since the 1960s, they've turned our colleges and schools—many of which are funded by our tax money—into an elite-run fiefdom of political correctness and anti-Americanism.

Earlier in this book, I emphasized that to qualify as an elite, one does not necessarily have to be a liberal or leftist. There are Republican senators and congressmen who are members of the elite, just as there are elite conservatives who believe in unlimited immigration, and business elites who care less about our country than about their personal bank accounts. But the elite Edu-Mafia is liberal/leftist to the core. The Ivory Tower *is* Red in tooth and claw. Do you remember when an obscure anthropology professor at Columbia named Nick De Genova said this to an "antiwar" "teach-in"?

- "Peace is not patriotic. Peace is subversive, because peace anticipates a very different world than the one in which we live—a world where the U.S. would have no place."

- "The only true heroes are those who find ways that help defeat the U.S. military. I personally would like to see a million Mogadishus." (He refers, of course, to the humanitarian mission to Somalia in 1993 in which eighteen American soldiers were killed—events depicted in the movie *Black Hawk Down*.)
- "If we really [believe] that this war [with Iraq] is criminal... then we have to believe in the victory of the Iraqi people and the defeat of the U.S. war machine."

For advocating the killing of American servicemen in combat, De Genova received loud and enthusiastic applause from the assembled crowd of three thousand students and faculty members. Students in his graduate seminar later staged a "silent, motionless protest" in support of his statements.

De Genova remains utterly unrepentant about his repulsive remarks. In fact, he defiantly amplified them in a March 27 letter to the Columbia *Daily Spectator* after the uproar following his remarks broke out. For De Genova, "imperialism and white supremacy" are what American foreign policy has always been about. "Vietnam was a stunning defeat for U.S. imperialism; as such, it was also a victory for the cause of human self-determination." And Columbia University president Lee Bollinger affirmed that lunatic America-haters are welcome at Columbia. "He has the right to say what he wants to," Bollinger said. "I won't fire him." De Genova, whom nobody before that time—at least outside of the bizarro world of higher education—had ever heard of, had in fact (like many of his academic colleagues) a history of leftist activism. Terrence Moore, now the principal of Ridgeview Classical Schools in Fort Collins, Colorado, recalled:

As a first-year student taking the Core course "Soc" (Social Sciences) [at the University of Chicago], I sparred over the economic theories of Smith and Marx with another student, a very thin young man who always wore a pea-green trench coat. To his credit, this young man knew Marx cold.... One day after class, this student politely and very insistently invited to take me back to my dorm in his car. . . . Few students on campus had cars, and he seemed very proud of his . . . because it allowed him to go to his "party meetings" on the South Side. . . . After hearing this business about party meetings several times, I finally took the bait. "What party?" I asked. "The Communist Party." "So are you a neo-Marxist, then?" I ventured further. "No, an orthodox Marxist." . . . The young man who gave me that ride was Nick De Genova. He was well known on campus, seemingly harmless, and most of us thought he was a flaky ideologue. For years I have figured that he had shed his pea-green jacket for a business suit and taken a job in a Chicago bank or on Wall Street, as did the hippies of the sixties.[1]

It's a pity he didn't. Now he's teaching your kids "anthropology."

David Horowitz, a former radical 1960s leftist turned conservative commentator, said that De Genova's phrase, "a million Mogadishus," reminded him of the time in 1967 when Che Guevara issued a call for his fellow revolutionaries "to create . . . two, three, many Vietnams" to defeat the Americans. Horowitz himself, in his radical days, edited "a book of anti-American essays with the same title, *Two, Three, Many Vietnams*." I wonder whether we'd find it on De Genova's bookshelf?

De Genova represents a blast from the past, amply demonstrating that the conservative wave of the last few decades has passed over our universities without leaving a trace. Only in academia is Marxism still a hot commodity. Just try getting hired at a Chicago bank or the local hardware store while wearing a pea-green trench coat and droning on about Marx.

## ANTI-AMERICANISM 101

It's well known that in the 1960s, leftists conquered the Academy. They're still in charge. The faculties of virtually all colleges are overwhelmingly leftist/liberal Democrat, as survey after survey bears out.

- John McGinnis (of Northwestern University) and Matthew Schwartz (Columbia) reviewed all federal campaign contributions over $200 by professors at the country's top twenty-two law schools from 1994 to 2000. Of professors who contributed, only 16 percent donated to the GOP, compared with 74 percent to the Democrats. That was on *average*. At Yale, for instance, almost 50 percent of profs donate, and 95 percent gave primarily to the Democrats. At Georgetown, in the six years studied, the Democrats received $180,000, the Republicans got $2,000 (!), and $1,500 went to the Greens (!!).

- At Ithaca College, according to Mark Finkelstein (chairman of the Tompkins County, New York, Republican Party) and Michelle Meredith (chairman of the Ithaca College Republicans) in a study published in www.frontpagemag.com, there are 117 registered Democrats or Greens (93.6 percent) versus only eight registered Republicans or Conservatives (6.4 percent). The Department of Politics has eight Democrats and no Republicans. The Department of History has seven Democrats and not a single Republican. The English Department has thirteen Democrats and no Republicans. The same fat "0" score for Republicans or conservatives goes for the departments of Psychology, Sociology, and Environmental Studies. We ought to be grateful that there's one Republican in the Department of Writing (twenty-five Democrats). Even in the Department of Business, thirteen professors were Democrats and just two were Republicans.

The leftists of academia aren't the centrist, fair-minded liberals who populated the universities until the 1960s; they are the radicals who chanted, "Hey, hey, LBJ, how many kids did you kill today?" and purged the centrist liberals, let alone conservatives. Now they run most colleges and universities with a rod of iron. Today, the Ivory Tower elites use their privileged—and unaccountable—positions to propagate extremist views designed to transform society into their own image.

Don't believe me? Listen to Richard Rorty, a well-known leftist professor of philosophy at the University of Virginia, who is quite open about the Elite Project's aims. According to David Horowitz, writing in www.salon.com (June 20, 2002), a few years ago Rorty bragged that "the power base of the left in America is now in the universities, since the trade unions have largely been killed off. The universities have done a lot of good work by setting up, for example, African-American studies programs, Women's Studies programs, and Gay and Lesbian Studies programs. They have created power bases for these movements."

Precisely. And it is your tax dollars that support the state university, the checks you write for your daughter's tuition, and your donation to your alma mater that fund the "power bases" for the left.

And these "power bases" don't remain idle. They are the springboards for countless radical, anti-American "movements." Indeed, Rorty has written and said that universities should be "centers of social protest" and act as "redistributionist social initiatives." Notice how Rorty didn't bother discussing the intellectual content of these dubious programs. That's because they don't serve the traditional purpose of a liberal arts education. They are not designed to teach students how to think for themselves, or how to recognize that an argument may have more than one side. No, students who take these courses are indoctrinated in the radical and anti-American agenda of a professoriate obsessed with "social protest." Many of these so-called "professors" award the highest grades not to those who have mastered the material, or who can best articulate their own independent views, but to those who best parrot the professor's ideology.

Oh, come on, Laura, I hear you saying. That must be an exaggeration. I wish it were, but it's not. Consider the fascinating story of

"Professor" Rosalyn Kahn of California's Citrus College. She taught a compulsory speech class, and she thought it would be a great idea to hand out extra credits to students who wrote antiwar protest letters to President Bush. Once she was caught, the college administration forced Kahn to apologize for such an abuse of her power, though it allowed her to keep her job. If you have to take her class, I would suggest that you not speak out in defense of the president.

In fact, it is becoming increasingly clear that there is almost no intellectual content to self-regarding fluff like Gay and Lesbian Studies, in the way most Americans would understand the term "intellectual content." These types of classes were largely created for the sole purpose of undermining traditional American society and its values. But where are the core courses? It's revealing that, according to well-regarded historian David McCullough (who won the 2002 Pulitzer for his biography of John Adams), the only three colleges that require students to take a course on the Constitution in order to graduate are the U.S. Military Academy at West Point, the Naval Academy at Annapolis, and the Air Force Academy.

## THE RAP ON AN IVY LEAGUE STAR

Instead of devoting their careers to enlightening their students and teaching them how to be better citizens, "professors" who inhabit the sundry Gay Studies and "Womyn's" Studies departments and many in African-American and other "victims-studies" departments in our nation's universities are political propagandists and/or academic frauds who exploit well-meaning white liberal guilt to garner huge salaries and lavish perks.

Perhaps the most famous of these fine scholars is Cornel West, formerly of Harvard's Afro-American Studies department and now resident at Princeton. He's no run-of-the-mill "professor": out of approximately 2,000 members of the Harvard faculty, West was one of only fourteen elite "University Professors." Until recently, West was untouchable. Cowed by his politically correct beliefs and extraordinary title, reviewers bent over backwards to give glowing notices of West's hilariously unreadable books. Well, at least I find them hilariously unreadable. Decide for yourself. Here's a taste of West's writing style:

> I believe that the major life-denying forces in our world are economic exploitation (resulting primarily from the social logic of capital accumulation), state repression (linked to the social logic of state augmentation), bureaucratic domination (owing to the social logic of administrative subordination), racial, sexual and heterosexual subjugation (due to the social logics of white, male and heterosexual supremacist practices) and ecological subjection (resulting, in part, from modern values of scientific manipulation), I entertain a variety of social analyses and cultural critiques that yield not merely one grand synthetic social theory.

Or how about this gem?

> Following the model of the black diasporan traditions of music, athletics, and rhetoric, black cultural workers must constitute and sustain discursive and institutional networks that deconstruct earlier modern black strategies for identity-formation, demystify power relations that incorporate class, patriarchal and homophobic biases, and construct more multivalent and multidimensional responses that articulate the complexity and diversity of black practices in the modern and post-modern world.

Don't you feel smarter? Actually, you should award yourself a gold star if you can make heads or tails of it. When you read phrases like the "social logic of state augmentation," you can't help but be reminded of those times in class where you couldn't really understand what the teacher was saying, so you just made up an answer that sounded as though you did. As an adult you know that more syllables does not necessarily mean more brain power.

That particular passage from Professor West says absolutely nothing. It's drivel. Yet still the official media outlet of the elite, the *New York Times,* religiously refers to him as "Dr. Cornel West" even when it uses plain old "Mr." for most people who also have doctorates. The *Times* also used to refer to Castro, with his absurd "law degree" from the University of Havana, as "Dr. Castro."[2] West himself certainly believes he is God's Gift to Knowledge. His *own* website refers to himself as a "genius" of "oratorical passion and unmatched eloquence." High praise indeed.

But West's self-proclaimed literary genius pales into insignificance compared with his musical talents as a hip-hop impresario. In May 2001 he released what must be a contender for the worst album of all time, *Sketches of My Culture.* (For $15, it's a pretty good deal—good comedy albums are hard to come by these days.) If I had to sum up *Sketches*, I'd have to say it sounds like Cornel amateurishly reciting his antiwhite lectures over a hip-hop loop. Move over, Eminem.

But this album brought Dr. West a few problems. Harvard's newly installed president Lawrence Summers (a friend of mine) reportedly did not see the academic value in *Sketches* and intimated as much to West. What a scandal! A Harvard president—and former Clinton Treasury secretary—who actually believes a Harvard professorship should mean something! Various media reports stated that Summers urged West to pursue more traditional scholarship, rather than trying to be a thinking man's 50 Cent. That request set off a chain of events that proved, fairly conclusively, that the PC movement was not just alive and well at Harvard—it ruled Harvard.

West was "outraged" that anyone would question his seriousness as a scholar, though he reportedly spends 150 days a year off-campus giving speeches and hasn't published a scholarly book through an academic press since 1989. (Note: Although Summers and I had never discussed West, some faculty members at Harvard speculated that I was somehow responsible for Summers' turn to the right. Anyone who knows Larry knows that is laughable—he's his own man.) Also outraged were West's allies at the *New York Times*, who put the story on their front page. The spin? Summers wasn't truly "committed to diversity." The idea that the president of Harvard would be motivated by concerns about academic excellence was never seriously addressed by any of the elites that attacked Summers. But the *Times* was not alone. Harvard faculty members, rushing to West's defense, hyperbolically called Summers' mild rebuke a blow to "academic freedom." Members of the Afro-American Studies "Dream Team" threatened to decamp en masse to Princeton (K. Anthony Appiah actually did, citing personal reasons). Jesse Jackson and Al Sharpton (West was one of Sharpton's presidential campaign advisors) of course stepped in with the usual charges that Harvard wasn't committed to affirmative action. The *Washington Post* wrote an adoring profile of West as a "man who believes that scholarship and street smarts are inseparable."

The elite assault ultimately was too much for Summers, who issued this statement: "We are proud of the Afro-American Studies program at Harvard, collectively and individually." The *New York Times*, happy to have Summers back in line, greedily reported that "in two interviews . . . he [Summers] seemed eager to refute any suggestion that he was too confrontational," adding that "even his critics seem to grant that Mr. Summers has learned from the disputes over the past few weeks."

This showdown demonstrated how difficult it is for anyone to take on the powerful nexus that exists between elites in the media (The *New York Times*) and the elites in universities (the Harvard establishment). In the end, not even Summers' rapprochement could make Dr. West happy. He flounced off to Princeton, which jumped at the chance to add such a brilliant star to its academic firmament. The *New York Times* put West's defection on its front page. (No, Jayson Blair didn't write the story.)

## HE'S A POET, AND WE DIDN'T KNOW IT

Another entertainer masquerading as a serious scholar is the Poet Laureate of New Jersey (yes, there is one, and it's not Bruce Springsteen), one Amiri Baraka. That's not his original name, by the way, which is the rather less flamboyant Everett LeRoi Jones. The *New York Times* adoringly describes Baraka as a "fiery poet-warrior." Since the 1970s, he's been a Third World Marxist-Leninist activist. He also left his white wife because, in the words of the *Los Angeles Times*, he was "unable to reconcile love across the racial divide with the struggle for black equality." (So much for tolerance.) With this background, it's not surprising that Baraka has had an extremely successful university career. He went to Howard University, did some graduate work at Columbia, and has taught at Yale, Rutgers, San Francisco State and the State University of New York at Stony Brook.

But then Baraka became poet laureate of New Jersey, a dangerous position for him because it increased the likelihood that normal people would actually read some of what he wrote. And sure enough, after September 11 he wrote a 227-line poem titled *Somebody Blew Up America,* which he read at a New Jersey poetry festival (and then read again at Yale). It's little more than a childishly written, illiterate, anti-Semitic, racist, anti-American rant packed with mad conspiracy theories. It is also unintentionally hilarious, and I highly recommend reading it (it can be found on several sites on the Internet). A sample "line": "Who knows what kind of Skeeza is a Condoleeza."

Press reports of the poem set off a controversy in New Jersey, with patriotic taxpayers (and their elected representatives) on one side, and the anti-American elites on the other. (You guess which side supported Baraka.) New Jersey governor James McGreevey tried to fire Baraka from his post, which he'd held for little more than month. But under New Jersey law (which apparently protects state-funded poets from the consequences of their own stupidity) he couldn't do so. So he asked him to resign. Baraka (apparently seeing no contradiction in taking state funds from a citizenry that he holds in contempt) refused. The only option left was for the state senate and assembly to vote to abolish the post of Poet Laureate.

## EXPOSING THE ELITES

The "tenured radicals," of our universities have little interest in actually enlightening students. And it shows. The National Association of Scholars, a higher-education reform group, conducted a survey in late 2002 that found that college seniors have slightly less cultural knowledge than *high school* graduates of the 1950s (i.e., before the radicals took charge). On average, on a battery of 15 questions assessing general cultural knowledge, today's college seniors gave 53.5 percent correct responses. In the 1950s, high school graduates gave 54.5 percent correct answers to similar questions, and college seniors scored 77 percent.

The point here is not that today's college kids are idiots. It's that the people who are supposed to be teaching them have dropped the ball. *Today's college seniors barely know as much as high schoolers did half a century ago.* In the 1950s, those who attended college could count on getting a good, well-rounded education that broadened their minds and made them *think*; today, in return for shelling out $35,000 a year, college students are subjected to "diversity" workshops and listen to professors drone on for hours about whatever "issue" is bothering them. Content has been replaced by politics.

It's not that it is *impossible* to get a good education, including a solid grounding in the great works of Western Civilization. The real travesty is that doing so has become much more difficult because radicals have consolidated their hold on academia.

Thankfully, some people are shining the spotlight on the left-wing infestation on campus. A great new website called www.noindoctrination.org collects anecdotes from students who "have experienced courses or orientation programs that advance one-sided social or political ideologies, denigrate alternative views, or create an intimidating atmosphere for expressing diverse opinions." Even when you consider that these are strictly personal opinions (which are verified by the webmaster), many of the descriptions of what goes on in college classes are harrowing.

- According to the course catalogue description, Professor David Presti's course at the University of California (Berkeley), "Brain, Mind and Behavior," is an "Introduction to human brain mechanisms of sensation, movement, perception, thinking, learning, memory, and emotion in terms of anatomy, physiology, and chemistry of the nervous system in health and disease." But science isn't the only thing on the professor' mind. According to a posting at www.noindoctrination.org, "today, March 18, 2003, the professor dedicated thirty minutes of a 1.5 hour lecture to letting about ten individuals speak out about the reasons students in this class should dissent against the war." Incidentally, "the professor also plays music of his choosing at the beginning of class. In the last five weeks or so the music selection has [often] been about a war topic by artists popular during the Vietnam War. He will make comments for about 5 minutes each class when there is a new development about war, an anti-war rally, etc." Instead of teaching a course about the brain, Professor Presti should get himself one.
- More California tax funds are being wasted at California State Polytechnic University at Pomona, by Professor Brian Dolinar who teaches the "History of the United States together with state and local materials from the Reconstruction (1865) to present." Here is one student's course review: "The instructor chose selected news stories to discuss every class period, but made sure that they were all about the L.A.P.D. using excessive force or any other story he could find attacking a white

politician. Although current events did not take up a significant amount of class time, they were never related to historical events. Most of them were from independent radical
newspapers protesting war, capitalism, or anything else usually associated with the conservative population. Whenever
a student tried to speak of another issue, the discussion was
ended." Dolinar "spent class time 'preaching' to us about such
topics as [why] crack should be decriminalized, and on several occasions praised gang members and graffiti writers as
'visionaries' or just expressing themselves. The majority of the
class were first-time freshmen and were obviously intimidated by the new college experience. After speaking to some
outside class, they acknowledged that they were refraining
from opposing the instructor for fear of negative repercussions." In short, "this class was not about the history of the
United States. The whole class was taught as a history of
minorities in the United States and how all their pain was
caused by white people."

- The stories about California professors kept rolling in. Here's
what one student wrote about Professor Adrian Novotny's
class at Long Beach City College on Physical Anthropology.
"Dr. Novotny uses his Anthropology class as a forum for his
excessively socialistic/political views. He would consistently
interject his personal views, i.e.: The white race should be
ashamed of itself, I'm ashamed to be white, The system
should be more socialistic, Take from those who have and
give to those who do not, Women are too lazy to breast-feed,
We should be ashamed of our government, Our government
is nothing more than a giant war monger, Democracy is nothing more than a disguise for colonialism, The rest of the
world has just cause to hate us, We should pay reparations to
all African-Americans, etc. The man is full of guilt....He
takes young and impressionable minds and attempts to bend
them into forming an anti-American ideology."

- In replying to the website, the good doctor seems to fully agree that these comments captured the spirit of his class: "Well, here we go again. I sometimes get such glib, knee-jerk patriotic 'you hurt my feelings' reactions to my lectures. For many of my students, I am their first encounter with the stark reality of the world at large. I expect to be attacked by people whose reality has been largely formed thorough [*sic*] indoctrination into unchallenged patriotism, unexamined Christianity, and a general absence of understanding of world history, especially the role of multinational corporations and the U.S. military in neocolonial ventures. Yes, I do occasionally 'soapbox' on topics involving our species' headlong plunge into self-destruction (after all, I do teach anthropology, the study of people). I am guilty of placing the Earth, all its living systems, and human well-being above corporate greed, national policy, hegemonic religion, and the 'comfort level' of students in my class."

Charming. Not all of America's professors think or speak like these snotty, sanctimonious dolts with doctorates. But the gems among the professorate who still value teaching over personal political invective are in the distinct minority. (To avoid trouble, they usually keep quiet, which merely allows the shenanigans of Novotny, Dolinar, and Pasti to continue.) Without any real accountability on campus, thousands of pseudo-professors around the country work as full-time propagandists of anti-American hate speech.

Remember, if any of this bothers you, you're a Neanderthal, a close-minded product of a repressive and racist culture. Plus, it's all protected by academic freedom anyway!

## AL QAEDA DOESN'T EXIST

Most Americans have long since given up on the academic world. It's almost as if we agreed to let these radicals have their cushy,

tenured jobs on the condition that we could ignore almost everything they said, wrote, or advocated. That arrangement hasn't
worked out too badly. Since the 1960s, the country has consistently
moved to the right as the universities moved more radically left.

But after September 11, it became clear that when it comes to
Middle Eastern Studies, we should pay more attention, because the
rampant radicalism is linked to actual terror.

Luckily the Middle East Forum, a Philadelphia-based think
tank, is paying attention and has established www.campus-
watch.org, to keep an eye on what's being taught about the war on
terror, militant Islam, the Arab-Israeli conflict, Syria, Iraq, Saudi
Arabia, and similar subjects.

Campus Watch found that Middle Eastern specialists—the
ones who not only teach students but also influence policymakers
and pop up on cable news—are in many cases leftist, extremist,
intolerant, anti-American apologists for terror and suicide
bombers. In fact, several of these Middle Eastern Studies professors have been accused of real terrorism. In February 2003, four
men were indicted at a U.S. District Court in Florida as "material
supporters of a foreign terrorist organization"—namely the Palestinian Islamic Jihad (PIJ). They were:

- **RAMADAN ABDULLAH SHALLAH.** Born in the Gaza Strip, he taught
  Middle Eastern Studies as an adjunct professor at the Univer-
  sity of South Florida (USF) in 1991. He is currently living in
  Damascus, where he acts as the PIJ's secretary-general. I'm
  guessing his students at USF didn't receive an objective edu-
  cation in American foreign policy and the Arab-Israeli conflict.
- **BASHIR MUSA MOHAMMED NAFI.** An Egyptian with two doctor-
  ates deported from this country in 1996 for visa violations.
  He had been a researcher at an institute associated with USF.
  He now teaches courses like "Social and Political Issues in
  Islam" at the University of London. (Hey, I never said we
  were the only country that has this problem.)

- **SAMEEH HAMMOUDEH.** Started at USF in 1995, where he taught Arabic. At the time of his arrest, he was working on a master's degree in "religious studies."

The biggest fish of all, however, was Sami al-Arian—a former USF professor who enjoys strong support from elite liberals. He was arrested for his alleged role in directing the American operations of the PIJ, criminal racketeering, conspiracy to kill and maim people abroad, extortion, visa fraud, perjury, the list goes on and on. Undeterred by the government's fifty-page, 121-count case against him (which was described by the judge as "substantial and convincing"), student groups at Georgetown University, where al-Arian's daughter Laila is studying, and various academic sympathizers (including philosophy professor Mark Lance and a chaplain from Howard University) held a fundraiser for his legal defense.

In June 2003, the American Association of University Professors condemned USF for firing al-Arian and violating his due process rights and—you got it—his "academic freedom." Sami claims he has no links to terrorism, so I guess that must be good enough for the AAUP.

Despite the official Ivory Tower principle that professors must be "tolerant" of "different viewpoints," Middle Eastern scholars and college activists display a disturbing tendency to sideline or censor views with which they disagree. At the November 2002 four-day conference of the Middle East Studies Association (an academic organization of professors in this field) more than 550 papers were presented. Out of this vast number, just one dealt with al Qaeda and one other with "fundamentalism." No one spoke about militant Islamism. Joel Beinin, the association president, even mocked studying terrorism in his speech, calling it "terrorology."[3] Before September 11, a Sarah Lawrence College prof, Fawaz Gerges, charged "the terror industry" with creating an "irrational fear of terrorism by focusing . . . on far-fetched horrible scenarios."

We should have a very rational fear of this kind of idiot teaching in a university.

The anti-American left on campus brooks little outside criticism. Consider what happened to Daniel Pipes, a well-known commentator on Middle Eastern issues (he founded Campus Watch). His lecture at York University in Toronto was initially canceled at the behest of the Middle East Students Association. Fortunately, the university president stepped in and said that Pipes had a right to be heard.

Even so, campus leftists and their professors (whose Faculty Association slanderously accused Pipes of being "committed to a racist agenda and a methodology of intimidation and harassment") did their best to run him out of town. Before the lecture, Pipes—a well-respected and knowledgeable writer—was taken aside by a detective from Toronto's Hate Crime Unit who warned him that he could be jailed if he advocated genocide or promoted hatred. Pipes's speech took place under locked-down circumstances, in a curtained-off section of the school's basketball court. Every attendee was frisked before entering. A hundred police officers, ten on horseback, were on hand to restrain the protesters.

This is what the Academy has become. An ideologically monochromatic place of false accusations and pseudo-intellectual thuggery. You can be sure that if anti-American apologists for terror like Nick De Genova or Edward Said (both of Columbia University) were invited to speak at York University, they wouldn't be hounded by the campus Hate Crime Unit.

But it is not enough for the left to try to silence men like Pipes. "Classes" on Middle Eastern affairs are often little more than propaganda rallies. Consider a course offered at Berkeley in 2002, "The Politics and Poetics of Palestinian Resistance." Here there were more politics than poetics in evidence, judging by the inclusion of three books (count them, three) on the reading list by Said, a Palestinian activist who broke with Arafat because Arafat was *too moderate!* The course description promised the course would cover "the brutal Israeli military occupation of Palestine, an occupation that has been ongoing since 1948, and has systematically displaced, killed, and maimed millions of Palestinian people."

Now, leaving aside the many factual errors and exaggerations in just that one sentence, it's pretty obvious that those students who opted for the course were not going to be getting a judicious, aesthetically oriented education in the poetics of Palestinian resistance. No, it was to be an exercise in brainwashing by the "teacher," Snehal Shingavi. That's par for the course in the Academy, and no one would have paid much attention, but Snehal's description went on to advise potential students that "Conservative thinkers are encouraged to seek other sections." *That* was being a little too frank, and following the resultant uproar, Berkeley conducted an investigation and "acknowledged...that there was a failure of oversight on the part of the English Department in reviewing section descriptions authored by graduate student instructors." Good for Berkeley, but how many more Shingavis are out there?

Part of the anti-American bias of Middle Eastern studies professors can be attributed to sordid self-interest. The Sultan bin Abdulaziz Al-Saud Foundation Arab and Islamic studies program at Berkeley, for instance, was given a gift of $5 million—courtesy of the Saudi royal family. Much of the money goes to scholarships, professorships, and grants, and very little of it, I'd imagine, goes to professors who are going to challenge the Saudis on any particular issue.

The rot spreads even beyond the cloistered world of Middle Eastern "specialists." Every elite anti-American professor seems to think he can score political points by drawing on his own, nonexistent expertise. Before the Iraq war, these self-appointed geniuses went to town. Daniel Pipes, in a column for the *New York Post*, helpfully reproduced some of their more inane comments:

- "We all know...what they're aiming at," said MIT professor Noam Chomsky. "Iraq has the second-largest oil reserves in the world." Chomsky, a virulently anti-American nut since the 1960s, teaches linguistics at MIT.
- The war against Iraq "takes us back to the notion of the rule of the jungle," crowed Columbia history professor Eric Foner, who compared Operation Iraqi Freedom to the Japanese sneak attack against Pearl Harbor. (Columbia *again*? What's going on there?)
- Tom Nagy, an associate professor of business at George Washington University, traveled (illegally) to Iraq, where he offered "estimates of the number of civilians needed to act as a human shield to protect infrastructure and buildings for Iraqi citizens."
- Mazin Qumsiyeh, an associate professor of genetics at Yale believed that a U.S. war against Iraq would be just a diversion created by "Israeli apologists" and Jewish officials in the Bush administration so that Israel could get away with inflicting "even higher atrocities" against Palestinians.

## SHUT UP, I'M TALKING

If their closed-mindedness, anti-Americanism, and idiocy weren't bad enough, the members of the Edu-elite are champion hypocrites. Back in the 1960s, they were the leading members of the Free Speech brigade (as they incessantly remind us). But that was *before* they gained control over the universities. Once they finally strengthened their hold in the 1980s and 1990s, they introduced censorious speech codes onto American campuses as a way of enforcing their own elite agenda. So today, because they've been exposed as America-haters and subjected to widespread derision, they now whine about being "censored."

So now the Ivory Tower elites circulate petitions supporting professors' right to express their opinions free of censure, citing the "American tradition of dissent."

Let's call a spade a spade: the only people who wish to stifle free speech—*your* free speech—are radical leftists and anti-American hatemongers—the elite, in other words. That's why they organize teach-ins and petitions to protest the "chilling of dissent" but don't raise a word in protest when conservative campus newspapers are torn up or stolen by leftists. Thankfully, somebody is fighting back against the elite suppression of free speech. The Philadelphia-based Foundation for Individual Rights in Education (FIRE) is a non-profit educational foundation devoted to restoring the principles of a true "liberal education" to our campuses by challenging unconstitutional "speech codes." In April, FIRE kicked off a major assault against the ongoing censorship at public universities by filing a lawsuit against the speech code at Pennsylvania's Shippensburg University. Over the course of the next year, FIRE will be filing challenges in each of the twelve federal appellate circuits, the aim being to establish legal precedents nationwide that will end the scandal of unconstitutional speech codes on public college and university campuses.

How bad are these speech codes? The Code of Conduct at Shippensburg bans speech that is "inflammatory, demeaning, or harmful towards others," as well as speech that could "provoke" others. Presumably the Declaration of Independence is inflammatory and provoking to some—why not ban it? Shippensburg also bans "subordination . . . on the basis of race, color, creed or national origin, communicated through words, attitudes, actions and/or gestures." And what does this sentence mean? Basically, it means that you're not allowed to do *anything* at Shippensburg: nothing that "annoys, threatens, or alarms a person or group," no "innuendo," "comments, insults," "propositions," "humor/jokes about sex or gender-specific traits," or, and this is classic, "suggestive or insulting sounds, leering, whistling, [and] obscene gestures." But even this is not enough. In language that clearly violates their freedom of conscience, students are officially directed to display a "commitment to racial tolerance, cultural diversity, and social justice . . . in their attitudes and behaviors."

Talk about "chilling" debate. So when will the members of the Ivory Tower elite get around to sending their tax-free donations to FIRE to support its passionate defense of free speech? Answer: Never.

## SCHOOL DAZE

Just as a fish rots from the head, American education is being ruined from the top to the bottom. First, the elites took over the universities. Now they've moved on to the K-12 grades, where their sympathizers control the all-powerful teachers' unions, specifically the National Education Association (NEA) and the American Federation of Teachers (AFT). Like their colleagues in the university faculties, union honchos put left-wing politics and power first, real education last.

The NEA's annual conferences are a wonder to behold. Like their counterparts in higher education, the 9,000 union delegates attending the four-day gabfest prefer to pontificate on issues wholly unrelated to education. Mike Antonucci of the Education Intelligence Agency, a private, for-profit contract research firm that supports no particular program or specific reform, compiled a report (August 2001) on the NEA's policies decided at its conferences. Here are some examples of how the NEA thinks we could improve "education":

- "Extension of Daylight Savings Time until the first Sunday in November."
- "A tax-supported, single-payer health care plan for all residents of the United States, its territories and the Commonwealth of Puerto Rico."
- "A mutual, verifiable nuclear freeze with cessation of testing,

production, and further deployment of nuclear delivery systems and other destabilizing systems."
- "Legislation to preserve and expand Native Hawaiian land ownership."
- "Federal initiatives to deal with the growing national concern relating to stalking."

Maybe, just *maybe*, we could live with such nonsense if our children were learning something. But, like, they're totally not. Like the college seniors I discussed earlier in the chapter, too many of today's schoolchildren are "graduating" with a sub-standard education. In the last fifty years, the average vocabulary of a fourteen-year-old has dropped from 25,000 words to 10,000. Many teachers are even making research papers a thing of the past. These writing projects once taught teenagers the rudiments of criticism and argument and forced them to acquire in-depth knowledge of a given topic, but these crucial skills are being lost. A survey in late 2002 found that 81 percent of 400 high school teachers never assign history papers that are twenty pages long (5,000 words), and 62 percent don't assign ones that are fifteen pages long (3,000 words). It's common today to ask students to prepare merely "summaries" of assigned readings. That "may very well mean that a majority of our high school students never read a complete non-fiction book on any subject before they graduate," said Will Fitzhugh, editor of the *Concord Review*, which published the survey. Moreover, the effect of such poor training on college admissions is alarming. More and more colleges now find themselves having to give classes on basic writing skills. That means increasing already steep college tuition fees and cutting back on other, more advanced courses.

The ignorance of basic American history among students is a scandal. The facts demonstrate that many teachers, for whatever reason, are simply not *teaching*. More than half—*half!*—of high school pupils, when asked which American Revolutionary general was in charge at Yorktown (when Lord Cornwallis surrendered) guessed—*guessed!*—Ulysses S. Grant. About 6 percent thought it might have been Douglas MacArthur. (Note to reader: If you don't know the answer to this question, go look it up right now! This book will be here when you get back.) Given this lack of grounding in high school, it's not surprising that our college students are so ignorant of even the most basic facts about our history. Another survey found that there were even some Ivy League college students who thought Germany and Japan were our allies in World War II. Didn't these kids even watch *Saving Private Ryan*? (Of course, France was our ally then, but it isn't now, so that might have confused them.)

At a Senate panel hearing in April 2003, the historian David McCullough testified that "we are raising a generation of people who are historically illiterate" and who are ignorant of how our constitutional free society came about. When committee chairman Senator Lamar Alexander asked the historian whether students should be taught that America is an "exceptional" country, he replied, "Yes, we're an exceptional people.... The American story is exceptional. The American Revolution was the first revolution of a people breaking away from a colonial power and establishing a free country."

Is it that many of our teachers don't believe that America is an exceptional country? Or is it that many are afraid of an edu-elite backlash if they dared to make a positive classroom statement about America's greatness? Probably, it's the latter. But unfortunately, most parents don't have other educational options for their kids. Why? Again, the unions are to blame.

The NEA and AFT devote tens of millions of dollars every election cycle to defeating school choice. These edu-elites know that as soon as parents are given a choice—among public, private, or charter schools—the union gig is up. They are protecting their political power base by robbing poor children of quality education. These same hucksters use pliant journalists to spin lies about the home-schooling movement. So the stereotype persists that home-schooling is purely the province of right-wing Bible thumpers. (They have a hard time, however, explaining away all these home-schooled spelling and geography bee winners!)

Unions line the pockets of anti-voucher pols, mostly Democrats, and have also nabbed votes among GOP elites like the milquetoast RR Arlen Specter.

The average teacher is obliged to have about $500 subtracted from his salary each year to keep the pigs at the top rolling in clover. In Michigan alone, there are 75 union officials being paid more than $100,000 a year. In Iowa, according to 2001 figures, 36 professional staffers of the NEA's state affiliate earn an average $117,072 in salary and benefits. (California: 179 staffers, $135,434; New Jersey: 101 staffers, $132,413, etc., etc.) No teacher earns that kind of money, nor does he enjoy the 100 percent coverage for health and dental insurance union bosses receive. It's a clear-cut case of the elites at the top looking after themselves and not caring enough about the people they're supposed to be looking after.

Even as they whine about "teacher shortages," the teachers' unions resist the very incentives—like merit pay, hiring bonuses, or certification waivers for highly experienced professionals—that could bring talented employees into the system. As it is, talented teachers are leaving or being forced out, fed up with the system and the union heavies. To make up the shortfall, we have even begun hiring foreign teachers under the H-1B visa program.

## COOKING THE BOOKS

With teachers' unions so busy playing politics, it's no wonder our public school textbooks have gone to hell. Coast to coast, our students' curricula are designed and dictated by the K-12 edu-elite. In years to come, these children will grow up and attend college, their heads filled with all sorts of anti-American, politically correct nonsense. At college, their prejudices will be confirmed, encouraged, by the Ivory Tower Reds. This is a surefire way of undermining America and eroding our national unity.

Curriculum manipulation takes place on two levels. On the first level, there is the K-12 equivalent of campus speech codes by means of censoring textbooks for incorrect thoughts. Diane Ravitch, a historian of education, says in her book, *The Language Police*, that "advocates for social change have set their sights on controlling reality by changing the way in which it is presented in textbooks."

Examples range from the silly to the bizarre to the nannyish to the antireligious. The thrust of the effort is to avoid controversy and offense (except to our common sense) at all costs. So in the government's National Assessment of Educational Progress tests (NAEP), which measure academic achievement in grades four, eight, and twelve, a passage about the inventor of peanut butter (George Washington Carver, if you didn't know) was excised in case children with peanut allergies felt left out. Because some Native American tribes regard certain birds as taboo, the NAEP deleted a scientific text about owls. References to dolphins have also disappeared as inner-city kids were assumed to be too stupid to know anything about the sea. (Does that mean youths living in fishing towns cannot be asked about skyscrapers?) In California, textbooks must not mention coffee, cream cheese, french fries, fruit punch, bacon, or butter, because these foods have been deemed unhealthy.

And, of course, references to God are being cut out—even when the religious aspect is crucial to understanding the reading in question. For instance, the Regents of New York State changed a passage written by Elie Wiesel about surviving the Holocaust from this: "Man, who was created in God's image, wants to be free as God is free: free to choose between good and evil, love and vengeance, life and death," to this, which has a completely different meaning: "Man wants to be free: free to choose between good and evil, love and vengeance, life and death."

The second level of curriculum manipulation is far more threat-ening because it focuses on *altering truth itself* (rather than "just" being concerned with censoring "offensive" references). In this respect, the American Textbook Council (ATC) has done sterling work examining what our children are being taught about Islam, its beliefs, and its impact on American values. While the large majority of the world's Muslims live peacefully, radical Islam has spawned murderous villains worldwide, including the September 11 hijackers. Only you wouldn't get that impression from many of the world history textbooks currently being used across the coun-try for grades seven through twelve. In fact, you'd be led to think that America was at fault for what happened to us.

A 2002 report by the ATC focused on four aspects of Islam (and Islamism, its radical political/military version). Its findings were disturbing, to say the least. They paint a picture of an educational establishment—the same establishment that fights every single day to keep any positive reference to Christianity out of our schools— bending over backwards to present everything about Islam in the most positive light possible. Here are some examples:

**JIHAD.** This is an extremely complex subject. Conventionally and traditionally translated, it means "holy war" by Muslims against non-Muslims until the whole world is Islamicized either by con-quest, slavery, or conversion. This is clearly the sense in which it is being used by many of the terrorists who are attacking us. Some modern Muslim theologians, however, interpret it in a spiritual and moral sense: it can refer to personal "striving in the path of God." Textbook editors have fastened exclusively onto the latter definition (using "guides" issued by Islamist advocacy groups). So American children are never told about the traditional meaning of *jihad,* and are taught only that this term means a form of self-improvement (quitting smoking, learning to read, etc.). For instance, Prentice Hall's *Connections to Today,* the nation's most widely used world history textbook, defines *jihad* as "an effort in

God's service." That's it. By ignoring *jihad's* other, more accurate, definition, textbooks present an image of Islam as the religion of personal betterment. Compare that kid-gloves treatment to how Christianity—with its "repressive" and "racist" past—is regarded by the elites.

**SHARIA.** It means "holy law." In Islamist states, there is no distinction between church and state, a separation that in the Christian West goes back to the New Testament teaching of rendering unto Caesar that which is Caesar's and unto God that which is God's, and to the separate offices of emperor (or later king) and pope. *Sharia* regulates all aspects of human life. According to one of the foremost historians of Islam, Bernard Lewis, "the principal function of the Islamic state and society was to maintain and enforce these rules" and "the idea that any group of persons, any kind of activities, or any part of human life is in any sense outside the scope of religious law and jurisdiction is alien to Muslim thought."

Our public school textbooks take a kinder, gentler approach to Sharia by glossing over *Sharia's* more oppressive aspects. Holt, Rinehart and Winston's *Continuity and Change* blandly says that "the *shari'ah* guided the personal conduct of all Muslims, including religious observances, marriage, divorce, business affairs, and inheritance. It also outlined the appropriate practices of Islamic government. Adherence to the *shari'ah* soon became one of the most important elements of the Muslims' sense of identity." While this is accurate as far as it goes, there is no discussion of the very real differences between Western legal traditions (separation of church and state, limited government, independent judiciary, personal liberty, freedom of religion, trial by jury, due process, etc.) and Islamic ones, which have no basis in Roman, British, or American constitutionalism. Islamic law is dictated by a repressive clerical class that can use it to control all forms of behavior by means of stoning, amputation, flogging, and beheading. Elite-written textbooks, however, don't dwell on these topics for fear of being seen as judgmental. If only the Ayatollahs and mullahs were so sensitive!

**SLAVERY.** Some of the textbooks briefly mention Arab and Muslim slavery (though devoting much more space to our own experience with it) but often they downplay it. In the words of the ATC, Muslim slavery is portrayed as "a benign institution, simply a part of economic life, even a route to influence and power, illustrating the inconsistencies and double standard of multiculturalized world history." In fact, Muslim slavery is central to the history of Islam, the Arabs having "invented" the African slave trade in the first place. From our school textbooks, however, you would be led to think this evil practice was employed only by Europeans and Americans.

**STATUS OF WOMEN.** History textbooks dwell obsessively on the "repressed" status of women in the West but pass over in silence their wretched, chattel-like status in Muslim countries, which continues to this day. *Connections to Today*, apparently unable to come up with any positive spin on this point, confines itself to saying that "conservative countries like Saudi Arabia and Iran have opposed the spread of many western secular influences among women." That must be the understatement of the century.

In short, a noisy band of elite multiculturalists (many based at universities—so completing the Ivory Tower–K-12 nexus) work to alter truth by painting a rose-colored picture of Islam and Islamism at the expense of American traditions and history. In the aftermath of September 11 and the continuing war on terrorism, it is vital that students gain a solid grounding in what is happening around them.

Unfortunately, thanks to the efforts of the elites at all levels of "education" to transform and subvert America simultaneously, they're not. In fact, just 10 percent of high school students scored as "proficient" on the history section of the 2001 National Assessment of Educational Progress. "Too much of the history taught in our schools is compressed and diluted within broader social studies curricula," said Eugene W. Hickok, undersecretary of education. Precisely.

## A SILVER LINING?

The damage the edu-elites have done to education at all levels is staggering. But there are signs of hope. Since September 11, Americans have been much more willing to challenge the elite orthodoxy "taught" in colleges and schools. As we have seen in this chapter, the citizen armies of freedom are on the march even in education. Brave students are standing up in class and telling their professors that they are way out of line when they call America a racist dictatorship. University presidents are being pressured by alumni to dump hate-mongering professors. The contents of school textbooks are being more closely scrutinized for blatant anti-American politicization. Websites have been set up to monitor radical professors for using their pulpits to preach Hate America sermons. Organizations are using the law to force universities to end their outrageous restrictions on free speech that does not meet the elites' approval.

Goaded by their students and alumni, universities are even downplaying their anti-American hatred of the military and relaxing their old Vietnam-era strictures against ROTC. It would be going too far to say that they're "welcoming them with open arms," but Yale, Harvard, and Columbia have begun to change their snobby, p.c., unwelcoming attitude toward student ROTC programs. It was a headline-making event when Harvard president Lawrence Summers attended a graduation ceremony for ROTC graduates (how sad that such a simple gesture was considered newsworthy). Baby steps, but steps nonetheless when Harvard decided to allow students to list their ROTC activities in the yearbook. It must have driven the anti-military zealots up the wall. Both the Harvard *Crimson* and the Yale *Daily News* editorialized in favor of a return to ROTC on campus.

Americans realize that educators in schools and colleges have a special role to play in our national life. Professors have a duty to uphold the truth and allow the free interplay of opposing views, even if—*especially* if—they conflict with their own. Their job is not to indoctrinate students with their own personal politics like some Soviet-era "reeducation camp" instructors. Their responsibility is to enlighten and broaden the minds of the young, and teach them *how* (not *what*) to think in a critical, lucid, rational way. While students should respect their authority and knowledge, professors are expected to be open to well-informed challenge. Good professors, no matter their politics, already do this. The bad ones, and there are far too many of them, ignore (or distort) the facts and let themselves be blinded by ideology. A student who expresses a nonconformist opinion (either liberal or conservative) in term papers or in lecture halls should not have his grades reduced, even if the professor or teaching assistant disagrees with his views. The crucial litmus test for gaining high grades should be whether the student can defend his arguments and hold his own in debate.

A first step to ending the outrageous liberal elite bias in our nation's colleges would be to reform university hiring procedures. Closed committees, composed of like-minded academics, tend to hire those who attain the ideal of "collegiality"—a code word for leftist groupthink. They should be replaced by open, fair hiring of the sort used by companies and the government to judge candidates.

As for the public schools, parents just shouldn't take it anymore. Their children are being shortchanged. Demand change by demanding an end to the public school monopoly. Buck the unions. Go to school board meetings and stand up for your values, for learning, for honesty. As for all the hard-working and dedicated teachers out there, they would be better off in a system that rewards merit and punishes incompetence. This, the vaunted NEA has not delivered.

We should demand an end to the elite politicization of education and return to what the great nineteenth-century thinker, Matthew Arnold, proposed: educators must cultivate the habit of scholarly "disinterestedness" that refuses to "lend itself to any... ulterior, political, practical considerations." In other words, the members of the edu-elite should heed the words of their own American Association of University Professors, which laid down this basic statement of principle nearly a century ago: "Institutions of higher education are conducted for the common good and not to further the interest of either the individual teacher or the institution as a whole. The common good depends upon the free search for truth and its free exposition." It continues, "the university teacher... should, if he is fit for his position, be a person of a fair and judicial mind; he should, in dealing with such subjects, set forth justly, without suppression or innuendo, the divergent opinions of other investigators... and he should, above all, remember that his business is not to provide his students with ready-made conclusions, but to train them to think for themselves."

# 10

# In Kofi We Trust?

A h, the "*United* Nations." Doesn't it have a lovely ring to it? It sounds so warm and friendly. The elites just love the United Nations. They love all that "consensus-building" and all those "multilateral initiatives." They adore the idea of the nations of the world getting together and sorting out their "issues." Most of all, they love how the UN is the only body that tells America what to do. Why? Because in their eyes it's the sole "legitimate authority" in the world today, and America is a rogue nation that needs to be brought into line. Most Americans, if they think about the UN at all, believe that it may be useful at controlling the most dangerous parts of the world. But to the elites, the UN has a much more important mission: controlling America. The UN needs to be disabused of this arrogant notion. It desperately needs to be reformed, reconfigured, and reoriented.

Why would any American—particularly elite Americans—want the United States to be subservient to any international organization, much less one as dysfunctional as the UN? To understand the answer to this question, you have to remember that elites think very differently from the way the rest of us think. For most Americans, being governed by our own elected officials is a *good* thing;

**267**

the fact that we elect them is the source of their legitimacy. The United Nations is an unelected body, most of whose members are undemocratic states. It is not an institution created of, by, and for the American people; it is not recognized by our Constitution; and therefore, to most Americans, it has no legitimate role in telling America what to do. Now if you're nodding your head at this point, and thinking "That makes sense," then you've given yourself away. You're not part of the elite.

As we've already discussed, the U.S. electoral process hasn't worked out so well for America's elites lately. The evidence is increasingly clear that American voters aren't buying into the elite agenda. Accordingly, the elites here and in Europe are increasingly convinced that all of this consent-of-the-governed stuff is becoming obsolete in this "interdependent world of open borders, easy travel, mass migration, universal access to information and technology, drenched in global media" (to use the words of Bill Clinton in his October 2002 address to Britain's Labour Party). American elites trust the wisdom of their fellow UN-ionized elites around the world far more than they trust the wisdom of the American people. As our former president added, "the prospect for a truly global community of people working together in peace with shared responsibilities for a shared future was not institutionalized until a little less than 60 years ago with the creation of the United Nations and the issuance of the universal declaration of human rights."

So if you're in the elite, you probably believe that America should really evolve beyond its musty old Constitution. A sitting Supreme Court Justice almost said as much recently. Justice Stephen Breyer, on ABC's *This Week*, said the big challenge for the future will be "whether our Constitution [fits] and how it fits into the governing documents of other nations." Undoubtedly, when Justice Breyer hobnobs at cocktail parties in Barcelona or Manhattan and says such things, he's greeted with nods of approval. But here in America we see the disturbing implications of this elite outlook—namely, that our democratic process is subverted if our courts interpret American laws so that they better mesh with the (more "enlightened") views of other countries.

This is precisely what happened recently in *Lawrence* v. *Texas*, where the Supreme Court struck down a Texas criminal statute barring homosexual sodomy. Writing for the majority, Justice Anthony Kennedy, cited as "significant," a decision of the European Court of Human Rights, which held that laws that prohibited homosexual sodomy violated the European Convention on Human Rights. In his dissent, Justice Antonin Scalia rightly blew a gasket over the Court's reliance on the reasoning of a foreign court to decide the constitutionality of an American law. Scalia dismissed the majority's citation of foreign authority as "meaningless dicta," even "[d]angerous dicta" since the Court "should not impose foreign moods, fads or fashions on Americans." Unfortunately, Scalia is losing this battle against his international elite colleagues. Justice Breyer seemed to indicate that there would be more decisions like *Lawrence* v. *Texas* to come, "We see all the time, Justice O'Connor and I, and the others, how the world really—it's trite but it's true—is growing together." You got the trite part right at least.

Everyone likes to moan about the abortion "litmus test" that Republican administrations use to screen its judicial nominees. But given what we've heard from Breyer and Kennedy, any litmus test should include the pledge that the prospective judge or justice will never rely on the decisions of foreign courts or the views of international organizations to decide American disputes or determine the constitutionality of American laws.

Remember, the international elites at home and abroad know that their views aren't succeeding in American ballot boxes, so they must do anything and everything they can to go over the heads of our voters to effect change. So it makes perfect sense that the elites desperately want to increase the role of the UN and why they just love judges who think like Breyer or Kennedy. In the elite dream world, America would be able to do little internationally and domestically without first clearing it with our "partners," a term that refers to these same international elites. They believe America needs "adult" supervision by the progressive thinkers abroad. "U.S. politicians should reflect on their country's selective approach to global standards of justice and decency," as Amnesty International warned in a recent press release.

## ANTI-AMERICANS OF THE WORLD UNITE!

Bolstered by the attitude of U.S. elites, America bashers around the world feel free to lecture us on any issue that grabs their attention. For example, in 2001 the Parliamentary Assembly of the Council of Europe adopted a resolution demanding we "put a moratorium on executions in place without delay and . . . take steps to abolish the death penalty." Why? Because the death penalty is allegedly "racist" and "discriminatory." But what about the fact, which even the Parliamentary Assembly's own report makes clear, that a majority of American voters and their elected representatives support capital punishment. Well, that doesn't matter, states the assembly, because a true democracy would take *world* opinion into account: "In continuing this barbaric and anachronistic form of punishment . . . the United States is out of step with other democracies and international human rights standards . . . and, in this aspect, 'undemocratic.'"

The Europeans were backed by our homegrown elite, desperate for their respect and acclaim. In January 2003 the outgoing governor of Illinois, Republican George Ryan needed a professional reputation resuscitation. He had run a calamitous administration. His poll figures had plummeted. He was mired in a corruption scandal. As one of his final gubernatorial acts he commuted the sentences of all 167 death row prisoners in his state. This brought him almost immediate cheers and accolades by top UN officials. Ryan's name was even forwarded for the Nobel Peace

Prize, and Rome's Colosseum was lit up to honor him. Amnesty International declared that "Governor Ryan has shown that change is possible and that principled human rights leadership is crucial. Such leadership has been sadly lacking over the past quarter of a century of judicial killing in the U.S.A." And lastly, "I congratulate George Ryan on his courage and his conviction," said Walter Schwimmer, the Council of Europe's secretary-general. "I sincerely hope that this is a step forward to the abolition of the death penalty in the whole of the United States."

What the elites never acknowledged were the views and opinions of the people of Illinois—most notably, what the families of the 250 victims of Ryan's death row inmates thought of this arrogant, unilateral, decision beloved by the elites. The international elite also didn't bother mentioning that the prisoners on death row had committed horrendous crimes—which was why they were on death row in the first place. The *Chicago Tribune* helpfully noted some of criminals and their acts:

- Anthony Brown: Already having served time for rape, he strangled and suffocated a sixty-seven-year-old woman in her home.
- Lorenzo Fayne: Stabbed or strangled four girls between the ages of nine and seventeen.
- Lenard Johnson: Stabbed an eleven-year-old boy to death and sexually assaulted three girls (ages seven, eleven, and thirteen) while he babysat them.
- Fedell Caffey and Jacqueline Williams: Shot a pregnant woman, cut the nearly full-term baby from her womb, resuscitated it, and stabbed her two children (incidentally cutting the throat of the woman's eight-year-old son and dumping his body in an alley).

Governor Ryan said he would "sleep well knowing I made the right decision" to spare these criminals the death penalty. The loved ones of these criminals' victims are probably sleeping less well because of him.

But to the Council of Europe and its elite American lapdogs, "democracy" is defined as "Do What *We* Want." For decades, poll after poll has found that the vast majority of Britons want the death penalty restored. Unfortunately for British voters, it's never going to happen, despite rising murder rates, because the Euro-elite hates the death penalty. And as Britain has to follow the norms set by the European Union, who cares what the voters think?

America's elites would like a similarly bureaucratic body here to see to it that America's voters either mend their ways or, better

# **Elite**speak **alert!**

O f course, if you really want to know what the American internationalist elites are thinking, you just have to listen to the guy who still sets their agenda—**Bill Clinton.** These gems were from his highly acclaimed British Labour Party conference in October 2002. Our esteemed former president went gung-ho for replacing our independent elected government with some type of global bureaucracy:

- "The number-one task of the world today is to move from interdependence, which can be good and bad, to an integrated global community in which there is a shared future, shared responsibilities, shared prosperity and, most important, shared values." Of course, international elites don't share the values of average Americans, so there's no chance our values will be reflected in the "integrated global community."
- "There are still people who vote in the United Nations based on the sort of old-fashioned national self-interest views they held in the Cold War or even long before, so that not every vote reflects the clear and present interests

still, get out of the way. But rather than pressuring America, why don't groups like Amnesty International demand that all dictatorships in the world reform themselves to reach *American* "standards of justice and decency." And why doesn't the Council of Europe mind its own business? Or perhaps our Congress should urge Europe to reintroduce capital punishment given that London and Paris are now more dangerous cities than New York.

For now at least, the United States remains a sovereign nation that still celebrates "Independence Day"—as opposed to "Standards of Justice and Decency Day"—and so we are free to ignore the counsel of the Council of Europe. But our sovereignty won't

---

of the world and the direction we are going." Imagine that! There are "still" people who think in terms of national interest, not the interests of the world community!

- "We must move from interdependence to integration because our common humanity matters more than our interesting differences and makes the expression of those differences possible; because every child deserves a chance, every adult has a role to play and we all do better when we work together." When you hear the elites talking about children, you know something wicked this way comes.
- And here it comes. "That is why we must build the institutions that will help us to integrate, that is why we must stand against the threats, whether they are from weapons of mass destruction, terrorists, tyrants, AIDS, climate change, poverty, ignorance and disease which would tatter this world and prevent us ever from coming together as one." When you hear the elites wanting to "build" institutions, you better duck and cover, because those institutions won't have your best interests at heart. ■

last long if the elites have their way, since they don't like independent nation-states. Independent nation-states are, well, too *independent* for the elites' tastes. They're sooooo 1950! They don't do what they're told by the elites. And that's why the elites are so adamant about preserving the UN's position on the global stage. The UN is the ultimate elite organization—unelected, unaccountable to anyone, free to pass whatever resolution it wants regardless of the opinions of any one state. It's the perfect vehicle for curbing the power of independent states, particularly the most independent state of all—America.

As Clinton's deputy secretary of state Strobe "The Globe" Talbott put it a decade ago (the elites always think long-term), "All countries are basically social arrangements... [that] are all artificial and temporary.... Within the next 100 years, nationhood as we know it will be obsolete. All states will recognize a single global authority." Now to you or me, these words sound like a prophecy of doom. But to Talbot, the idea that all states will recognize "a single global authority" is something to celebrate. We should be looking *forward* to America's becoming obsolete because then—at last!—the UN can run the show.

Come on, Laura, you say, that was just one liberal bloviator popping off. That can't really represent elite thought in America. If you think I exaggerate, here's then Vice President Al Gore introducing his foreign-policy vision of the new "Global Age" in April 2000. "The traditional nation-state is changing as power moves upwards... [to] supra-national institutions." That's why America needs to champion "reinvigorated international and regional institutions" dedicated to, among other thing, "stabilizing population growth... the protection of children against sweatshop labor and the protection of the environment... [and] promoting the stable flow of investment around the world." In other words, the world would be great if the elites were allowed to manage everything through unaccountable, unelected "supra-national institutions."

Democracy be damned.

Current Democrat candidates for president are echoing the international elite sentiments on America's role in the world. They think our glory days are behind us. America needs to change because America cannot possibly remain a dominant force forever. Howard Dean, the former governor of Vermont, said at a New Hampshire yogurt factory in April that "we have to take a different approach" to diplomacy because "we won't always have the strongest military." Dean tried to backtrack but we know that the truth came out. John Kerry's staff saw a potential campaign issue and responded angrily. "No serious candidate for the presidency," said Kerry's spokesman, Chris Lehane, "has ever before suggested that he would compromise or tolerate an erosion of America's military supremacy." Tough talk and certainly no one can question Senator Kerry's own brave service to his country during the Vietnam War. But if only Kerry himself weren't coopted by the international elites. In his first major policy address after announcing his intention to run, Kerry took his cue from *The Dummies' Guide to Global Governance*. Kerry obediently declared that America must:

- Embrace "a bold, progressive internationalism that stands in stark contrast to the too often belligerent and myopic unilateralism of the Bush administration."
- Reject "the narrow vision of those who would build walls to keep the world out" in favor of "forging coalitions and step by step creating a new world of law and mutual security."
- Make "[a] choice between those who think you can build walls to keep the world out, and those who want to tear down the barriers that separate 'us' from 'them.'"
- Eschew the Bush administration's "blustering unilateralism," which "is wrong, and even dangerous."
- In January, Kerry clarified that "in a world growing more, not less interdependent, unilateralism and arrogance are formulas

for isolation and for shrinking influence. And as much as some in the White House may desire it, America cannot opt out of a networked world."

• And, "working through global institutions doesn't tie our hands, it invests U.S. aims with greater legitimacy and dampened the fear and the resentment that our *preponderant* power sometimes inspires in others."

And there you have it. If you won't knuckle under to the French and their toadies at the UN, you're guilty of "blustering unilateralism." If you don't agree with Kofi Annan's interpretation of international law, you're accused of building "walls to keep the world out." It apparently never occurs to Kerry that Americans might be right and our so-called "allies" might be wrong. Like all liberal elites faced with any conflict between the American people and European bureaucrats, he'll go against the American people every time.

The globalists' strategy should be obvious by now: advocate a foreign policy that favors international institutions over American power, independence, and old-fashioned common sense. Sadly, Kerry is a voice of reason compared with other Democrats who think they should be president, such as congressman, and part-time ventriloquist, Dennis Kucinich of Ohio. He told *Meet the Press* (February 23, 2003), "I think there may be a point that if Saddam Hussein continues to be noncooperative, the world community has to make a decision." Kucinich is a caricature but it should be obvious how dangerous someone who thinks like him would be in the White House—someone who needs to check with the "world community" before doing the right thing for American security. For the Kucinich types, it's perfectly fine send American soldiers to fight and die for the "security of the world" (or in a place like Liberia), but not when we make decisions on our own about *our* security.

## SELLING THE GLOBALONEY LINE

Internationalist elites have their own "think-tanks" and lobbying outfits, including the Washington-based World Federalist Association. The organization has high-power elite backers who take "world federalism" very seriously—people such as Walter Cronkite, Kurt Vonnegut, and Joan Baez. Way back when, Albert Einstein was a supporter. "Antiwar" bores Martin Sheen and Mike Farrell serve on its National Board of Advisors and help sell a global elite agenda.

According to the WFA's Statement of Goals and Beliefs (the italics are mine):

- "The nations of today need to transform the present weak United Nations system into—or replace it with—a *truly effective global institution* or family of institutions having the authority to maintain world peace...and the capacity to promote a more just world society."
- "As steps toward achieving our goal, World Federalists support efforts...to hold a convention to draft *a world federal constitution*, and also efforts to create new global institutions."
- "We also seek to gain acceptance of the concept that each individual is a *citizen of the world as well as a citizen of his or her own city, state, and nation.*"
- "We believe that a *world federation should be given adequate powers* to...deal with those other urgent global problems that clearly are not manageable by nations acting separately in an ungoverned world. Those problems include air and sea piracy, terrorism, slavery, weapons proliferation, narcotics trade, money laundering, and pollution that crosses national boundaries." In other words, the world federation could poke its nose into almost any issue it cared about.
- "A world federation would have jurisdiction over non-national

areas: the oceans, the polar regions, and outer space and would operate transitional authorities to oversee the recovery and democratization of failed political units whose people have been unable to govern themselves." In other words, the world federation could take over any "failed political unit" not strong enough to fend it off.

- "Such a federation must have limited but adequate sources of revenue." And you think the IRS is bad news.
- "It must be able to establish a world peacekeeping force which would replace national military establishments capable of conducting international war." In other words, the world federation would have a stronger military force than the United States. But don't worry, because we are assured that the world federation would be subject to a "federal Bill of Rights."[1]

You don't need to be a member of the "UN Black Helicopter" crowd to be left shaking your head in either shock or amazement (or both) at these bald statements. Remember, just because it sounds funny doesn't mean it's a joke. Stupid ideas have a way of turning into bad policy, especially when the elites get involved.

If you think the UN wastes money and resources, imagine what this "new and improved" world bureaucracy would cost us. If you think the UN runs roughshod over American interests and values, just imagine how the WFA would trample all over us. Then there's the small matter of preserving our national sovereignty, laws, and Constitution. The elites in the WFA think we can scrap 'em all.

Marguerite Peeters, who has exhaustively chronicled the rise of "the movement for global governance" in her paper *Hijacking Democracy: The Power Shift to the Unelected*, says it is "already well underway." "Its norms and standards are neither marginal nor reversible: they already affect us all. Even as this movement gathers momentum, its course has been set and its concepts have matured. Scholarship of a high intellectual caliber supports the movement. That scholarship, in turn, has energized recent reforms and current attempts to strengthen the UN, which are identified clearly with the values and principles of the global governance movement."[2]

## WHO'S PULLING THE STRINGS?

By itself, however, the UN and its elite champions cannot achieve the elite goal of global governance. At the end of the day, the UN is still a talking shop. It lacks democratic accountability, territorial responsibilities, independent financial resources, and any way of enforcing its will. But the UN is not alone—we must also contend with the *agents* and *tools* of UN globalism. I'm talking about nongovernmental organizations (NGOs), nascent international institutions, and "special conferences" aimed at controlling the way we live.

NGOs are nonprofit, voluntary citizens' groups organized on a local, national, or international level. Outfits like Amnesty International, Human Rights Watch, Women's Environment and Development Organization, the Earth Council, Greenpeace, and the International Planned Parenthood Federation seem like cuddly charitable organizations to many Americans. But in fact many of them seek to demolish American sovereignty, erode our independence of action, interfere in our domestic affairs, and denigrate our values and traditions. Unfortunately, these groups have already made deep inroads into American life. Since the end of the Cold War, the influence of NGOs has skyrocketed. In the past decade alone, the number of NGOs worldwide has exploded from 6,000 to *26,000*.

For those of you who have access to the Internet, and who can steel yourselves for a shock, check out this http://www.unhchr.ch/html/racism/05-ngolist.html. What is it? It is a list of NGOs "accredited" to attend the disastrous World Conference against racism, racial discrimination, xenophobia and related intolerance held at

Durban, South Africa, in the summer of 2001. (You might remember the Durban Conference as being an exercise in racism, racial discrimination, xenophobia, and related intolerance—in which case, you'd be remembering right.) There are *thousands*—I stopped counting at 200, which is roughly the number of NGOs whose name begins with the letter "A." Keep in mind that this list only includes *accredited* NGOs; there is a whole separate list for NGOs with "consultative status." No doubt some of these are legitimate organizations, like B'nai B'rith or the Helsinki Committee. But the NGO list also includes the absurd agendas of—to take some random examples—the International Association of Peace Messenger Cities ("devoted to creating an active culture of peace within cities around the world"), the Multicultural Council of Saskatchewan ("organizations and individuals dedicated and committed to enhancing the multicultural reality of Saskatchewan"), and the New York–based Third Wave Foundation (which, among other things, runs an "education campaign" called I SPY SEXISM that encourages activists to send postcards to general-interest magazines that don't carry enough stories about "women/people of color/lesbian and gay people" for the Third Wave's tastes).

It's true that many NGOs do a great deal of good. NGO staffs volunteer for dangerous jobs in war zones and provide aid for those subsisting in impoverished nations. Some do not fall into the anti-American trap. Despite all the positives, however, there is huge potential for abuse and manipulation inherent in the system. Those employed by the big international NGOs can be suspected of having a conflict of interest: are they loyal to their country of origin or to the cause of globalism?

By their very nature, NGOs are *nongovernmental*, which means they do not identify with the policies of any government, though many of them gladly accept financial patronage from them. Neither are they accountable to any government, let alone answerable to a democratic electorate, as Western governments are. In fact, NGOs owe their allegiance to no one but themselves and their friends at the UN. And although it is rarely noted, nearly all of them, and certainly the larger ones, are profoundly left-wing groups that regularly shill for the UN.

How does the NGO-UN axis against independent nation-states work? NGOs lock themselves into a UN bear hug by gaining "UN accreditation" for international conferences and summits. For instance, when former UN Secretary-General Boutros Boutros Ghali declared that NGOs' participation in UN activities was a "guarantee of the latter's political legitimacy," he was echoed by NGOs rushing to fulfill the UN's criteria for accreditation. These are:

- "Share the ideals of the UN."
- "Have a demonstrated interest in United Nations issues and proven ability to reach . . . educators, media representatives, policy makers and the business community."
- "Have the commitment and means to conduct effective information programs about United Nations activities through publication of newsletters, bulletins, backgrounders and pamphlets; organization of conferences, seminars and round tables; and enlisting the cooperation of print and broadcast media."[3]

In other words, if you oppose giving more power to the UN, don't bother asking for accreditation.


## DEFINITION OF HELL: THOUSANDS OF MINI–UNITED NATIONS

As these quotes prove, NGOs do have their own private agendas— they just so happened to almost always coincide perfectly with the cause of UN globalism. For instance, at the UN International Conference on Population and Development in Cairo in 1994, the committee chairman drafting the conference declaration just happened to be the president of International Planned Parenthood. It was a fix, in other words, and effectively cut out any pro-life principles advanced by the other side.

The vaunted "independence" of many NGOs is merely a moralizing cover for their anti-American activities. NGOs derive their legitimacy by insisting that they act for the "good of us all" or "in the public interest," even as they refuse to submit their policies to public accountability at the ballot box in any country. This assumption that they are too high-minded and moral for any democratic supervision whatsoever is elitism at its most abhorrent.

# By Any Means Necessary

The NGOs are the UN's agents and tools. They assume a variety of forms, each of which is designed to rip power away from the American people and hand it to the internationalist elites. Let's look at how the NGO-UN axis works:

1. Collect a gang of UN bureaucrats and elite NGO activists together in a "special commission."

2. Think of an issue that you intend to use to undermine and humiliate America—let's say "children's rights." (Don't laugh: UN committees are examining legislation that will give minors the right to privacy, even at home; the right to professional counseling without parental consent; the right to abortion; the right to full expression at home and at school, including the right to receive all information (e.g., pornography); the right to challenge their parents in court.)

3. Organize a conference in a pleasant resort. Make sure that a high-ranking representative of every government attends, as well as about 17,000 NGO delegates.

4. Use your friends in the elite media to "report" that President Bush has decided not to attend. Ask them to take the opportunity to bash Bush for being in favor of child slavery.

Now let's go to a real-life example like the International Criminal Court (ICC).

## STAR CHAMBER AT THE INTERNATIONAL CRIMINAL COURT

President Bush's refusal to join the International Criminal Court (ICC) is cited by the elites as Exhibit A to prove America's unyielding "unilateralism." But any honest assessment of the ICC reveals its mission is not to advance and safeguard human rights but to

Provide the press with dossiers "proving" that in capitalist, imperialist America child labor and child abuse have reached "epidemic proportions."

5. At the conference, don't forget to put representatives of the worst offenders in charge of the various committees discussing aspects of "children's rights."

6. Ensure that any NGO with any kind of grievance against America is allowed to exploit the issue of "children's rights" and turn it into an anti-American orgy of hate against this country. Ban or impede NGOs that are not inherently anti-American.

7. Remind the media to quote only spokesmen for anti-American NGOs.

8. At the end of the conference, issue a rabidly anti-American, anti-Western "communiqué" that world leaders must sign or face the wrath of the NGOs.

9. And last, from now on, treat the communiqué as "international law." Always remember to highlight the fact that America is "violating international law and unilaterally ignoring the world community" by not signing it. ■

take power away from sovereign states. In fact, its founding treaty, the 1998 Rome Statute, claims jurisdiction over the citizens of nonparty states (like the United States). That means that American soldiers, or the American president, can be charged with alleged war crimes and crimes against humanity. Do you trust the French, Belgians and other countries to judge Americans fairly in such a trial? Do you even trust them to enforce to the rule of law (or should we say "world law"), and not trump up new charges as they see fit? A president who would sign on to the ICC would be acting not in America's interest, but in the interests of an indignant, anti-American elite.

Geoffrey Robertson, an über-elite European lawyer, has openly proposed that "the law of war may come to resemble the law of tort, with combatants liable to be sued for negligence if they miss their approved military target." Some war crime! The ICC is nothing more than a forum for politically inspired allegations by our enemies. But don't hold your breath waiting for Fidel Castro or Kim Jong Il to be hauled off to The Hague anytime soon.

And on what possible grounds can the ICC claim the right to sit in judgment on Americans? It lacks any democratic accountability to this people or country. It is a permanent, supranational court based on non-American legal practices that can try our elected officials if they do not conform to "codes" of behavior by an elite class that is openly contemptuous of this country. With a stroke, the ICC would erase the American tradition of self-government and popular sovereignty if the elites get their way. To the elites, this is the whole point of the exercise. Let us hear from Mr. Robertson again: "The movement for global justice has been a struggle against sovereignty."

The ICC violates our Constitution, but to the elites, the Constitution violates the principles of a "just world." They don't care that the Bill of Rights' guarantees are not observed by the ICC in its deliberations and actions. The ICC also challenges the Declaration of Independence, one of the cornerstones of the Republic. In the Declaration, the reasons we rebelled are laid out. Three of them are:

- Britain subjected Americans "to a jurisdiction foreign to our constitution and unacknowledged by our laws."
- Britain had "depriv[ed] us, in many cases, of the benefits of Trial by Jury."
- Britain had "transport[ed] us beyond [the] Seas to be tried for pretended offences."

The ICC strikes out on all three of these. Under an ICC regime, Americans could be transported to The Hague for "pretended offences" and barred from being tried by a jury of their peers in a "jurisdiction foreign to our constitution and unacknowledged by our laws." In every respect, the ICC strikes at the heart of our traditions. Which is why the elites worship it.

## FROM OUR COLD DEAD HANDS

Another disguised attempt to extend elite internationalist power into American life was the UN's Conference on the Illicit Trade in Small Arms and Light Weapons in All Its Aspects, held in July 2001 (with a follow-up scheduled for 2006, along with biennial reviews in the meantime). These types of UN conferences are a cover for the very worst kind of elite manipulation to ram through anti-American policies.

Regarding the trade in illicit small arms, we are all in favor of banning it, and rightly so. Smuggling illegal weapons to guerrillas and terrorists is like selling Glocks to drug dealers in Los Angeles and New York. But just as we already have dozens of tough gun control laws, America already has the strictest export controls on guns in the world. Laws and export controls need to be enforced to be effective. So the conference should have focused on tightening up controls around the world. The problem is, the UN conference wasn't interested in stopping just the "illicit" trade: attendees (from both the UN and from 170-plus NGOs like Human Rights Watch, Worldwatch, the Federation of American Scientists, and the International Action Network on Small Arms) quickly turned it into a venomous attack on *legal* gun ownership in America.

Small wonder that our own elite gun controllers leapt onto the bandwagon. Some outfit called the Eminent Persons Group (if they do say so themselves), which includes such luminaries as Senator Dianne Feinstein and former Secretary of Defense Robert McNamara, declared their support for heavy restrictions on private ownership. These Eminent Persons were joined by Eminent Dictatorships like Cuba, Syria, and Zimbabwe, who also called for outlawing gun ownership. Too bad they didn't also call for outlawing terrorism and stopping repression.

As always, the UN, dictatorships, and internationalist elites walk hand in hand. The UN delegate from Ireland announced that "all states must suppress private ownership of small arms and light weapons." To antigun advocates, the mere ownership of a gun implies latent criminality. Rey Pagtakhan, a Canadian secretary of state, said that "the excessive and destabilizing accumulation and uncontrolled spread of small arms" in private hands leads to violence.

In fact, the UN based the entire conference on that premise. According to its own draft protocol, the UN believes in "tighter control over their [firearms and ammunition] legal transfer," more closely regulating "civilian possession," and "enhancing accountability, transparency and the exchange of information at the national, regional and global levels." In other words, a global database of your gun collection, owned and operated by the UN.

But for once, instead of lying back and doing what the elites tell us to do, America fought back. And we torpedoed the elites on gun control—at least temporarily. Undersecretary of State John Bolton laid down the bottom line. "The United States will not join consensus on a final document that contains measures abrogating the constitutional right to bear arms." He also pointed out that the UN was meddling in our domestic affairs: the U.S. "believes that the responsible use of firearms is a legitimate aspect of national life." And further, "We do not support the promotion of international advocacy activity by international or nongovernmental organizations," adding, "particularly when those political and policy views advocated are not consistent with the views of all member states." Bob Barr, the Georgia Republican legislator, backed up Bolton: "The UN Conference is an effort by its many liberal members to accomplish through the international arena what they and other gun-control advocates have been unable to achieve domestically: expanded registration and control of lawful, non-military firearms. If these nations are serious about combating illegal firearms trafficking, they should strengthen their export laws to parallel those of the United States, instead of attacking our nation's Second Amendment rights."

The NGOs and UN junkies were taken aback, so accustomed were they to getting their own way. In the horrified words of Tamar Gabelnick of the leftist, antigun Federation of American Scientists in Washington, "the United States wanted qualifications for, or exceptions to, calls to action, deletions of requests for financial support of conference initiatives, and a limited role for the United Nations in follow-up activities." Imagine that! American officials standing up for America. Shocking. Who woulda thought?

In the end, the UN blinked. The draft document from the conference proposed ways to curb illegal trafficking while protecting the Second Amendment. That's how it should be done. But sadly, it's all too rare to see us standing up against the elites. And we can only wonder at what sort of a treaty President Kerry, or President Dean, or President Kucinich would have agreed to.

## WHO'S THE BOSS?

Infatuation with the UN is so embedded in their souls that the elites can't grasp the idea— believe it or not—that countries ran their own affairs for many centuries before the UN was invented in 1945. America, for example, was founded on the very premise that a foreign body (the British Parliament) did not have the right to make laws interfering in the domestic affairs of the North American colonies. Our argument was that since we were not represented in the British Parliament, parliamentarians had no authority over here. To this day, we believe—in the words of the Declaration of Independence—that governments "derive their just powers from the consent of the governed."

As Americans, we looked to no one else but ourselves to defend our borders, fight our battles, make our laws, and decide domestic policy. America is an independent entity. When the elites criticize our hardheaded independence and call it "obsolete" or "isolationist," we should retort that it is they who are willing to toss out the American traditions and principles, which have kept us on the winning side of history, in favor of the whims and personal preferences of an unelected gang of Euro-elites and UN bureaucrats.

That's not to say that Americans work alone and ignore the world around us. We never have and we never will. Ask the citizens of Paris or Berlin who stood with them when they fell under the long shadow of tyranny. Americans are not isolationists—that term is nothing more than a bogeyman the elites drag out when they get backed into a corner. Instead, we are American exceptionalists who oppose the elite's unthinking "multilateralism" in the name of some airheaded "globalism." After all, who was being multilateralist on North Korea? Bush, who urged North Korea's regional neighbors—South Korea, Japan, Russia, and China—to urge Pyongyang to back down and stop its nuclear games-playing. Or the elites who savaged Bush for not immediately agreeing to talks with Kim Jong Il?

Americans have long been willing to form alliances, cooperate with other countries, intervene in foreign wars, and create international institutions when circumstances and our national interest require it. For instance, it was FDR who coined the phrase "United Nations" during World War II. It was first used in the "Declaration by United Nations" [*sic*—not *the* United Nations!] on January 1, 1942, when twenty-six countries asserted that "complete victory over their enemies is essential to defend life, liberty, independence and religious freedom, and to preserve human rights and justice in their own lands as well as in other lands, and that they are now engaged in a common struggle against savage and brutal forces seeking to subjugate the world."

Later, we helped create NATO, which was a voluntary association of like-minded Western liberal democracies pledged to defend each other against Soviet attack. The operative word in the "coalition of the willing" that fought in Iraq is "willing." We didn't strong-arm anyone to join, and many countries proved themselves unwilling (and unworthy, in the case of France). In other words, it is possible to act multilaterally while not acting as the UN's lackey, but the elites can't get their head around that.

It all comes down to a difference in trust. We, the people, put our trust in God; the elites trust in Kofi Annan. We think we can choose our own elected government to run the country and conduct foreign policy; *they* think the unelected membership of the UN should be running our country as part of a world government. That's the crucial difference between the elites and us when it comes to the UN.

An entire book could be written just about what the UN does badly. The elites have never come to grips with the fact that the UN is, rightly, toothless. Sometimes their blind love leads to self-deception. Timothy Wirth, a former Democrat senator from Colorado and now president of the United Nations Foundation, actually wrote this: "Outside Iraq, we will need the UN to continue and win the war on terrorism." No, it is the military forces and intelligence services of the allied powers that will win the war on terrorism. The UN is part of the problem. Every terrorist state in the world is not only represented there but is treated as the moral equivalent of democratic nations such as the United States and its allies.

Wirth also wants "the United Nations to respond in future crises" and "maintain the peace by setting the foundation for the rule of law, democracy and civilian control of government." Like other members of the elite, he seems oblivious to the fact that the UN's "response" to the Iraq crisis was to do nothing, and that it was happy to allow Saddam and his thugs to maintain "control of government."

When it comes to "setting foundations," the UN's track record is nothing to brag about, especially under the disastrous leadership of Kofi Annan, a man who wants his own private UN army. Annan was given the post of secretary-general in 1997 and he hasn't enjoyed any success yet. But the elites still love him as a counterweight to the United States and as a sophisticated ditherer in the name of diplomacy. Look at what happened in Rwanda when Annan was undersecretary-general in charge of peacekeeping back in 1994. Annan refused to do anything about the impending massacre there, despite being warned by UN representatives in Rwanda that the Hutus were about to attack the Tutsis. Some 800,000 Tutsis were ultimately killed. (This genocide wasn't entirely Annan's fault, of course. Bill Clinton ordered the State Department never to use the word "genocide" publicly and told Madeleine Albright, then our UN ambassador, to block any action being taken to stop the "nongenocide.")

Four years later, Annan was still banging the drum about the "illegal" use of force by NATO to push the Serbs out of Kosovo. If we hadn't taken the initiative, precisely nothing would have been done, and today Slobodan Milosevic would still be in power. Three months *after* the end of the Kosovo war, Annan was *still* bleating that "the greatest threat to the future of international order is the use of force in the absence of a Security Council mandate."

## SECRETARY GENERAL TODAY, PRESIDENT OF THE WORLD TOMORROW

You'd think that Annan might have learned from his mistakes—but no. It was he who thought that Saddam was "a man we can do business with" and then undermined the UN weapons inspections team, UNSCOM, by cutting a deal with him in 1998. And what was the deal? That Saddam's "presidential palaces" would be off-limits to inspectors. Saddam could certainly do business with Kofi Annan, but it is hard to see what those opposed to the proliferation of weapons of mass destruction got out of the deal. And when the United States and Great Britain said that our coalition of the willing would enforce the teeth of binding United Nations resolutions against Saddam Hussein's weapons programs, Annan thoughtfully warned us that if Bush "launch[es] action without the support of the Council, the legitimacy of this action will be widely questioned and it will not obtain the political support required to ensure its success in the long term, once the military phase is over." In other words, the enforcement of UN resolutions violates the UN Charter. In an attempt to undermine the allied coalition from acting decisively to *uphold* Resolution 1441, Annan then encouraged the chief weapons inspector, Hans Blix, to grandstand on the world stage and act as if Iraq was actually "cooperating" with the UN. Annan was doing the anti-American hustle by giving verbal ammunition to our rivals on the Security Council who blithely ignored seventeen of their own resolutions ordering Iraq to get rid of its illegal munitions.

In collaboration with the French and the Russians, Annan lobbied for the UN to take over postwar Iraq, despite the UN's abysmal record in building democracy. As the French foreign minister, Dominique de Villepin, put it, "The UN must steer the process and must be at the heart of the reconstruction and administration of Iraq." Kofi and his elite UN friends think of it as a way of teaching us a lesson for launching our "illegitimate" war. The

French and the Russians—*especially* the French—think of it as a way of undermining America's success. Even with all the difficulties the U.S. faces in Iraq, it was right not to turn the keys over to Kofi. Just what Iraq needed—to go from life under a repressive dictator to life under a repressive international bureaucracy.

But as much as the UN would like to hold itself out as a moral arbiter and champion of oppressed peoples everywhere, its record on advancing freedom, democracy, and human rights is rather pitiful. It has played almost no role in the dozens of democratic transitions that former dictatorships have undergone over the last twenty years. These occurred *in spite of*, not because of, the UN.

Though you never hear this from the elites, *we* can take a huge amount of credit for helping countries oust their repressive regimes and become functioning democracies. Non-UN, American-funded institutions like the U.S. Agency for International Development and the National Endowment for Democracy have worked alongside freedom-minded groups and movements in these dictatorships to liberate enslaved peoples. If that's unilateralism, then we need more of it.

# The UN Scam Continues

From the Inmates Running the Asylum Department: In January 2003, at the height of the Iraq crisis at the UN, Iraq was still on schedule to chair the UN-established Conference on Disarmament, a body that reports to the General Assembly. It touts itself as "the single multilateral disarmament negotiating forum of the international community." When queried by reporters, UN officials said Iraq's chairmanship was a procedural matter. The chair rotates in strictly alphabetical order, so every country gets to have a turn—and it happened it was Iraq's turn. ■

If you doubt this, compare our actions after the fall of the Iron Curtain, and our work in Africa and South America, with the behavior of the UN during the Iraq crisis. Egged on by the elites, France and Russia despicably used the UN to further their own sordid ends. President Bush was right in not rewarding them after the U.S. and its willing partners committed hundreds of thousands of troops and after hard working Americans contributed billions of their tax dollars.

Bush pledged that the UN will play a "vital role" in Iraq. Fine. But that "vital role" does not mean establishing an interim government and setting Iraq on the path of democratic progress. That is eventually for the Iraqis themselves to do, with our help. Bush wisely wants the UN to play to its strengths, which means throwing all its politicized baggage overboard and doing what it does best—organizing and providing humanitarian aid through UNICEF and the World Food Program.

## THE UN'S SKELETONS IN THE CLOSET

The UN's anti-American bias is nothing new. George W. Bush didn't trigger it, contrary to what a lot of the elites claim. For the most part, it's less of a global forum and more of a bully pulpit for anyone with a grievance, real or imagined. In the 1960s and 1970s, the UN was so crammed with Arab, Latin American, and Third World stooges of the Soviet Empire, it effectively turned into a mouthpiece of the Kremlin and a haven for terrorists.

Back in 1974 the world witnessed a classic UN moment when Yasser Arafat showed up to address the UN General Assembly. He arrived in full guerilla warfare garb—wearing a holster at his hip (he had to leave the gun outside). Accompanying him as bodyguard was Ali Hassan Salameh, the commander of Force 17 and operations chief of Black September, the group that perpetrated the 1972 Munich Olympics massacre. Arafat of course received a standing ovation from the "diplomats" after his speech extolling violent "revolutionary" warfare against "oppressors."

To his eternal credit, the late Democrat senator Daniel Patrick Moynihan, who was appointed to the post of UN ambassador in 1975 (soon after Arafat's appearance), waged a ceaseless war inside and outside the UN chambers in defense of liberal democracy and American values. He refused to apologize for America's success, and defended us and our allies. After the UN's infamous Zionism-is-racism resolution (manufactured by the Third World, Arab, and Soviet blocs), Moynihan denounced it in the harshest of terms. He saw in it the seeds of anti-Americanism. In a New York speech, he said it was part of "a general assault by the majority of the nations in the world on the principles of liberal democracy." His strong words and countercharges against the dictators and tyrants manipulating the UN made him a hero. *Time* cited a poll that found that 70 percent of Americans wanted him to continue on the offensive, even if he had to be "undiplomatic" about it (as usual, the State Department was having conniptions at the effects Moynihan's words were having).

Sadly, Moynihan's influence was not permanent. Even now that our Soviet friends have disappeared, their former clients still spend their time bashing America and scoring points. (Though of course they keep demanding that we pay the lion's share of the budget.)

## HUMAN RIGHTS? NO. AMERICA-BASHING? YES.

One of the UN's many failings is that apart from the five permanent members of the Security Council, it treats every country equally, no matter how abusive, corrupt, or murderous they are. Rather than sidelining some of the worst regimes in the world, the UN refrains from expressing "judgment" and arranges for them all to chair various commissions "in strict alphabetical order." One of the reasons America gets so little respect at the UN is because its commitment to human rights, democracy, and the rule of law is a *rarity* at the UN. There are so many nondemocratic governments represented at the UN that they can gang up on us. Fewer than half of the 191 governments represented at the UN are "liberal democracies." One of our big problems is that while Western democracies are powerful countries, they rarely work together (see "France"), while the nondemocracies frequently collaborate to ram their agendas through.

So what has happened at the travesty known as the UN Human Rights Commission should really come as no surprise. The anti-American malcontents on the Commission stuck it to the Americans a few years back when they tossed the U.S. off the Commission in a secret ballot. (We were also thrown off the UN's International Narcotics Control Board.) Rather than heap scorn on the cheap maneauver by the Commission, the elites were nearly unanimous that it was all *Bush's* fault. It was Bush's America that wanted to insert anti-abortion provisions into proposed UN declarations, wanted out of the obsolete 1972 Anti-Missile Defense Treaty (ABM), wanted to reform the UN's AIDS policy in Africa so it reflected reality, wanted to keep land mines in South Korea (to prevent a North Korean invasion), wanted to ensure that the ICC couldn't frivolously try American "war criminals" (like Bush, for example), and wanted a level playing field for implementation of the Kyoto Treaty. Yet again, American "unilateralism" had apparently caused a massive backlash.

This is poppycock. There are fifty-four members of the Economic and Social Council (ECOSOC) who vote to nominate which countries will serve on the Human Rights Commission, where we've played an active role since it was established in 1947 (Eleanor Roosevelt chaired it). Of these, forty-three had promised in writing to back America's candidacy, but mysteriously, only twenty-nine voted for us. In other words, somebody fixed the election from the inside.

Then came the final insult to us, and the frosting on the cake for the elites—at the same time we were voted off, Sudan—one of the most egregious human rights abusers on earth—was elected. This is the same "Human Rights" Commission that allows China, Cuba, Zimbabwe, Saudi Arabia, Libya, Syria, Vietnam, Sierra Leone, Uganda, and Algeria to serve on it, no questions asked. Today, about two dozen of the commission's members are seriously repressive regimes. (Cuba, for instance, recently sentenced seventy-five political dissidents to jail terms of up to twenty-seven years.) If anything, the trend *away* from the democratic countries on the Human Rights Commission has grown stronger in recent years. Today, human rights groups like Christian Solidarity International, Freedom House, the International Organization of Human Rights, and PEN International find themselves constantly harassed by ECOSOC and the Human Rights Commission.

Not surprisingly, many of the countries on the so-called Human Rights Commission don't like America's full-throated criticisms of their dismal human rights records. We devote more resources to investigating and exposing human rights abuses around the world than any other country. Each year the State Department releases a blistering report describing exactly what we've found, and we keep up the pressure through the U.S. Commission on Religious Freedom and the Commission on Security and Cooperation in Europe.

So the Human Rights Commission and our other fair-weather friends, like the French (who were also re-elected to the Commission with a huge fifty-two out of fifty-four votes), got together and "taught us a lesson." The French—as usual—dug the knife in a little deeper. According to a *New York Times* report, the French ambassador, Jean-David Levitte, "attributed the overwhelming vote for France to its policy of approaching human rights issues with cooperation and dialogue rather than confrontation, a system he said worked well with China." Yes, I'm sure it did—just ask all those Chinese people enjoying their human rights. When France uses words like "dialogue" to distinguish itself from the American tradition of "confronting" human rights violators, you can be sure that China and Cuba approve of the French approach. After all, if you were Castro, would you rather have America or France sitting next to you on the Human Rights Commission?

In the same week that we were ousted from the Human Rights Commission, Herbert Okun, the American candidate for reelection to the International Narcotics Control Board, was defeated. Again, the members of ECOSOC got together to stick it to America. And again, France found favor in their eyes.

Earlier this year, things only got worse with the Human Rights Commission, even though we managed to get back on board after furious negotiations by the Bush administration. Proving that the humiliation in 2001 was not a fluke but was a deliberate piece of anti-American trickery, the commission decided to elect Libya—Libya!—as chairman. Libya, a police state, has one of the world's most appalling human rights records and is strongly suspected of being behind the bombing of Pan Am Flight 103 over Lockerbie in Scotland in 1988. But it has one saving grace: it's violently anti-American, which appears to be all that counts at the UN.

## TAMING THE UN BEAST

Now the instinct among many conservatives is to simply quit the UN and send all those stuck-up elite diplomats living on the East Side of Manhattan packing. As tempting as that is (and humorous to contemplate—after all, what would they do without all those lunches at the Four Seasons?), it is unrealistic and unwise. For all its horrid faults, the UN does a lot of helpful things internationally—like organizing humanitarian aid and food packages. It manages to do good in setting up hospitals, sending observers to monitor democratic elections, overseeing AIDS prevention, and eradicating diseases. It's good at promoting literacy in poor countries. Amazingly, it's even getting a *little* better at not wasting as much money as it used to.

Even if we did pull out, the UN wouldn't disappear. Ignoring a bad odor doesn't make it go away. In the UN's case, it would get even worse without us looking over its shoulder and paying the bills. The UN would become *more* anti-American, *more* radical, *more* dedicated to world government if we couldn't keep our eye on it. At the moment, at least, we can exert some control over the insanity that goes on in the UN's committees and commissions. Without us there, the lunatics would take over the asylum. At the moment, at least

Some of my listeners wrote in to suggested alternative uses for the UN building in New York City. Here are a select few:

1. Turn it into a livestock yard. After all, it's so full of crap already, what's a little more?

2. Turn it into a mental hospital. Half the patients are already there.

3. Transform it into the Mother of All Anti-Terror command posts. It would be the first time that building was ever used to solve problems instead of create them.

4. Level the building! Too much bad, anti-American karma to overcome. ∎

there's a warden around. Should we care? Yes. What the UN does affects us, even if we're absent from the room. We could find, for example, that a "UN Army" is established, which would be deployed in opposition to American forces around the world.

Withdrawal is not a realistic option. What we should do instead is reform the UN from top to bottom. Believe it or not, we can achieve this. (Of course we can, we're America.)

The first thing to do is to take a long, hard look at the UN Security Council, which has five permanent members (America, Britain, Russia, China, and France). On the one hand, the Security Council helps America because, by threatening or using a veto, we can stop the UN from interfering in *our* business. The last thing we want is for France, China, and Russia to outvote us and approve putting, for instance, a UN "peacekeeping" force on the U.S.-Mexico border. In addition, if the Security Council works together, the five members can quickly decide on military intervention where it's really needed. To stop another massacre in Rwanda, for example, the Security Council can cooperate and approve a force consisting of soldiers drawn from mostly African nations.

On the other hand, certain countries (e.g., France) can abuse the veto system to try to prevent America and its allies from taking decisive action to defend their interests. The best example here is the Iraq war, which France attempted to torpedo for no reasons apart from pure anti-Americanism.

So what should we do? We have two options. We can propose enlarging the Security Council to include other great powers, like India (whose population grows more in a week than the entire European Union does each year) and Japan. Or perhaps drop older members in favor of new ones. As it is, the Security Council reflects the position of the world in 1945, not 2003. After all, why on earth is France still there? And let's face it, Russia is not a superpower anymore.

Since Britain and France are both members of the European Union, wouldn't it make more sense to combine their places and just have one "European Union" seat? Or perhaps allow Britain to keep its seat, but ask that France—as a proud member of Old Europe—share hers with Belgium and Germany?

Unfortunately, this option is simply not viable. Dropping France would be immensely satisfying. Just seeing the panicked expression on Chirac's face would be worth all the trouble it would cause. But unfortunately, it's pretty unrealistic. France would destroy the Security Council before it relinquished its seat. And she could count on Russia to back her up, because Moscow might suspect it would be next. China would instantly veto Japan or India from getting on (Beijing's terrified of the competition) and we could end up with a distinctly unfriendly "regional superpower" like Iran or Egypt being voted on board instead.

For the moment, there's another reason why we should be wary of enlarging or changing the council too much. At least we know the current members and what their views are. We can *usually* arrive at a compromise. But what is Japan's view of the Middle East or African peacekeeping? As it is, it's hard to get the existing members to agree on a common definition of what constitutes "terrorism," let alone getting everyone to agree unanimously that terrorism must be fought. Last, the more members on the council, the more difficult it will be to pass any resolutions at all without watering them down so much that they mean nothing.

So instead of enlarging it or withdrawing from it, we need to make the Security Council work more effectively. The biggest item on our agenda must be to stop paying lip service to the elite myth that the American president must do what the UN Security Council wants. If the French threaten us with a veto, then so be it. Let them veto—and destroy any authority the Security Council has left. No matter what the elites say, Paris cannot stop us from doing what is right because Chirac disapproves. In short, the UN Security Council does *not* decide whether America goes to war to protect our interests. It also doesn't decide whether France can intervene in her former colonies in Africa (and even if it did, France would ignore it). In other words, the council was not established to judge its members, which is what the elites mistakenly believe. The council exists for two main reasons:

1. Because all of its members are major powers and they all have interests around the world, it is inevitable that sometimes these interests will clash. The council can serve to defuse military tensions through diplomacy in secret session. During the Cold War, America and the USSR often fought their "battles" behind closed doors at the UN.
2. Because its five members have a shared interest in maintaining peace in the world, the Security Council can work together to prevent little wars from breaking out. Few dicta-

tors are as clever as Saddam Hussein, who exploited divisions within the council to get away with ignoring seventeen resolutions. Most other troublemakers are unwilling to face down the collective will of the Security Council, backed up by the threat of force if they do not mend their ways.

To make it work more effectively, we need to refocus the council on doing what it does best—overseeing peace and security throughout the world while allowing its members the freedom to act like Great Powers in their own spheres of influence. We must stop the elite drive to turn the Security Council into a kind of International Supreme Court that judges and condemns our actions. We must make it clear that we do not require its approval to use force to defend our interests and protect our citizenry.

The next thing to do is reform the General Assembly. When it began, the UN was an "equal opportunities" institution: any state could join and be treated equally, whether it was a fascist dictatorship, a Communist tyranny, an authoritarian monarchy, or a genuine democracy. I think those times should come to an end. We need to introduce a good-government element into the UN, as laid out in its own Millennium Declaration. That document stated that democratic government is the best way to advance human rights, but did not make it a condition of membership. Well, it ought to be.

We're sick of the elites helping out their buddies in Cuba and North Korea by allowing them equal status with the free, open states of the world, like Israel, Poland, or Australia. There's no reason why the Cuban or Libyan or Syrian "ambassadors" should be treated as the legitimate representatives of responsible, decent countries. They're the representatives of, and apologists for, regimes that practice murder, repression, and torture on an inhuman scale. They are an affront to civilization. We need to make a stand for democracy, liberty, and our way of life.

We should take our cue from the Organization of American States (OAS), which was established three years after the UN.

According to Chapter II, Article 3(d) of the OAS Charter, membership is restricted to countries "on the basis of the effective exercise of representative democracy." The OAS takes its charter seriously: Cuba was suspended from voting and participating in OAS activities in 1962.

We should create a new tier of constitutional democracies that will show up the General Assembly as an anti-American hangout for kleptomaniacs, psychopaths, and authoritarians. At the very least, we should stipulate that only democracies be allowed to sit on the Security Council as rotating members. We could even start up a "democracy caucus" dedicated to advancing democratic principles, upholding human rights and fighting terrorism. Is that such an impossible dream?

Thirdly, we need to reform the "special committees" and "special conferences" that are manipulated by dictatorships and leftist NGOs into denouncing America and our friends. The first thing we should do is turn the tables on them by encouraging more reasonable NGOs to participate in their activities. These pro-American NGOs would denounce the denouncers and expose them for the frauds and hypocrites they are.

A group based in Paris called Reporters Without Borders had the right idea. When the Libyan-chaired Human Rights Commission opened on March 17, hundreds of leaflets were dropped from the balconies overlooking the chamber. They read: "Disappearances, torture, arbitrary arrests, detention without charge, pervasive censorship. Libya... knows a thing about human rights violations."

At the same time, we should be loudly pointing out to the world that although these unelected, manipulative "special committees" *hold no power*, the elites treat them with more respect than they give to electoral democracies. It's the *respect* that lends these committees power and influence.

We need to highlight the globalist, anti-American agenda of the UN, which is exerted by means of the committees and through the conferences with the help of NGOs. Even in the face of international criticism from the elites and their acolytes, we need to stand firm and refuse to ratify these absurd declarations that impinge on our sovereignty. We should counter with proposals of our own: we will help any country that wants to adopt American-style practices, and offer aid and support for NGOs based in those countries that are not beholden to a radical globalist, anti-American agenda. Essentially, we need to offer smaller and less powerful countries and NGOs another option apart from the UN, which forces them to come into line or face cuts in funding and a torrent of abuse.

And last, we need to reorient the UN to what it does best: providing humanitarian aid where it is needed efficiently, effectively, and above all, *nonpolitically*. In recent decades, the internationalist elites who have taken over the UN and its agencies have forgotten their primary responsibilities. Instead, they've spent their time and their energy—and a lot of money—attacking America.

We need to take back the UN.

# 11

# Europe vs. the Cowboys

▶ The European Elites

n the past, Europeans emigrated here to escape the Old World. They wanted to leave behind its suffocating snobbery, hypocrisy, and arrogance, and experience freedom and openness for the first time. In America, it didn't matter what creed you held, what class you were born into or what country you came from. In America, you were expected to make your own way in the world and other people minded their own business.

Over here, the Frontier Spirit counted for something. America was—it still is—a culture that embraced risk-taking, direct action, and innovation. Americans adore rough-hewn heroes who stand up for their beliefs and possess a clear vision of what they want, and need, to do. We love mavericks. We're genetically disrespectful of authority, democratic by instinct, and entrepreneurial by choice.

On the other hand, Europe was hidebound and decrepit, subsisting on its fading glories, and envious of our advantages. Over there, the Ideal Man was an aristocratic "gentleman of leisure"; i.e., someone who doesn't need to work. Over here, Teddy Roosevelt was our hero. Theirs was Friedrich Nietszche.

From colonial times, America prided itself on the fact that it was *different* from Europe. We were established as a republic in a world of monarchies. Though we admired its cultural riches and shared many of its ideals, we regarded "Europe" as the very opposite of our pulsating, frenetically energetic nation.

The elites have other ideas. They're ashamed that we're different. They want us to be more like Europe and act less like Americans. They think we're crude and rude and behave like gun-toting cowboys—unlike those sophisticated Europeans, who "favor diplomacy over military solutions" and love the UN. They can't stand that we're Number One at pretty much everything we do. We're the richest, the strongest, the most technologically advanced; and we're the most confident country on the planet. We enjoy so much freedom that even if, as the ACLU loves to intone, "John Ashcroft erodes our freedoms with his religious police-state tactics," we'd *still* be the freest country on earth by a long shot. For regular Americans, these achievements are a matter for pride. We are an exceptional nation, and we're not embarrassed to say it.

But to the elites, being rich, successful, free, and happy are things to be *concerned* about. They suspect that we must have cheated to get ahead. They feel that others should judge our way of life, as if there was something shameful about our doing well by being different and standing by our own values of enterprise and freedom. To elites, American values are low-brow and passé. You know, all the frontier stuff about patriotism and faith and High Noon and apple pie and self-reliant rugged individualism is just so *American*.

Susan Sontag, the high priestess of elite Europhilia, summarized it in an interview with a Spanish newspaper, *La Vanguardia*, in December 2002. Asked "what is the America of Susan Sontag," she swooned: "My America is called Europe. It is my place of dreams." When the plucky interviewer interjected, "The United States has saved Europe several times, it's provided solutions..." the diva cut him off. "Today the United States isn't a solution, it's a danger! A world dominated by the United States would be horrible, and Bush's imperialism frightens me. I hope Europe will show us a road to follow." [1] Ah, Europe, this century's Shangri-La.

Elites have a kind of nervous tic that kicks in whenever the subject of American greatness comes up in conversation—especially when there are Euro-elites in the same room. You'll find American elites bemoaning the fact that they're American and assuring the Euros that not everybody here is like George W. Bush. As an expatriate malcontent named Gary LaMoshi wrote in the *Asia Times* (March 20, 2003): "For U.S. citizens living overseas, President George W. Bush's unilateral ultimatum to Iraq makes us all ugly Americans.... Now we are representatives of the world's leading bully. Our flag, which stood for the hopes of humankind now stands for disdain for diplomacy in favor of military intimidation."

I remember reading that just before Operation Iraqi Freedom was launched, there was some graffiti written in one of the army latrines in Kuwait that read: "If you'd voted for Gore, you wouldn't be here now." That anonymous vandal had perfectly satirized the collective Euro-Am elite view of the war. Gore is the kind of cosmopolitan that pseudo-intellectual, dovish, pro-abortion liberal elites on both sides of the Atlantic love. Ditto for Clinton and the rest of the Democrat presidential candidate clones. Bush is the Ugly American. It's as simple as that.

So we shouldn't be too astonished that the Euro-elites, who pride themselves on their "subtlety" and "intelligence," pour vitriol down on his head and ridicule his faith. Referring to a Bush speech laying out a clear moral line between right and wrong, Jörg Lau, a *Die Zeit* correspondent, opined: "I mean it was just so stupid, they [Americans] are always talking about good and evil, in quasi-religious terms, and it gives us a strange sense of relief. Bush is always showing himself to be utterly stupid." As for Bush's campaign against Iraq, the French newspaper *Liberation* haughtily wrote it off as "simply the old American cocktail of missionary zeal and crude realpolitik."

Or how about the attitude of Jacques Rupnik, who once served as an adviser to Jacques Chirac: "Americans are fond of saying, 'The world changed on September 11.' But what has changed is

# **Elite**speak **alert!**

The elites don't seem able to make up their minds about how stupid Bush is. It's usually taken for granted that (like all Republicans) he's a moron. But even when they're denigrating him, the elites believe that he's somehow also diabolically clever. The famous spy novelist, John le Carré, recently wrote a rabid hate-screed about Bush in *The Times* of London (a pro-Bush paper that printed it just to show everyone how hateful the elites' anti-Americanism has become). Le Carré talks about "Bush and his junta" and how they managed to obtain the White House fraudulently in 2000. Even now, he says, "the American public is not merely being misled. It is being browbeaten and kept in a state of ignorance and fear. The carefully orchestrated neurosis should carry Bush and his fellow conspirators nicely into the next election." If Bush has managed to pull the wool over our eyes for so long, then how can he be as "utterly stupid" as the elites think? So, which is it: genius or idiot? It's a trick question. There's no correct answer. For the elites, Bush-hating is synonymous with America-bashing. His intelligence doesn't matter.

What we *should* call into question is the intelligence of the elites. The fanatical Bush-basher, Mark Crispin Miller, a "professor of media ecology" (don't even ask what it is; it's not nuclear

America. The extraordinary moral self-righteousness of this Administration is quite surprising and staggering to Europeans."

Every poll and survey that has examined European attitudes post–September 11 has found that our "approval" rating has fallen. "Overwhelming majorities disapprove of President Bush's foreign policy, and the boost in ratings he enjoyed post–September 11 in Western Europe has dissipated," said Andrew Kohut, director of the Pew Research Center for the People and the Press. But notice physics) at New York University thinks the president is "illiterate, bone-ignorant and generally illogical." He wrote an entire book called *The Bush Dyslexicon*, which is devoted to attacking the "extraordinarily shrewd" Bush's "cabal, which was un-democratically installed and whose aims are wholly, dangerously anti-democratic." (Notice the typical elite inability to decide whether he's "shrewd" or "bone-ignorant.") On a British radio show, Miller loudly complained that Bush "only speaks gibberish when he tries to sound compassionate or idealistic or altruistic."

He then offered this reason why: "My favorite example of Bushspeak was his statement in New Hampshire: 'I know how hard it is to put food on your family,' which was a perfect example of Bush's difficulties in trying to convince an audience that he cares about the have-nots because he doesn't and because of his indifference and his failure to cover that up he can't say things like, I know how hard it is to put food on your family table. Whereas he's clear when he's speaking as a punisher, when he speaks vindictively or vengefully which I think helps explain his seeming transformation after 9/11...."

So it's *Bush* who "speaks gibberish"—and *not* the brilliantly incisive "professor of media ecology"? At least I could understand what Bush was saying. ∎

that all the criticism is ostensibly directed at Bush, not America. As Kohut added, "Western Europeans mostly see Bush as the problem, rather than America more generally." Not true. Bush is seen by the Euro-elites as a *symbol* of America.

Sometimes, the Euros use the codeword, "Texas," to disguise their anti-Americanism. Explaining why he disapproved of Bush, Hans-Ulrich Klose, the vice chairman of the Foreign Relations Committee in the German Parliament, said that "much of it is the way he talks, this provocative manner, the jabbing of his finger at you." In other words, "it's Texas, a culture that is unfamiliar to Germans. And it's the religious tenor of his arguments."

Often, this decline in our approval ratings is highlighted by the elite media as evidence that Bush must begin acting more like an urbane European and less like a "toxic Texan." Their theory is that if Bush starts taking his cue from the Swedes or the Belgians, our approval rating will rise. Sure, they'll like us as long as we become more like them! Talk about a raw deal. I'd rather be hated. And why should we be so concerned about how they view us? It would be one thing if they seemed the least bit worried about ticking us off, about how Americans view *them*. But they never care until after the fact—until their political or economic power-base is harmed. (Compare France's post- and pre-war attitude toward us.) Hey, France, I have an idea! Act more American and maybe we'll start vacationing in Paris again!

Basically, the Euros despise Bush because he acts exactly like an American president should by following his constitutional duty to safeguard the lives of American citizens. This is virtually guaranteed to tread on the Euro-elite's toes and put their noses out of joint, but so what? Our safety is more important than their comfort level. The elites merely use their "disapproval" of Bush as an excuse to attack America.

The Euro-elites are so desperate to pretend that they're only "anti-Bush" not "anti-American" that they rewrite history to prove their case. *Le Monde*, the virulently anti-American paper beloved of the French elites, went so far as to say that Reagan was a *good* president. Alain Frachon, who writes on foreign affairs for *Le Monde*, had the temerity to argue that Europeans had identified with Reagan. "When Reagan was President, we never had the impression he was motivated by fundamentalism. He was divorced. He had worked in Hollywood. But this George Bush is totally foreign to us. He quotes the Bible every two or three sentences. He is surrounded by Christian fundamentalists. There was a dose of charm, humor, of Hollywood to Reagan. But not to Bush. It's another world and one we find extraordinarily hypocritical. No one told us that the Republicans had moved this far to the right."

Wait a Munich minute. Did we imagine the gigantic "antiwar" marches in Western Europe during the 1980s? All those placards denouncing ("Ronnie RayGun") as a worse warmonger than Stalin? I can't remember any Euro-elite saying at the time, "Give Ronnie a break, he's divorced and worked in Hollywood!" This is taking revisionist history to new heights. The Euro-elites like Reagan as much as they liked Margaret Thatcher—not much.

Of course the Euro-elites and their expat American friends living amongst them grow positively misty-eyed whenever the name "Clinton" is mentioned. After all, Bill wasn't just our first black president—he was our first European president. He studied in Oxford, steered clear of the military, believed in projecting a sensitive type of American power, and loved the UN—and yes, he was even unfaithful to his wife! How French! Susan Neiman is an American who heads something called the "Einstein Forum" in Germany. Saint Bill, she swoons, "was the thinking person's American Dream. Alive, unpretentious, he played the sax. For seven years in Europe, it was suddenly unbelievably cool to be American. Bush, on the other hand, is the American nightmare: a spoiled frat boy who doesn't know or care about the rest of the world." You have to love that "thinking person" line. (If you just ate before reading the foregoing, accept my apologies.)

*Le Monde Diplomatique* is a foreign-affairs newspaper known for being even more left-wing and anti-American than its associated outlet, *Le Monde*. It too goes crazy for Clinton. Serge Halimi, its editor, wishes Bill were still in charge post-September 11. "The hostility to U.S. policy would be lessened with Clinton in the White House, even assuming that these policies were exactly the same as Bush's. Clinton's 'I feel your pain' worked well in the international arena too, much better in any case than Bush's 'I don't give a damn what you think.'"

Europe loves Bill because, like them, he's uncomfortable with America's superpower status. They hang on his every word because he says things like America should strengthen the UN and other "mechanisms of cooperation" because "we need to be creating a world that we would like to live in when we're not the biggest power on the block." Whereas most Americans would probably prefer that Bill Clinton just go away, the Euros just can't get enough of him. He was the keynote speaker at Britain's Labour party conference in October 2002 and the crowd could barely control itself. He played to the crowd with gems like: "We live in an interdependent world that is not yet an integrated global community," and "The UN is still becoming," and also we need to stand up against WMD but do so "in the context of building the international institutions that in the end we will have to depend upon to guarantee the peace and security of the world." Bravo!

He really had 'em wowed when he crassly took after the Republicans when discussing Iraq. "This is a delicate matter but I think this whole Iraq issue is made more difficult for some of you because of the differences you have with the conservatives in America over other matters," Clinton said. "[Matters like] the [international] criminal court and the Kyoto Treaty and the comprehensive test ban treaty. I don't agree with that." (When in office, Clinton did nothing to force a vote on Kyoto in Congress, ditto on the ICC.) The audience was mesmerized. So much for politics stopping at the shoreline.

Bush talks in terms of American interests, American sovereignty, American security, and the Euro-elites roll their eyes. Clinton refers to himself as an American *and* a "citizen of the world" and they sit in awe. (They even excused his love of McDonalds!) Bush symbolizes the "differentness" of America to Europe. He knows his mind and what's right. No politician in Europe would assert, as Bush did, that the United States has the "sovereign authority to use force in assuring its own national security." Euros prefer to hide in Kofi Annan's skirts, so scared are they of what they call "unilateral action."

They weren't always so wimpy. It wasn't so long ago that the Euros pioneered "gunboat diplomacy." In those days, if some brash dictator stepped out of line, the next morning he'd find the Royal Navy blasting away at his palaces. But in the last few decades, the Euro-elites have become so scared of their own shadows that they've lost the will to fight against bullies and gangsters. We're the can-do culture; they're the can't-face-doing crowd. Plus, as long as our people are willing to do all the heavy-lifting, why not free-ride on our strength and determination?

## WE LOVE THEIR CHEESE, THEY LOVE OUR CHEESEBURGERS

How exactly is America different from Europe? Let's start with their similarities. Leaving aside their congenitally anti-American elites, ordinary Europeans and Americans *like* each other.

When we express our irritation with the French—those "cheese-eating surrender monkeys," as Willie the Scottish groundskeeper from the *Simpsons* once put it—we're really criticizing the French elites, not the French people as a whole. It's the French elites and their leftist allies who espouse the virulent anti-Americanism we see in the streets of Paris. In 2002, for example, at the height of the "antiwar" hysteria, the Pew Research Center conducted a major poll in forty-four countries of "national attitudes" toward America. *Voila!* No fewer than 63 percent of the French said they have positive views of America. In Britain, the number was 75 percent and even in pacifist Germany it was 61 percent. Another poll conducted in Britain in November 2002 (by the respected MORI research foundation) found that 81 percent of Britons "like Americans as people." That's a figure even higher than during the Cold War. Yet the results of these polls hardly get an airing in the media, so obsessed are they with the "Europeans Dislike Americans" theme.

There are also surveys by the German Marshall Fund and the Chicago Council on Foreign Relations bearing out similar conclusions. For instance, the six Western European countries gave America 64 positive marks out of 100, which was more than they gave to France. Between two-thirds and three-quarters of Europeans backed "the U.S.-led war on terror," and we received universally high scores for our achievements in science, technology, and popular culture. We also share a broad belief in the virtues of democracy and the free market thanks to our common Western heritage.

None of this diminishes the deep differences between the Europeans and us. Many Europeans, for example, are repulsed by our "gun culture" and our "extreme" views on religion. We, in turn, cringe at the thought of paying $6 dollars a gallon for gas and being forced into a nationalized health care system. Yet one senses that regular Europeans, like regular Americans, basically take a "live and let live" attitude toward each other. Not so with the elites at home and abroad who are prone to bouts of uncontrolled rage and hatred toward American culture, traditions, and laws. The elites seethe at America for what they see as its *moral shortcomings*, especially its "schoolyard bully" approach to foreign affairs, its disdain for international institutions, and its support of the death penalty, limited government and SUVs. They feel this desperate desire to force us to change our ways. If we don't, then there's something wrong with us. And in that case the elites feel perfectly justified in insulting and mocking America.

It's completely alien to the elite collective that we in America insist not only on our rights and freedoms, but that we also vigorously protect our traditions. We are the most modern society in the world, but we go to church. We don't let the government establish religion, but we want don't want the words "under God" removed from our Pledge of Allegiance. Among the European elite, it's taken for granted that secularism, atheism, opposition to the death penalty, and prohibiting people from owning guns are all good things that "modern" people understand. The only way you'd get a Euro-elite into church on Sunday is if Michael Moore were giving a guest sermon.

It's America's unique mix of tradition and modernism that throws the elites' off-balance. They can't understand it. And what they don't understand, they treat with utter contempt.

## PLAYING COWBOYS AND IRAQIS

Like the miniature Lilliputians in *Gulliver's Travels*, the Euro-elites aim to tie the American giant down. Why? Because Europe is weak and scared, as well as poisonously jealous of our status. They have been bred to believe that we're the stupidest bunch of people on the planet, yet somehow we're richer and more successful than they are. (Domestically, Bush and the Stupid Party—the GOP—keep beating the Democrats, which drives them insane with bitterness.)

Strip away all the bombast and the preening arrogance, and Europe—especially what the great Donald Rumsfeld dismissed as "Old Europe" (basically, France and Germany)—is in decay. Because they can't even get their voices heard in places like the Middle East, European elites need to control "unilateralist" America by tying us into arrangements like the Kyoto Accords, the International Criminal Court, and, especially, the United Nations. These multilateralist bodies and treaties bind America's hands and constrain our freedom of action. To make things worse, our own homegrown elites will always chime in with a kindly word for them. From reading the *New York Times* and other elitophile newspapers, you'd think UN Secretary-General Kofi Annan was President Bush's boss.

The Euro-elites repay the compliment by backing up their American cousins in their prejudices. Here's what Will Hutton, a well-known writer in Britain, had to say in his book bewailing American dominance. According to Good Will Hutton, we're in "the extraordinary grip of Christian fundamentalism" and our "democracy" is an "offense to democratic ideals." Conservatives are "very ideological" activists who propagate a "tenacious endemic racism." Our free-market economy "rests on an enormous confidence trick." He claims our "citizens routinely shoot each other" due to our absurd affection for our Second Amendment. Hutton's statement could just as well have been pulled off Handgun Control, Inc.'s website.

The Europeans paint America as the world's biggest bully, one needing the kind of adult supervision that can only be provided by—you guessed it—multilateralist Europe! Only by impressing us with their supposedly "superior" values can the Europeans still hope to awe us trailer-trash Americans with how classy they are. Though collectively there are 375 million of them (outnumbering us by about 100 million), studies are showing that the continent's pitiful birthrate heralds an almost irreversible population decline. If the downtrend continues, as seems likely, by 2050 Europe's population is predicted to fall by 88 million. And that decrease is in spite of the tens of millions of Muslim immigrants to Europe. Old Europe is on life support. As for us, we go from strength to strength.

The Europeans can't speak softly and carry a big stick, as we can. A wet twig, maybe, and a condescending lecture are about all they can rustle up. Under the influence of the pacifist left, and the financial burden of their swollen welfare-state bureaucracies and inefficient state-run industries, the Euro-elites have let their militaries atrophy into near irrelevance. Europe can only call on a quarter of our deployable fighting strength—despite their significantly larger population—and even then, without our lift capabilities their troops and equipment aren't going anywhere. Germany has actually cut its defense budget from a measly 1.5 percent of GDP to a useless 1.1 percent. It's getting to the point where the German Army can't even defend Germany from an attack by Poland—I'll bet it's the first time in history *that's* ever happened. There's a Marine Corps saying: "nobody likes to fight, but somebody better know how."

To get a sense of how lopsided our comparative military strength is, each annual defense *increase* for the Pentagon exceeds the entire defense budget of any individual European country (indeed, more than Europe, China and Russia combined). In fact, at more than $350 billion, America will this year (in fact, every year) be spending vastly more on defense than the rest of Europe put together. For next year, the Pentagon is asking for $380 billion. Currently, Germany spends about $25 billion, Russia $9 billion, France about $28 billion, and Britain $37 billion. But compared to the relatively high levels seen during the Cold War, America is spending just a small percentage of its GDP on defense, between 3 and 4 percent. Our technology is at least one generation ahead of any other country's. Despite what you're hearing from the anti-military elite, we're not even breaking a sweat paying for our military. If anything, we should be spending more to keep it in peak condition.

As for their economies, the European countries are relatively well-off, but they're constrained by severe structural flaws. It's virtually impossible to fire anyone, no matter how incompetent, in Old Europe. Top jobs are unofficially reserved for clones graduating from particular schools. And labor costs are sky high while unemployment keeps on rising (as does the lavish welfare spending). Thanks to the terrifying taxes, workers' take-home pay is far smaller than ours.

Between the built-in costs, the taxes, and the inefficient industries, it's a wonder that anything gets done in Europe. Even when unemployment is higher than we'd like it to be, our free-market policies have helped American businesses create millions of jobs over the past decade. Meanwhile, in continental Europe (according to the Organization for Economic Cooperation and Development), the number of private-sector jobs hasn't increased since 1970. No wonder they gush over big government. It's their perpetual jobs program.

Like so many of Europe's welfare programs, France's pension system is threatening to implode. When the prime minister, Jean-

Pierre Raffarin, proposed pension reform, French workers took to the streets, shut down air traffic and schools, and refused to pick up the garbage. The revolutionary change? All state workers would be required to work an extra 2.5 years to qualify for a *full*, and very generous, pension. A whopping 25 percent of France's workers are employees of the state!

The situation is only going to get worse—from the Euro-elite angle, of course. Even in the aftermath of a huge stock market meltdown, American economic superiority is staggering. A country with just five percent of the earth's population produces 25 percent of the world's economic output. We're the world's largest economy by a long shot: add together the next four (Japan, Germany, France, and Britain) and they would equal ours. Indeed, the Euros are in a panic right now. According to a report issued in May 2003 by the respected French Institute of International Relations, over the next fifty years, Europe's share of world output will almost halve from today's 22 percent to 12 percent. As the report pessimistically concluded, "a slow but inexorable movement onto history's 'exit ramp' can be foreseen" for the EU. It also predicts that we will remain at our current level (China is actually our main rival, not the EU) and that the North American population will rise from 413 million to 584 million. Even now, half of the world's research and development is performed here, and we're responsible for 40 percent of all high-technology production. Columnist Charles Krauthammer had it right (as usual) when he wrote: "The fact is no country has been as dominant culturally, economically, technologically and militarily in the history of the world since the Roman Empire."

Because their militaries are so weak and their economies so relatively shaky, the Euro-elites can't lift themselves up to our level. So how can they drag America down to their own level? Simple. Focus on our *strengths* and turn them into *weaknesses*. Hey, our own elites will only be too happy to collaborate. And so will our rivals in the UN and other international institutions.

Our strengths are military power and economic muscle. The Euro-elites are determined to undermine them. They and their elite cousins over here are convinced that our military might makes us rich: we terrorize small countries so our corporations can sell them products. And then once we dominate them commercially, we need our military to protect our economic assets.

Our critics call this the "American Empire" and accuse us of wanting to impose a "Pax Americana" on the rest of the world. To the elites, it's understandable why the rest of the world allegedly "hates us." After all, it's only natural for oppressed people to rise up against their oppressors.

The thing is, just because we're the most powerful country *since* the Roman Empire doesn't mean that we *are* an American Empire. President Bush was clear about this when he told West Point graduates that "America has no empire to extend or utopia to establish." Acting "imperially" implies that we wish to conquer other countries and rule over them by force. What is the last country we've conquered and held under our thumb? We have never been an agressor seeking land or treasure or revenge. We don't take money from defeated or exhausted countries; we throw money at them—hundreds of billions of dollars' (like France and Germany after World War II, and now Iraq).

Colin Powell eloquently described America's foreign policy during an MTV "Global Discussion" on February 14, 2002. When a participant asked him how he felt representing the United States, "the Satan of contemporary politics." He answered:

> [F]ar from being the Great Satan, I would say that we are the Great Protector. We have sent men and women from the armed forces of the United States to other parts of the world throughout the past century to put down oppression. We defeated Fascism. We defeated Communism. We saved Europe in World War I and World War II. We were willing to do it, glad to do it. We went to Korea. We went to Vietnam. All in the interest of preserving the rights of people.

And when all those conflicts were over, what did we do? Did we stay and conquer? Did we say, 'Okay, we defeated Germany. Now Germany belongs to us? We defeated Japan, so Japan belongs to us'? No. What did we do? We built them up. We gave them democratic systems which they have embraced totally to their soul. And did we ask for any land? No, the only land we ever asked for was enough land to bury our dead. And that is the kind of nation we are.

When we dealt with Iraq and threw Saddam's Ba'athists into the gutter, we didn't do it because we wanted to own its territory. We did it to stop a tyrant from amassing WMD and to liberate a people crushed under his boot. Why on earth would anyone want to conquer Afghanistan? Thanks to the Taliban, its most plentiful resources are opium and rubble. We won't stay in Iraq a day longer than we have to. Neither Iraq, nor any other foreign country is ever going to be the fifty-first state (well, okay, maybe we could make an exception for Canada).

That makes us unique in history. We're the most powerful nation of all time and one that could rule the world if we wanted, but we don't want to. Yes, sometimes we assume the responsibility of global sheriff, but that's because no one else can or will do it. But intervening occasionally in foreign countries is not the same as conquering them. All we wish for is that other countries share in the benefits that freedom and democracy have brought us. We don't have territorial ambitions. We're not the Roman Empire, nor the Soviet Union. We're America. No "Empire" needed.

Our complete lack of interest in ruling the world disproves the silly elite theory that the reason why we're "hated" is because we are, allegedly, aggressively expansionist, that there is something scary about America. In a long article for *Newsweek* revealingly headlined "The Arrogant Empire," my friend and occasional radio guest Fareed Zakaria wrote that "what worries people around the world above all else is living in a world shaped and dominated by one country—the United States. And they have come to be deeply suspicious and fearful of us."

Of course, if we were "isolationist" instead of "imperialist," the elites would criticize us for our "aloofness," for "looking after Number One," and for "locking ourselves into Fortress America." We can't win. One day, they're pushing for us to send troops to Liberia. The next it's "End the Occupation!" The latter is the view of musician Brian Eno who in *Time* magazine writes: "America as a gated community won't work, because not even the world's sole superpower can build walls high enough to shield itself from the intertwined realities of the 21st century. There's a better form of security: reconnect with the rest of the world, don't shut it out." Make up your minds, kids. Are we hated for being a closed "gated community" or an expansionist "arrogant empire?"

## THE EMPIRE STRIKES OUT

Most of the time, the elites would say "arrogant empire" because that's what they've been taught in their elite schools. The whole "Empire" fixation is just an old conspiracy theory dredged up and polished off for modern consumption. It all started before World War I, when the British liberal economist J. A. Hobson "explained" how capitalism creates financial surpluses at home. Since there's so much spare money around, the cash is invested overseas and protected by the armed forces. In a kind of vicious circle, as the capitalist nation becomes ever richer it needs to expand further in order to find new opportunities, leading to increasingly large colonial empires based on military domination.

Since then, Hobson's theory has been disproven dozens of times (why should surplus money be invested overseas when it can be spent here on home renovation, new cars, or 401(k)s?). It would be forgotten today if it weren't for Lenin. Before the Russian Revolution, Lenin grafted Hobson's theory onto Marxism in order to "prove" that Capitalism plus Militarism equaled War. Though

Lenin and Marx and the evil system they invented are dead, their spirit lives on in the hearts and minds of the elites. They still believe in this stuff, only now they direct their ire toward America, which they identify as the world's Number One capitalist, imperialist, militaristic superpower.

That's one of the reasons why they declare repeatedly that our economic system is "unfair," "exploitative," and "harsh." The implication is that we need the kind of heavy-handed government intervention they have in Europe. At a major European Union summit in February 2002, finance ministers disparaged Bush's $690-billion tax cut plan, saying it "endangered the world economy." Why? Because the very fact that Bush was cutting taxes showed them up as a bunch of tax-loving Euro-elitists presiding over stunted economies. For them, it was as natural as breathing to believe that high taxes "stabilized" the world economy.

The Euros have always had a problem with our ability to make a lot of money. They're insanely jealous of our success, and so they get snobbish about it. Americans have always been stereotyped as being money-obsessed by their poorer European cousins. It's their way of getting back at us. Even in the 1790s, when the Frenchman Francois La Rochefoucauld-Liancourt was touring the country, all he noticed was that "the desire for riches is their ruling passion." It was Charles Dickens who coined the phrase, "the almighty dollar," as in the stuff Americans were frantically chasing after. The German philosopher Oswald Spengler thought the sure sign of an American was his adoration of "technical skill, money and an eye for facts." Yes, that "eye for facts" has always been our problem in European eyes.

It is true that we Americans do like our dollars and our home equity loans and our credit cards. The Euro-elites think we are crass and superficial because we spend our wages on super-huge plasma televisions, super-powerful cars, and super-thin laptops—and once in a while on a lark we'll throw good money away in some tacky casino. Although things can get pretty crass and superficial, the

Euro-elites forget that this is also the country that produced Ernest Hemingway, Philip Roth, Bruce Springsteen, Mark Twain, Herman Melville, Nathaniel Hawthorne, Saul Bellow, Tennessee Williams, *Citizen Kane*, Irving Berlin, Louis Armstrong, the New York Philharmonic, and George Gershwin. Maybe we're a little more cultured than they give us credit for. And speaking of crass and superficial, have you ever watched Euro-television? It's even more raunchy and vulgar than ours.

The Euro-elites also forget that over here we expect our young people to work their way through college. In Europe, students in higher education receive lavish government subsidies for as long as they want. So, if our crass and superficial kids buy a lot of clothes and DVDs, or own a car, it's partly because they have an income derived from pulling double shifts at the 7-Eleven. As for ourselves, we work longer hours and get much shorter vacations than Europeans. We deserve a break today, in other words.

No amount of arrogant elite-grousing can change the fact that no other country in history has developed such that its working- and middle-classes could afford the kind of lifestyle ours enjoy here. This is a place where a construction worker can afford a nice car and a decent house in a safe neighborhood. Regular Americans buy electronics and cars—the latest in-things—because, well, they *can*. And, for all of their egalitarian rhetoric, the elites can't stand the fact that Joe Smith of Peoria can watch the Super Bowl on his 7,000-inch Sony flat-screen, pick up some Chinese food in his SUV, get his news on the Internet instead of from the *New York Times*, and take the kids to the beach or the lake in the summer. The elites think he ought to *know his place* and do what he's told—as the proles do in Europe.

They've been thinking that for a long time—and it's still irritating them. As early as 1904, Europeans were getting worked up over what Paul Dehns, a German, termed "the Americanization of the World." Dehns defined Americanization as "the uninterrupted, exclusive, and relentless striving after gain, riches and influence." To this day, whenever you hear jibes about how "cheap and tacky"

McDonald's is, or how Mickey Mouse is "taking over the world," they're just updates of the old anti-American sneers. In this vein, the once-great novelist Norman Mailer let loose with a salvo of loathing for America and its "all-pervasive aesthetic emptiness" in the *New York Review of Books*—the fountainhead of Elite Opinion in America—that proved once and for all that he and his elite pals don't have anything original to say.

As I mentioned in a previous chapter, whenever they make a crack about "Southern rednecks," the American elites think they're making some brilliantly insightful comment, when all they're really doing is recycling old stereotypes from the Civil War era. Same thing goes for the Euro-elites' "insights" about large-eared, helium-voiced rodents, our love of doing business, and America's "aesthetic emptiness." This hackneyed stuff goes back more than two centuries. The elites really aren't as clever as they think they are.

And as usual, the Euros don't bother shouldering any responsibility themselves for the fact that we don't force Britney Spears, Coke, and bad Hollywood flicks down their throats. Regular Europeans love American movies and eating Big Macs. It's only the elite snobs who make an issue of "Americanization."

Another Euro-elite riff on the Capitalism = Imperialism theme is to blame "American corporations" for creating "poverty in the Third World." Again, they never blame themselves for any of the world's problems. In fact, with the sole exception of the basket case of Liberia (which was independent and created for freed slaves), if you look at a map of sub-Saharan Africa, the poverty-stricken and war-ravaged countries there were once controlled by European states like France, Belgium, Germany, Portugal, and Britain, not us. It was Belgium's brutal rule that created the Congo civil war, not General Electric's products. And who drew all those borders in the Middle East randomly demarcating Iraq, Syria, Saudi Arabia, Jordan, and Israel that have caused trouble from the very beginning? Was it Microsoft, or Amazon? No, it was France and Britain. We're still trying to clear up the mess they left behind.

Because the Euro-elites are socialist sympathizers, they also never blame themselves for supporting genocidal or tyrannical Communist regimes in the Third World. When Robert Mugabe grabbed power twenty years ago, he was hailed by the Euro-elites as *the* bright light of the future who would turn Zimbabwe into a workers' paradise. And he has, with all the charm of a Communist paradise: politically induced starvation, oppression and brutality. Same goes with mass-murderers like Pol Pot and the Khmer Rouge. The anti-American left idolized them as "liberators" of the Cambodian people. They "liberated" them from their very lives. But all that history is forgotten in the rush to blame America first.

In truth, the only way to mitigate Third World poverty is by helping those countries move to the free-market, strengthen their laws of private property, and introduce democratic reforms. But you try telling that to the Euro-elites without being howled down as a "heartless capitalist." What's their solution? They don't have one, apart from trying to squeeze more money out of us to prop up their favorite Third World strongmen.

Lastly, the Euro-elites circumvent their impotence by emphasizing "diplomatic solutions" and "Security Council consensus" over "unilateralist military action." In the words of arch Euro-elitist Chris Patten, "smart bombs have their place but smart development assistance seems to me even more significant." He *would* say that. The Euros don't have any smart bombs in the first place.

Then there's good old Hans Blix, the UN weapons inspector who spent more time worrying about American "unilateralism" than Iraqi disarmament. Now he's complaining that we're "bastards" for daring to criticize him. In an interview in the lead-up to Operation Iraqi Freedom, Blix bizarrely opined that "to me, the question of the environment is more ominous than that of peace and war. We will have regional conflicts and use of force, but world conflicts I do not believe will happen any longer. But the environment, that is a creeping danger. I'm more worried about global warming that I am of any major military conflict." Again, he *would* say that. If there is any major military conflict, Europe's going to be (French) toast. So why not change the subject so that the Euros can focus on what they're really good at: sanctimonious moral posturing at our expense?

Of course, going to war must be the last option available—but it must be available. As George Washington so wisely said, "if we desire to avoid insult, we must be able to repel it; if we desire to secure peace, one of the most powerful instruments of our rising prosperity, it must be known that we are at all times ready for War." But the Euro-elites instead fetishize "peace." During a 2002 speech in London, the Finnish prime minister Paavo Lipponen summed up Euro-pacifism when he said that "the EU must not develop into a military superpower but must become a great power that will not take up arms at any occasion in order to defend its own interests." Euro-elitists like Lipponen believe that a just war— even in self-defense—is never the answer. They have no intention of ever using force, even if every other approach has failed. Lipponen's one saving grace was that he genuinely believed what he was saying, even if it was absurd.

## LE DOCTEUR EVIL ET MINI-MOI

In contrast, other Euro-elites are viciously cynical about using their "desire for peace" to disguise their real motive: Get America, by any means necessary. The French, for example, were never going to approve any UN resolution authorizing any sort of action against Iraq. No matter what Jacques Chirac said in media interviews, he wasn't concerned about "the potential loss of civilian lives" in an Iraq war, but just wanted to help out his cronies at TotalFinaElf, the French oil company with strong regime contacts. It is thought that 15 percent of Iraqi oil reserves had been earmarked by Saddam for TotalFinaElf.

Having sold Saddam a great deal of his illegal weaponry in the first place by violating UN-imposed sanctions, the French knew perfectly well that he was armed and dangerous. But they were willing to drag out "negotiations" with Saddam for another dozen years to make a lot of money (talk about "Gain! Gain! Gain!"). From the Euro standpoint, if they can delegitimize any military option, then they've tied our hands. The cost of this approach is that the Europeans are only too willing to appease every tin-pot tyrant they can find just to get one over on us.

France, despite being a third-rate power, still clings on by its fingernails to its veto-wielding UN Security Council seat. The French elites know that without that precious chair, Paris would be shown up for what it is: a bit-player with pretensions to world power. Chirac's moral posturing about giving peace another chance, and then *another* one, is a fig-leaf for his own imperial ambitions.

The Euros are good at that—moral posturing, I mean, especially when they accuse us of being greedy, narcissistic, and corrupt. Mysteriously, the Euros, and particularly the French, always seem to forget about their own towering greed, narcissism, and corruption. Chirac, for example, had to stand for a second term as president simply to avoid (by gaining immunity as a head of state) half a dozen corruption and ethics charges—ranging from illegal party funding to jobs-for-his-pals dating back to his eighteen-year stint as mayor of Paris. Then there are the accusations of using public money to fund trips to exotic locales and blowing about $2 million on good meals.

As for his friends at TotalFinaElf, thirty-seven former bosses are now on trial for corruption. They're accused to skimming hundreds of millions of dollars to use as bribes for African governments to secure contracts. A couple of years ago, the entire European Commission (a bunch of unelected has-beens who control the European Union) was forced to resign amid a flood of corruption and fraud scandals (one Commissioner was handing out lucrative contracts to her dentist). The closest American equivalent would be if the entire Bush cabinet (plus the president) stepped down in disgrace.

## WHO YOU CALLIN' "UNILATERAL?"

And why are we always accused of heavy-handed "unilateralism"? Can you name the only country that has ever, in history, asked the UN (or anyone else, for that matter) for "permission" to go to war to protect its interests? No, it's not France. In fact, it's the bullying, unilateralist, aggressive, imperialist, genocidal USA.

We've done it twice. The first time was in 1950, when we brought together a coalition of countries to fight the North Korean invasion of South Korea. The coalition flew a UN flag. The second time was in 1990, when the administration assembled an alliance under UN aegis to defend Kuwait. Both times, we operated out of principle.

France and Britain never asked before they took on Egypt in the Suez Crisis, nor did the Soviet Empire go cap in hand to the UN before it invaded Hungary, Czechoslovakia, or Afghanistan. China didn't jump through diplomatic hoops before crushing Tibet. India and Pakistan have fought three wars since 1947 without being threatened with a "French veto." And let's ask to see the Arabs' permission-slip to go to war with Israel—or Israel's to go to war with the Arabs—in 1948, 1956, 1967, and 1973. And what's more, even when all these wars erupted, the UN did nothing to stop them. (The exception is Suez, but that's only because President Eisenhower took the lead.)

So much for Chirac's earnest plea in March, "France calls upon others to understand that the law must be upheld. France calls upon others to hold together the unity of the Security Council over Resolution 1441. To privilege force over the law is to take on a heavy burden of responsibility." We should remind him about that next time France uses force to get her way, as she often does, without asking UN permission, in her former African colonies.

France talks a big game about how committed she is to diplomatic solutions, international law, morality, and Security Council consensus, but Paris doesn't hesitate for a second when its own interests are threatened. In the lead-up to the recent Gulf War, even as France was trying to isolate President Bush as a warmonger, France "unilaterally" dispatched troops to Africa to quell a rebellion in the Ivory Coast. I don't remember the issue coming up in the Security Council.

In fact, since 1964, when it sent its troops to overturn a coup in Gabon, France has "militarily intervened" in Africa thirty-five times. That's nearly an average of one intervention per year. France invariably backs its favorite dictators (men like the "Central African Empire's" Jean-Bedel Bokassa, who was a cannibal), or protected genocidal psychopaths like the French-armed Hutu leaders in Rwanda who murdered hundreds of thousands of Tutsis. The French record in Africa is nothing short of despicable.

So it's just fine for France to act "imperially." Its Foreign Minister is Dominique de Villepin—his last name translates as "Pine Village"—who was the subject of a glowing *New York Times* profile. He "is the Energizer bunny of diplomacy, a hyperactive force who sleeps no more than four and a half hours a night, enjoys waking up aides to discuss matters of state, runs marathons by day and writes poetry by night." Wow, if only our own president were as in touch with his feelings as Dominique!

But buried deeper in the profile was the fact that he is the author of a biography of Napoleon, the megalomaniac tyrant. Says Monsieur de Villepin, "There is not a day that goes by without me feeling the imperious need to . . . advance further in the name of a French ambition." He approvingly quotes Napoleon's philosophy as: "Victory or death, but glory whatever happens."

Why is it that a French foreign minister can declare that he adores a violent imperialist like Napoleon, that he supports "French ambition" and "Victory or death," but when an American president defends Americans and American interests—in a war where victory is crucial to our survival—he's dismissed as arrogant, stupid, greedy, corrupt, and a unilateralist?

At the same time, Jacques Chirac can obnoxiously chide the leaders of pro-American countries in Europe (like Poland) that defied France by signing a letter in support of Bush's policy on Iraq by saying, "It is not well-brought-up behavior. They missed a good opportunity to keep quiet." Not only does Chirac get away with this outrageous remark, but he's backed up by a chorus of liberal American elitists. Robert Scheer of the *Los Angeles Times* said that European countries supporting the United States on Iraq were ones "you can buy on eBay." Mark Shields, the CNN host, sarcastically declared, "Everyone's feeling better. Albania signed on."

They sided with us in the lead-up to war. And at least the eastern Europeans and the Albanians—a Muslim country, by the way—know something about what it's like living under a murderous tyranny for decades. Ask yourself, if you're in a foxhole, taking enemy fire, would you want pampered Frenchmen or liberty-loving Albanians watching your back?

But the important point here is that the "internationalist" elites, who are normally so quick to lecture Bush about his so-called "arrogance" toward other countries, gave Chirac a rousing cheer. Can you imagine what the elites would have said if Bush had told France, when it loudly threatened to veto any American or British UN resolution on Iraq, that "it missed a good opportunity to keep quiet?"

As for Monsieur Pine Village, let's take a closer look at his behavior. A couple of weeks into the war, Chirac's Mini-Moi traveled to London to try to repair relations with the British and ourselves. His charm offensive was not a success.

In fact, de Villepin's fence-mending speech at London's International Institute for Strategic Studies was a complete disaster. During it, he said he hoped for "a swift conclusion with the minimum possible number of casualties," but when pressed afterward by a reporter to say whether he hoped coalition troops would defeat Saddam Hussein, de Villepin sniped, "I'm not going to answer. You have not been listening carefully to what I said before. You already have the answer." When he had the opportunity to back our servicemen against the fedayeen and the Republican

Guard, he balked. Nor could he even say that he looked forward to the liberation of a people from tyranny. Nice. At least he was being honest—for a change.

De Villepin couldn't even use the excuse that he was answering questions in a foreign language. He speaks excellent English. Tellingly, when he discussed the liberation of France from the Nazis, he mentioned Winston Churchill and Charles de Gaulle but omitted FDR. Nothing new about that: French history books devote one paragraph to Omaha Beach and don't even bother to mention the Marshall Plan. After Operation Iraqi Freedom began, some of our gallant French allies daubed graffiti on a British war memorial in Etaples in northern France. The slogans read "Death to Yankees" and "Rosbeefs Go Home" (Rosbeef—"Roast Beef"—is French slang for the Brits), as well as "Saddam Hussein will win and spill your blood." These were smeared on the very graves of men who had died to liberate France. That very same week, a *Le Monde*/TF1 poll of 946 people found that 25 percent—25 percent!—supported Iraq, another 31 percent backed "neither side," and just 34 percent wanted the American-led forces to defeat Saddam. In other words, de Villepin is nothing out of the ordinary. He represents Euro-elite opinion at its most meretricious.

All things considered, France would rather have had Saddam and his murderous sons stay in power. You know the old French saying, it's better to deal with the brutal dictators you know, than support American forces you hate. Indeed, two weeks into the war, de Villepin told an international conference (attended by Colin Powell) in Brussels that France was deeply concerned "about the risk of divisions, the shocks between cultures and societies and religions" because of the war. To avoid these "shocks" and "divisions," de Villepin proposed that once order was restored in Iraq (courtesy of the allies, not that he bothered mentioning them), "we believe the UN. should have a central role to play" in its political and economic development. For de Villepin, the "United Nations is the tool of international legitimacy." For him and his international elite cronies, the UN, properly functioning, acts like a permanent restraining order against that big bucking bronco called America.

The Euro-elites' pals here in the U.S. are totally on board with this mindset. Walter Cronkite, "the most trusted man in America" (it was a disturbing thought thirty years ago and even more frightening today), takes delight in tearing into America's "arrogance" in foreign affairs. At a speech at Drew University in New Jersey, Cronkite confidently predicted that a war in Iraq would have cataclysmic repercussions world-wide. "Every little country in the world that has a border conflict with another little country...they now have a great example from the United States." I can't begin to unpack the stupidity of that statement. Just for starters, we didn't have a *border* conflict with Iraq, which isn't a little country in the first place. And secondly, any little country considering launching a "border conflict" with another little country may now think twice—thanks to the thrashing we gave Saddam. It's the "example" set by the vacillating UN and perfidious France that *encourages* little countries to attack each other.

## DEM-ELITES AND THE FRENCH CONNECTION

"Kerry looks French," an unnamed Bush White House aide remarked in the spring of 2003, about senator and presidential candidate John Kerry. The senator's wife Teresa Heinz Kerry likes to recount how he impressed her at one of their first dinners together when, after she muttered something in French under her breath, he answered her in French. *Trés magnifique!*

Kerry does have a certain affinity for the French, but then so do so many of his colleagues in the U.S. Senate. A few weeks before the war, Kerry pledged to refrain from criticizing the Bush foreign policy, given how close we were to the start of Operation Iraqi Freedom. For many months Kerry had been trying to walk a microscopically thin tight-rope on the wisdom of taking out Saddam—stressing the importance of the UN and the views of the "global community" while talking tough on Saddam himself. Undoubtedly, Kerry was worried that he'd be perceived as Bush-lite by the left-wing Democrat base, so he had made a point to jab at the administration whenever possible. Just two weeks into what was one of the most successful military campaigns in history, Kerry just couldn't help himself. In a speech he charged that President Bush had committed a "breach of trust" with the UN by going to war in Iraq. Kerry mouthed the tedious antiwar mantra, saying "What we need now is not just a regime change in Saddam Hussein and Iraq, but we need a regime change in the United States." Preferably so we can have the President Kerry running to Paris to pay homage to his mentor Jacques Chirac.

Then there was Joe. Before the Iraq war, Demohawk Senator Joe Lieberman, even more concerned than Kerry about the "Bush-lite" charge, tried to balance his support for the war with the requisite outrage about America's refusal to act like a responsible superpower in other areas. "By pulling out of the Kyoto global warming treaty, arms control treaties and other international pacts," he cautioned, "and by issuing an unnecessary and divisive policy of military pre-emption, George W. Bush has separated us from most of the rest of the world and weakened our alliances just at the time when we need them more than ever." Lieberman was auditioning for a starring role among the elites, but his heart wasn't in it.

Then there was Robert Byrd, the ancient senator from West Virginia with the penchant for florid language. He doesn't seem to be happy these days unless he's giving the Euro-elites comfort by calling America a bully. During one of his usual long-winded speeches on the Senate floor (in this one, he covered buying Slim-Fast at the supermarket, playing the harmonica, and the advantages of giving bubble gum to your sweetheart), he bemoaned the fact that "this administration has turned the patient art of diplomacy on its head [with] threats, labeling and name-calling." Then he sounded another distinctly Euro-elite note (not on the harmonica) by calling us "evil" for our "crude insensitivities." A few days before the war started, Byrd delivered a line that could have come out of an editorial in *The Guardian*, saying, "We flaunt our superpower status with arrogance." In Byrd's world, dealing with ruthless troublemakers like Saddam would be a heck of a lot simpler if we weren't so insensitive. (I wonder: Between 1992 and 2002, which self-adulating lawmaker had more parks, highways, libraries and monuments named after him? Saddam or Bob?

One of the most revealing moments for the future of the Democrat party involved its *former* majority leader Tom Daschle. How a South Dakotan can become so tangled up with the elites is frankly mind-boggling, but Daschle has managed to do so—especially since the Dems lost the White House in 2000. Sensibly, Daschle endorsed the notion of regime change five years ago and approved of then-President Clinton's decision to launch air-strikes in December 1998 (without French or UN permission!). But with George W. in the White House, Daschle made it up to the elites at home and abroad by suddenly seeing things differently—or at least pretending to. On the eve of hostilities, he told union workers, "I'm saddened that the president failed so miserably at diplomacy that we are now forced into war." In Tom's eyes, Bush would have "succeeded" at diplomacy only be avoiding the war at all costs. (And Daschle Democrats wonder why conservatives have branded them the "Blame America Coalition.")

Obviously, the Iraqi ambassador to the UN, Mohammed al Dhouri, wholeheartedly agreed. "The path of war chosen by Bush embodies the gravest failure of American diplomacy throughout the century," he said at a press conference the next day. Do these guys use the same speechwriters?

Although neither the EU nor any of its member countries can challenge America militarily, the Euro-elites have found other ways to meddle constantly in our affairs and throw roadblocks in our path. The Euro-elites won't be satisfied until America becomes, well, less American. They need Democrats like John Kerry or Howard Dean to take back the White House. Then they can appoint more people to the Supreme Court like Stephen Breyer, who is fond of saying that in the future we need to harmonize our laws with those of Europe. The Euro-elites are enthralled when Justices Breyer, Sandra Day O'Connor, Anthony Kennedy, and Ruth Bader Ginsburg make annual pilgrimages to European conferences of international scholars and jurists (many of whom are disturbed by recent trends in American law). In July 2003, at a conference in Florence, even my old boss (and decidedly non-elitist) Clarence Thomas joined the internationalist gaggle.

The Democrats return the Euro-elite love by backing them on issue after issue. Like their European cousins, the Democrats believe the best way to protect against terrorist attacks is to act less like a dominant force and more like a domesticated global partner. This essentially requires that we sign on to treaties such as the one creating the International Criminal Court, or remain bound by accords like the ABM treaty, regardless of whether they serve our national interest.

To sum it up in stark terms—the Democrat Party of today is the European Party. The GOP is the American Party. This is not to say that the Republicans get it right every time—far from it. But more often than not, Republicans, not Democrats, are more in tune with what's in America's interest. The Democrats are much more in sync with European sensibilities. But when it's in their interest, they still fall over themselves to suck up to us. They need us more than we need them, and they know it.

Who can forget the priceless footage of President Bush doing "rabbit ears" behind Jacques Chirac in the official G-8 photograph of world leaders during his visit to Europe? Okay, so he didn't do the rabbit ears thing—but we knew he could have. After all, he was Bush of Afghanistan and Iraq, and Chirac had made a fool of himself. Unlike his French counterpart in the lead-up to the war, Bush acted with great magnanimity and grace. "They greeted each other with polite smiles, a brief handshake, and small talk before walking into a luncheon with other presidents and prime ministers," in the words of the Associated Press report. Chirac was forced to be polite. After all, he had had to suffer the insult of Bush deciding to visit Poland—our allies in the Iraq war, the ones Chirac had obnoxiously told "to keep quiet"—before a very quick stopover in France, that great superpower. While in Poland, Bush pointedly remarked, "I think it's unfortunate that some of the countries in Europe will try to bully Poland for standing up for what you think—what they think is right." The Euro-elites didn't like that— but so what?

We were right.

# Conclusion

L
et them continue to think we're stupid. Let them continue to proclaim their superiority. Let them continue to seethe. We should be happy. On most issues, the elites are either losing or are on shaky ground. In a democracy, bad ideas and destructive policies can only survive for so long.

We must directly confront and oppose any attempt to change the nature of our system of government by weakening or circumventing our democratic process. That means fighting against an activist judiciary that supplants our will for theirs. That means resisting any attempt to give international institutions authority over the will of our people. That means turning back attempts to create super-bureaucracies that concentrate power in the hands of unaccountable bureaucrats. That means using our purchasing power to send messages to those people or companies who aren't doing right by the people who make their prosperity possible. That means writing letters to congressmen, senators, and the editors of your local paper when we feel strongly about an issue.

We are riding the truth train. The elites will continue to try to derail us by offering false promises of a better alternative to the old

**337**

ways of thinking. But we will keep chugging forward, regardless. We know that obstacles lay ahead on the track. But we'll smash through them with a positive, optimistic momentum.

The struggle to give voice to what the average citizen wants has been going on for centuries. Never forget how the Preamble to the Constitution begins: "We the People." It was an incredible statement of who we are—a bold pronouncement for a new nation. "We the People . . . establish Justice, insure domestic Tranquility, provide for the common defense, promote the general Welfare, and secure the Blessing of Liberty." We get our "inalienable rights" not from Kings, or an aristocracy, or from a few big corporations—we get them from our Creator. Our Declaration of Independence establishes that governments exist merely to secure those rights, "deriving their just Powers from the consent of the governed."

The elites of today are playing the same cynical game that elites have always played: attack the people, tell them how dumb they are, tell them they don't understand the complex issues of the day, tell them they're too eager to listen to demagogues, and that they don't have the type of specialized knowledge necessary to decide critical issues. This is the same pack of lies that Americans have heard for centuries. We heard it from King George III, we heard it from the old Soviet Union, and we're hearing it from the elites of today. We've ignored it in the past, and we should ignore it now. Of course the American people make mistakes—we are, after all, human beings. But history shows that over 200 years ago a small and weak collection of colonies decided to trust the people more than any government in history—and that country became the mightiest, freest, and richest nation the world has ever known.

The elites will always fail to understand America because they fail to recognize the true source of its greatness. America is not great because of its dot-com millionaires, or its Hollywood starlets, or its brightest intellectuals. America is great because of the millions of so-called "average" Americans who get up every day and do the best they can to build a better world for themselves and their children. We are the hardest working people in the Western world. We generate the wealth that supports U.S. power. We pay the taxes that allow us to project force worldwide. We provide the soldiers for the finest military on earth. We serve on juries, vote in elections, respond to calls to help those in need, and educate our children. After more than 200 years, our record of success speaks for itself. We should not listen to anyone who tries to tell us we "can't understand" something, or that we should trust the "expert" judgment of the "international community."

My first real job after college was in the Reagan Administration. It was a great time to be young and to be in Washington, because we had a President who believed in this country, in its people, and in its possibilities, with a faith that is too rare among American elites. At a time when many nay-sayers had given up on the American people, he insisted that a new morning was at hand. The nay-sayers are still there—and I've tried to expose them in this book—but the American people are still there as well, and if I learned nothing else from President Reagan, I learned that only a fool trusts the nay-sayers more than the people.

We will overcome the elites of this time—just as we have overcome so many more dangerous elites in the past. And we will continue pursuing the American dream of building a nation where, as Lincoln said memorably so many years ago, government of the people, by the people, and for the people shall not perish from the earth.

# Acknowledgments

I am blessed with a wonderful family and a circle of close friends, who helped me keep my life in balance as I wrote this book. My brother Curtis kept me laughing, my brother Jim and his wife Stephanie kept me grounded, and my brother Brooks kept checking in on me, even from 10,000 miles away. My dad, James Ingraham, was always there for me in these crazy months, and remains my biggest champion.

Neither blizzard nor an impossibly busy law practice could stop Pat Cipollone, my godfather, from providing invaluable insights. Alex Rose steered me in the right direction when I veered off course, with immensely useful editorial contributions. As he has been for so many years, Stephen Vaughn was a meticulous editor and literary counselor. Finally, Marshall Coleman's comments on the European elites were spot-on.

In my effort to dissect the entertainment industry, I was fortunate to receive key insights from Lee Habeeb, my friend of fourteen years, and collaborator in the crazy unpredictable business known as talk radio.

There are many others who make up my larger "family": Chuck and Ina Carlsen, my neighbors and the coolest seniors I know; Lia Macko, who is as talented as she is beautiful; Karen Macko, who is wise and giving; Joe and Jill Robert, whose door is always open; the Cipollones (Becky and Pat, and the kids Elisa, Frankie, Joey, John Paul, Anna and Julia), who are inspirational in every way; the Sidaks (Greg and Melinda, and their boys Gunnar, Christian, Colin and Lachlan); and Danielle and David Frum, who are gracious hosts and generous friends.

Others to whom I owe so much: Wendy Long, Deborah Colloton, Katie and Brian Sexton, Patty Coleman, Alex and Jennifer Azar, Julie and Bern Altman, Jon Ledecky, Maryann O'Donnell, Amy Downing, Wesley Neal, Pam and Darren Cooke, Joe and Lorraine Martynowicz, Nate Segal, Wesley Neal, Matt Drudge, and Kevin DeLany.

I am forever grateful to Monsignor Peter Vaghi of St. Patrick's Church in Washington, who guided me on my spiritual journey.

When I need advice, Sean Hannity is always there. David Limbaugh also gave key advice as I started this project. Don Imus is a friend indeed. And Conrad Black is forever reminding me of how fortunate I am.

Regnery, my publisher, continues to put out first-rate books for a public hungry for the truth. I thank everyone who helped shepherd this book to completion: Al Regnery for initially believing in me; Marji Ross for seeing the project through; Harry Crocker and Miriam Moore, my editors; Stephanie Marshall, in publicity; Rich Kershner, for all the art and design work.

Finally, I want to thank God for showing me the way.

July 2003
Washington, D.C.

# Notes

## CHAPTER 1

1. William O'Rourke, "Bush's Yahoo Nation," *Chicago Sun-Times*, November 14, 2000.

2. Interview with Spanish newspaper *La Vanguardia*, December 30, 2002. Quoted on www.andrewsullivan.com, January 10, 2003.

3. See, for instance, Robert Bartley, "Open NAFTA Borders? Why Not?" *Wall Street Journal*, July 2, 2001.

4. See "The GOP's Immigration Foul," *Wall Street Journal* editorial, August 1, 2002; and Michelle Malkin, "The *Wall Street Journal*'s Immigration Foul," syndicated column of August 2, 2002.

5. David R. Francis, "Tax Revenues Vanish as Firms Move From US to Bermuda," *Christian Science Monitor*, May 22, 2002.

6. See Terence P. Jeffrey, "Clintonites Run Some Corporations, Too," *Human Events*, July 15, 2002; Patrick Buchanan, "Patriotism in the Boardroom," *New York Post*, July 1, 1998; Donna Kolvin, "Corporate Pledge Struggle," letter in the *Progressive Populist*, August 1996; Krikorian, "July Fourth in Post-America," *National Review Online*, July 3, 2001.

7. Quoted in the *New York Times*, December 11, 2002.

## CHAPTER 2

1. Karlyn Bowman, "The South: Still Distinctive," *The American Enterprise*, March 2003.

2. John Judis and Ruy Teixeira, *The Emerging Democratic Majority* (New York: Scribner, 2002).

3. David Brooks, "One Nation, Slightly Divisible," *The Atlantic Monthly*, December 2001.

4. Michael Barone, "Puzzled By the State Poll Results? So Are the Candidates," *Jewish World Review*, October 30, 2000, originally published in *U.S. News & World Report*.

5. Andrew Leonard, "Is Bill Gates a Closet Liberal?," www.salon.com, January 29, 1998.

6. Barone, "Puzzled By the State Poll Results? So Are the Candidates"

7. David Brooks, "Patio Man and the Sprawl People," *The Weekly Standard*, August 12, 2002.

8. Oralandar Brand-Williams, "Better Attitudes, Jobs Court Blacks Back to the South; Younger Generation Is Leading the Trek from Northern Cities," *Detroit News*, January 1, 2003.

9. Stephanie Simon, "The Old South, Up North," *Los Angeles Times*, December 30, 2002.

10. James A. Barnes, "Homing Instincts," *National Journal*, October 26, 2002, and "Democrats See Red," March 16, 2002.

11. Bruce Fein, "Dominance in the Oval Office," *Washington Times*, December 31, 2002.

12. Ronald Brownstein, "Democrats Couldn't Defend Against Surge of Bush, GOP," *Los Angeles Times*, November 11, 2002.

# CHAPTER 3

1. This section relies on the brilliant work of John Fonte of the Hudson Institute.

2. See Roger Kimball, "The Elephant in the Gallery or the Lessons of 'Sensation,'" *New Criterion* (November 1999); and "Postscript to 'Sensation,'" *New Criterion*, January 2000.

3. For the full story, see Rick Pender, "Almost Paradise," *Cincinnati CityBeat*, January 22–28, 2003.

4. This remarkable statement is quoted in John O'Sullivan, "The Folly of Tolerance," *National Review*, October 24, 2001.

5. Ellen Malcolm, "EMILY's List Must Compete in Primaries to Elect Women," op-ed in *Roll Call*, undated, reproduced at www.emilyslist.org.

6. EMILY's List press release, July 19, 2001.

7. Richard Johnson, Paula Froelich, and Chris Johnson, "Stars Are Two-Faced on SUVs," *New York Post*, January 13, 2003.

8. John O'Sullivan, *Conservatism, Democracy and National Identity*, (Centre for Policy Studies lecture, 1999), p. 24.

9. Quoted in John Fonte, "Liberal Democracy vs. Transnational Progres-

sivism: The Future of the Ideological Civil War Within the West," *Orbis*, Summer 2002.

10. John Fonte, "Will Liberal Democracy Survive?," originally published in Spanish in *Perfiles Liberales*, April 1999.

11. Quoted in John Fonte, "The Progressive Challenge to American Democracy," *The American Outlook*, Spring 2000.

12. Quoted in Daniel Pipes, "God and Mammon: Does Poverty Cause Militant Islam?," *The National Interest*, Winter 2002.

## CHAPTER 5

1. The Wisdom of the Popes: A Collection of Statements of the Popes Since Peter on a Variety of Religious and Social Issues, Thomas J. Craughwell (Editor), (St. Martin's Press, 2000)

2. NBC News Transcripts, Dateline NBC (July 6, 1999); see also Kilpatrick, J., Tulsa World (Dec. 13, 1999).

## CHAPTER 7

1. On Novick, see Robert Locke, "The Open-Borders Conspiracy," www.frontpagemag.com, July 15, 2002. http://www.frontpagemag.com/Articles/ReadArticle.asp?ID=1880

2. Quoted in Tom Tancredo, "Bordering on Insanity," San Diego Union Tribune, March 24, 2002.

3. On May 22, 2003, the House of Representatives passed an amendment (250-179) to the Department of Defense authoriziation bill (H.R. 1588) that would allow for the use of our troops on our borders. A similar measure died in the Senate in 2002, and the Pentagon flatly opposes it. Marine Lt. Col. Michael Humm, a Defense Department spokesman, insisted that the defense secretary already has the authority to assign troops to assist the Department of Homeland Security on the borders.

## CHAPTER 9

1. Terrence Moore, "More Than a Million Mogadishus, We Need One Good Chicago," April 2003.

2. The *New York Times* isn't the only organ that regards Castro as a sensitive, learned man. *Foreign Policy* magazine, a journal widely read by Ivory Tower foreign-affairs specialists, published a book review by him at the same time as he

was jailing dissidents. One (unreadable) paragraph runs as follows: "As a public man forced to compose speeches and narrate events, I share the illustrious writer's delight in searching for the precise word, a sort of mutual obsession that is unappeasable until the phrase is just right, faithful to the sentiment or idea we wish to express, even as we remain firm in the belief that it can always be improved." Thanks, Fidel.

3. According to *real* Middle East expert Martin Kramer, who wrote a terrific book, *Ivory Towers on Sand*, which is devoted to dissecting America's Middle East scholars, Beinin is of the "far-left, blame-America-first, Zionism-is-colonialism school."

## CHAPTER 10

1. *WFA Statement of Goals and Beliefs*, at http://www.wfa.org/about/.

2. Marguerite Peeters, *Hijacking Democracy*, AEI (2000).

3.Cited in James M. Sheehan, *Global Greens: Inside the International Environmental Establishment*, Capital Research Center, Studies in Organization Trends No. 12, 1998, p. 5.

## CHAPTER 11

1. This gem of an interview was picked up by Andrew Sullivan at his blog, www.andrewsullivan.com, in early January 2003.

# Index

ABC, 84, 147, 231, 268
abortion issues, 11, 21, 40, 51, 59, 66–67, 114–15, 119
*About Schmidt*, 93
Abrams, Floyd, 53, 56
*Absalom, Absalom!*, 30
Ackerman, Gary, 125
ACLU. *See* American Civil Liberties Union
actors/actresses. *See* celebrities
Adams, John, 128, 240
Adams, Ryan, 76
Aetna, 25
Afghanistan, 71, 110, 140–42, 154, 158–59, 328, 335
Africa, 96, 100, 329
African-Americans, 31, 36, 42, 49, 57–58, 61, 149, 195, 210, 239–40, 245
Aideed, Mohammed, 163
al-Akhras, Ayat, 54
al-Arian, Sami, 250
al Dhouri, Mohammed, 335
al Qaeda, 64, 158, 176, 248–50
Albania, 330
Albright, Madeleine, 168–69, 290
Alexander, Lamar, 257
Algeria, 296
*All in the Family*, 63
Allen, Woody, 6
Alterman, Eric, 159, 160
*Amazing Adventure, An*, 11
Amazon, 19
America
    culture of, 305–36
    defending, 178–79
    definition of, 47–48
    foundation of, 126, 137

    hatred of, 18, 71–74, 95, 146, 165, 166, 194, 248, 263, 314
    love for, 1–3, 13, 73
American Association of University Professors (AAUP), 250, 265
*American Beauty*, 93
American Civil Liberties Union, 6, 33, 34, 53–54, 56, 114, 119, 127, 185, 186
American Federation of Teachers (AFT), 255, 257
American Immigration Lawyers Association (AILA), 191–93
American Nazi Party, 177
American Revolution, 256–57
American Textbook Council (ATC), 260, 262
American workers, 7–8, 10, 13, 20, 183, 184–85, 187, 198–200, 210, 226–27, 323, 338–39
Americans United for Separation of Church and State, 6, 119
Amnesty International, 26, 270–71, 273, 279
Anheuser-Busch, 25
Aniston, Jennifer, 78
Annan, Kofi, 163, 276, 289–92, 313, 315
ANSWER, 141, 155, 173–75, 177
anti-Americanism, 1–4, 16, 18, 23, 26–29, 39, 65, 71–74, 100, 106, 140–41, 144, 149, 153, 158, 160–64, 167, 171–78, 193, 207, 235–39, 2464–58, 263, 270–76, 280–85, 291–303, 308–13, 324–25
anti-Bush sentiments, 1, 15–16, 76–81, 84–89, 101–2, 108, 112, 139, 149, 165–67, 307–10, 333–35
anti-Israel sentiments, 16, 192